More Advance Praise for *Trump's World: Geo Deus*

"Malloch understands Trump better than anyone and should be his next Secretary of State."

Daniel Kawczynski, Conservative Member of the UK Parliament

"Malloch presents perhaps the strongest argument for the Trump Administration's foreign policy: period."

Sam Clovis, Trump 2016 National Policy Director

"A persuasive analysis of the huge impact President Donald Trump has had at home and abroad—a revolution in politics that will be influential long after he has left power."

Tim Newark, political commentator for the *UK Daily Express*

"A stirring and persuasive argument that Trump has put paid to years of amoral liberal pieties, and that this marks a turning point in world history."

Francis Buckley, *New York Post*

"No book spells out in such fine nuance and grainy detail how our great President Trump has transformed the world. Read it and take note."

Ed Martin, Phyllis Schlafly's Eagle Forum

"This is the best treatment of Trump's thinking—it captures the worldview, policies, and implications of America First."

Charles Herring, OANN

"Most critics of Trump's foreign policy treat it as, in Lionel Trilling's phrase, a series of 'irritable mental gestures.' Instead, Malloch makes a lively case both for its coherence, salience, and efficacy."

Paul Marshall, Wilson Professor of Religious Freedom, Baylor University

"This is the first complete and positive exposition of Trump's world view and his entailed policies; it exhibits precisely the level of discussion that his critics try to block by attacking him rather than discussing his world view. A masterful explanation of why Trump has earned the enmity of globalists, elites, and technocrats around the world, while simultaneously earning the support of common people."

Nadia Nedzel, D., LL.M., Reilly Family Professor of Law, Southern University Law Center

"Christ said: Do not be afraid. Pope St. John Paul II said: Do not be afraid. This book explains U.S. foreign policy under Donald Trump, rationally and in great detail. Those who prefer freedom have nothing to fear."

Ingrid Detter Frankopan, Lindhagen Professor of International Law, Stockholm University and advisor to Pope John Paul II

"This is an important book to understand the thinking of this President as he navigates world leaders' views toward the United States of America. He intends to have the country he leads be great and by his actions, and words, not only will the American people benefit, so too will people across the globe who love freedom, free enterprise, human rights, and economic growth. Elitists, statists, and totalitarian sympathizers will be unhappy as their globalist intentions are disrupted."

Becky Norton Dunlop, Ronald Reagan Distinguished Fellow, The Heritage Foundation

"Donald Trump is the voice of American conservatism and a terrific commander in chief. In this book, Ted Malloch brilliantly explains to the whole world what American Greatness means and how it is being enacted in foreign policy."

Ben Boychuk, Managing Editor, *The American Greatness*

"In *Trump's World: GEO DEUS*, Ted Malloch captures the Zeitgeist—Donald Trump's fight for national sovereignty in a world that wants to do business, not wage war."

Douglas Macgregor, Colonel (ret), USA, PhD.

TRUMP'S WORLD

GEO DEUS

THEODORE ROOSEVELT MALLOCH

FELIPE CUELLO

Humanix Books

www.humanixbooks.com

Humanix Books

Trump's World

Humanix Books, P.O. Box 20989, West Palm Beach, FL 33416, USA
www.humanixbooks.com | info@humanixbooks.com

Library of Congress Cataloging-in-Publication Data is available upon request.

Humanix Books is a division of Humanix Publishing, LLC. Its trademark, consisting of the word "Humanix," is registered in the Patent and Trademark Office and in other countries.

ISBN: 978-163006-131-9 (Hardcover)
ISBN: 978-163006-132-6 (E-book)

Printed in the United States of America
10 9 8 7 6 5 4 3 2 1

In hoc signo vinces.
                    —CONSTANTINE

We reject the ideology of globalism, and we embrace the
doctrine of patriotism. We will never surrender America's
sovereignty to an unelected, unaccountable, global bureaucracy.
                    —PRESIDENT DONALD TRUMP

Contents

FOREWORD

Europe has been awakened from its somnolence by the vigor and determination with which U.S. President Donald Trump has changed the face of America and indeed the entire world.

Since the fall of the Soviet Union, mainland Europe has been stuck in the old politics of the twentieth century. The annihilation of the European socialists in the European Parliament and the European Council (where they count only a handful of heads of state) is birthing a new European era.

Many leaders still do not know how to react to President Trump, to his decision to control immigration, to 3+ percent economic growth, and especially to the absolutely justified desire to implement a pro-U.S. policy. America's ideological leadership has been correct since 1945, and a resounding final rejection of socialism is coming on both continents.

Winning—this is true greatness.

Europe, like the rest of the world, needs Trump in order to relearn how to do politics instead of letting the elites spin endless tales in which no one understands anything and nothing is decided. The postpolitical age of the 1990s with its Blairite and Clintonian effect is over. The sophistry of pretending to rule with facts while sneaking leftism in the back door has been arrested.

A phrase has come into the zeitgeist: calling people the "Trump of their field." Elon Musk is the Trump of business. I am called the Trump of Italy. It is a phenomenon that recalls the great Caesars. The name of Gaius Julius Caesar became a title, honorific to the extreme of deification, copied a thousand years after the last Caesar fell in titles such as "tsar" and "Kaiser" and providing a deep common root among Western peoples, including Rome, where it originated.

The Trump of America must lead the world in uniting Western civilization against an onslaught of weak, feeble centrists and leftists at home and abroad. Europe needs Trump in order to wake up from its zealous overconfidence in its capacity to assimilate millions of non-Europeans into Italy and the rest of Europe. We have a common interest in controlling borders and will work together on that issue.

The world also needs Trump and America to learn the value of the nation-state and policies based on the community called the "nation," a concept without which Italy wouldn't exist. Leaders in Brussels want the nation forgotten for one big euro blob. Swearing fealty to any office, from councilman to prime minister, means we are honor-bound to fight for the idea of the nation.

Every nation in the world needs a president or prime minister like Donald Trump pushing it toward its greater destiny. All nations need presidents that put their nation first and fight for the interests of those who voted for them!

The European Union as a whole needs a European Commission president on the very same model. One who is not afraid to save Europe from the endless waves of non-European immigrants.

One who is not afraid of our Christian tradition. One who will keep the promises made to voters and encourage real economic growth.

One who understands that Europe needs the United States as it always needed it throughout the twentieth century. Finally, one who does not fear adversity and challenges when reforming and putting it on the right path.

God only knows there are enough influential people and bureaucrats who would like things to remain unchanged and frozen over time even if this would mean a bankrupt Europe and an impoverished world. They want their own power more than anything. These globalists need to be removed from the levers of power. That is why elections are essential, because then we the people will build a future in *freedom*.

All countries must learn from President Trump the true values of politics and the way in which just one man, when he is backed by the legitimate wishes and expectations of millions of citizens, can change the course of history for the better.

Citizens across the European Union and everywhere else expect change. They demand nothing less. We just have to find leaders who are willing to take us ahead on this overwhelming but achievable task.

Thank you, President Donald J. Trump, for setting the example. We owe you "hugely" to use your own words.

It all started with Trump—an American Caesar—a Geo Deus. We follow his lead.

He has bent the arc of modern history in his native land and with other partners will do the same thing around the world as popular sovereigntists win the day.

MATTEO SALVINI
Former Deputy Prime Minister and
Interior Minister of Italy

Introduction

The past does not have to define the future.
—PRESIDENT DONALD TRUMP

For over two years the world has been trying to figure out Donald Trump: what makes him tick, what guides his view of the world and America's place in it, and the extent to which he is a transformative global leader.

Many blatantly don't like him (almost everyone who has actually met him likes him a lot); some resist his presidency; others try to depose or impeach him from office. Some are bemused, others are captivated, and most are simply constantly reacting to all that his presidency implies. Foreign leaders are dumbfounded and have never encountered anyone or anything quite like Donald J. Trump.

They characterize him as a buffoon, a fool, or an idiot. They try to say that he has no ideas or that his base is deplorable and irredeemable. They mock him, laugh at him, and paint him as un-American, treasonous, and naive.

Nothing could be further from the truth. None are so blind as they who don't wish to see. Trump may be unconventional and his views not consonant with elitist foreign policy or the Davos mainstream, but he is quite understandable.

Trump was elected president in the United States because he is an outsider, not because he represented more of the same. That makes his worldview and foreign policy altogether different from those of his recent predecessors.

He is most definitely a *disrupter* on every front. This is what he ran on, promised, and is delivering. Such views and traits disrupt many established plans and ways of thinking and affect a great many people and institutions both in America and in foreign capitals.

His management theory, if you want to call it that, is best termed "chaos management." Chaos is a ladder, and fortune favors the bold. What this means is that he tends to listen to various points of view intently, playing one off and against another to see which fits best with the situation: less order, more flexibility.

This "principled realism" is not unheard of in the business sphere, where the bottom line is paramount. It is quite rare in politics. Trump is not liberal or a Democrat in the least. In that sense, he represents a complete break with the immediate past, be it Obama and Clinton or the Bush neocon dynasty, all of which were rejected by the voters.

It looks messy, but in the end it often delivers results—measurable results. It leads to a lot of turnover, bluster, and posturing, and it isn't always pretty. It makes great fodder for the investigative journalist types who are always trying to put down the president and his team, or their process of governing or Twitter communications, as well as his unconventional diplomacy.

Trump is an ENTJ on the Myers–Briggs Type Indicator. That means he is extroverted, intuitive, thinking, and judgmental. He is self-driven, motivated, energetic, assertive, confident, and competitive. He typically knows what he wants and mobilizes others to help them attain their goals. He generally takes a big-picture view and builds a long-term strategy that is felt, "perceived," not reasoned or argued.

ENTJs often are sought out as leaders because of their innate ability to direct groups of people. Unusually influential and organized, Trump sometimes may judge others by his own tough standards, failing to take personal needs into account. This is Trump to a T.

ENTJs are natural-born leaders. People with this personality type embody the gifts of charisma and confidence and project authority in a way that draws crowds together behind a common goal. But unlike their Feeling (F) counterpart, an often ruthless level of rationality characterizes ENTJs, who use their drive, determination, and sharp minds to achieve whatever goal they've set for themselves.

Perhaps it is best that they make up only 3 percent of the population lest they overwhelm the more timid and sensitive personality types that make up much of the rest of the world. However, we have ENTJs to thank for many of the businesses and institutions we take for granted every day. That is why they are called "commanders."

Trump is the American commander-in-chief, a mantle he wears comfortably. But he has also, if reluctantly, taken on the role of the leader of the free world, if not the whole wide world. That is why we subtitled this book *Geo Deus*.

Trump is in many ways akin to Saint Michael slaying the dragon, executing a hostile takeover of the Republican Party and daily wrestling down the whole world. "Miraculous" barely covers what the man gets away with and achieves on a daily basis.

Trump is theologically best seen as the defender of God's people. On so many counts, in his defense of Christians in war zones and America's commitment to religious freedom worldwide, America and its leader are a shield of the Cross. Saint Michael would be his patron, watching over warriors and mariners, along with the sick and suffering. America is ill, and Trump is its healer.

The later Roman emperors borrowed heavily from divine iconography. Trump might pass for a fourth-century emperor like Commodus, with the full power of the church and the state behind him in that united Leviathan that Hobbes spoke of over a thousand years after Rome fell.

Trump likes to command. He is quite transactional in his dealings and has set out an articulate *Art of the Deal* that shows how he operates and what to expect. He is foremost a deal maker, a negotiator by habit, and is willing to go to great lengths to get what he wants. He wants to *win*.

Building the country is Trump's political and economic imperative. As a patriot, he sees where America has been crippled and wants to fix that. As a world leader by extension, he sees America retaking its rightful place as the dominant player in world affairs even if his views, like those of the first president, George Washington, do not include having America entangled or overextended in foreign alliances.

As a sovereigntist Trump believes it is a job that we as a nation are up to and not one for multilateralism, the United Nations, or any form of globalism.

Trump seeks to restore the hegemony and prosperity of the American prowess of eras in which Washington's heroic power was at its zenith. Those past generations of Americans slew the dragons of their time—fascism and communism—and Americans must remain ready to do so again if the world ever needs it.

For Trump, no longer does the world have to demean America, knock the dollar, have ultimate allegiance to corrupt international organizations, and think that globalization or its attendant trade deals will solve all our ills.

In effect, according to Trump, globalism as an ideology and an economic process has created many discontents. It has disenfranchised extensive swaths of our population. Those groups have seen their median incomes fall in the last decade and a half and their costs rise while disproportionately suffering from under- and nonemployment. For the forgotten people, Trump is their man.

Thanks to blue-collar populism, these working people have spoken and have found a voice in Trump, the Manhattan populist who now represents them as president and world leader. But his administration and what it will build are ultimately more about hope than rage.

Trump will not buy the house that the Democrats built and broke. He will not, like Obama, make apology tours decrying America; quite the opposite.

Instead, here is the core of the Trump program, revolving around the p in public-private partnerships, namely, private capital. Trump is a capitalist for every man, woman, and child, not just the superrich or Wall Street titans. He is a capitalist for every citizen and wants the same thing for all people the world over.

The concept involves returning to a private enterprise model to develop not just America but the world. It includes deregulation and tax reform that reduces government involvement in our lives and our pocketbooks. Trump puts America first but not alone. He wants other sovereign countries to experience their own greatness as well. He seeks peace and prosperity that begin on our shores but travel the world over.

Ever since Harvard's John Kenneth Galbraith published *The Affluent Society* in 1958, the political left in the United States and around the globe has been locked into the notion that "public goods and services" must be taxpayer-funded and government-operated.

Trump doesn't buy this line and attacks socialism wherever it shows its ugly head.

The McKinsey Global Institute and others have made the economic case that investments pay off by expanding the economy and increasing the tax base. We all agree on that much. The real questions are: Who pays, how much, and where? For Trump this is an American saga, but the model can be adopted elsewhere to great benefit for all people.

The American voters have spoken, and the last thing they want is more government, costly fiscal policy, added bureaucracy, and old-style cronyism for politicos and big-city mayors with their hands out. Remember that ultimately money comes out of the public purse, as Trump says. Not this time; no thanks.

Trumpism is spreading. It is the rage in Europe, India, and Brazil. Our closest ally, the United Kingdom, started this phenomenon in its Brexit from the monolithic European Union.

Donald Trump is now saying, "Can we fix it? Yes, we can." Here's how.

If you want to go inside Trump's world and his populist outlook, you need an open mind. Put the invective away and try to understand where he is coming from and what shapes his mind and his policies, notably in foreign affairs.

Trump is a formidable force with a huge following that is growing worldwide, and the pendulum of history is swinging in his direction. He is not going away and has already said he will run for reelection in 2020 on the tagline Keep America Great.

Trump also has plans for foreign policy and America's place in the world as a safer, more secure, and more prosperous place.

If you take a close look, you can make sense of where Trump wants to go and his primary motivations, and then you can comprehend his political thinking, economic model, direction, and various foreign policies better.

Let the tour inside Trump's world begin.

1

Trump's View of the World

This is the most deceptive, vicious world. It is vicious; it's full of lies, deceit, and deception. You make a deal with somebody and it's like making a deal with—that table.
—PRESIDENT DONALD TRUMP

Trumpism versus Globalism

When you take the 30,000-foot view, you can see the larger context and the significant stakes in the contest between Trump and the globalists.

Globalism was Clinton's core belief, and it remains that of the entire Democrat elite and the party of Davos: open borders, diminished sovereignty, multilateralism, multiculturalism, and everything defined as "worldwide" or "global" in scope. World government is the ultimate long-term end.

Nationalism is its polar opposite. For Trump, the nation-state is supreme and sovereign, borders matter, bilateralism is preferable, national and ethnic identities are rooted in tradition, cultures count, and the intermediating institutions of society—family, church, civic association, and place—come first. Issues are settled by sovereign nation-states, which are not going away any time soon. This is patriotic in Trump's view of the world.

The battle lines are set as never before. One ideology is pitted against the other, one set of institutions against the other, one cultural outcome against the other. It is a war.

Truth is, globalization has been ebbing while economic and political populism has been surging. Globalists no longer provide the accepted set of rules for the political and economic order. Transnational, multilateral, and supranational organizations and their networks, experts, and regulators are everywhere on the defense. Cosmopolitan and globalist values are not ascendant as they were in the 1990s.

This is what made Trump's candidacy viable. It is the defining mark of his presidency.

As a matter of fact, national sovereignty has soared back and is growing stronger week by week and month by month. We see it most clearly in President Trump's principled realism that he calls "America first." Like the nineteenth-century version of populism that rallied against the gold standard, today's economic populism is antiestablishment, antielitist, and opposed to all forms of globalization and globalist governance. Economic history and economic theory both provide strong reasons to suggest that the advanced stages of globalization are proof statements for the populist backlash in both its right- and its left-wing variants and everywhere from Brexit and the Trump effect, to current European politics (Italy), to Brazil and throughout Latin America.

Whether along ethnocultural cleavages or along income-class lines, these forms of populism are a predictable and logical result.

It should surprise no one, including globalists, that the pendulum has swung so far away from them.

There are two sides to populism: *demand* and *supply*.

Economic anxiety generates a base for populism but does not determine its particular political narrative; that story line is left to various populist politicians and movements, which are on the rise worldwide.

National greatness in one place does not diminish it in another place. There is no reason why all nations cannot articulate their individual greatness and in their self-interest (national interest) interact in the world in a peaceful and benign fashion.

It is the economics of trade and financial integration that provide the politically contentious backdrop to all globalization.

Trade theory, such as the well-known Stolper-Samuelson theorem, shows that there are sharp distributional implications in open trade. In other words, free trade is not a win-win for everybody.

Losers are inevitable. Those who lose are generally low-skilled and unskilled workers.

Trade liberalization raises the domestic price of exportables relative to importables. Go to any Walmart if you want to check out this phenomenon firsthand. Where is everything made? There is an inherent form of redistribution at work here: the flip side of the benefits of trade. The surplus from lowering wage costs and the tax bill is unevenly divided between corporate executives and badly paid foreign laborers who work in appalling conditions—in violation of International Labour Organization (ILO) and World Trade Organization (WTO) standards, it must be said. Globalists never met a rule they didn't want a special exception for.

Overall, as globalization advances, trade agreements become more about redistributing and less about expanding the economic pie. The political fallout is clear: Globalization, the opposite of national interest, has become more and more contentious, if not unsustainable. The empirical evidence bears this out. From

NAFTA, which has cost the United States some $3.5 trillion over the last decade, to the widening United States–China trade deficit, the American economy has enjoyed few overriding efficiency gains from globalization.

What we have instead are large trade imbalances, income stagnation among middle earners, and other nasty social side effects. Talk to any middle-class family or visit any town or factory in the affected areas and you can gain firsthand knowledge, up close and personal. The overall benefits of globalization are zero to negative. Trade was supposed to be based on reciprocity and growth, but that turned out to be a sham. The benefits of international trade as originally argued by Adam Smith and its subsequent canonization ignore important historical differences.

A displaced worker in our modern technological age (unlike a day laborer or farmer in the eighteenth century) already has a home mortgage, car payments, tuition costs for his or her children, and lots of other overhead. Merely switching careers or retraining is not so simple for many people. Truthfully, it is more than difficult, especially for middle-aged workers who have worked one job in one place.

The share of U.S. imports in gross domestic product (GDP) went from less than 7 percent in 1975 to more than 18 percent in recent years, but the imbalance hasn't been corrected by what's called trade adjustment assistance. Why? Because it is very costly and because politicians on all sides of the spectrum make a lot of promises they do not keep. All economists know that trade causes job and income losses for some groups. The same economists deride the notion of "fair trade" as a kind of fiction, but that's clearly not the case, as we see with antidumping rules and countervailing duties.

These fixes are dubbed "trade remedies" for a reason. And don't forget what might be called "social dumping," in which one country literally dumps its unemployment potential elsewhere or subsidizes inefficient production forever, regardless of the cost.

What about operational mobility and the so-called benefits of financial globalization? The distinction between short-term "hot money" and financial crises and long-term capital flows such as foreign direct investment is significant. One is disruptive, and the other is enhancing. One is patient, and the other is imprudent. So why is it that the timing of financial globalization and the occurrence of banking crises coincide almost perfectly?

Recurrent boom-and-bust cycles are familiar to less developed countries but appear to have spread to the European Union and the United States. Financial globalization has, like trade, exerted a downward pressure on labor's share of income.

Has anyone ever heard this line? "Accept lower wages or we will move abroad!"

A gentleman in Ohio was interviewed who ran a large battery-manufacturing unit and had recently moved, as the boss, to Mexico. He was asked about the thousands of workers in Ohio. "They are gone," he said. "We hired far cheaper Mexican ones in Juarez at just a fraction of their hourly wage."

Those with lower skills or qualifications are the least able to shift or move across borders and are most damaged by this sort of risk shifting. But soon, so too will accountants, architects, engineers, software developers, and every other type of white-collar worker.

It also has become harder to tax global mobile capital. That is the case because capital moves to the lowest-rate tax haven and uses transfer pricing to disguise profits. Taxes on labor and consumption are much easier to collect, and they have gone up and up.

Globalization, we were told, had a big upside. This is the bill of goods the public has been sold for decades. In fact, globalization has helped only the few: exporters, multinationals, and the large international banks as well as certain professionals and the very top management.

It is a question of foreign policy, not just economics. It surely helped some countries, such as China, which rapidly transformed peasant farmers into low-cost manufacturing workers, thereby reducing poverty. But all those jobs were at the cost of "old jobs" in America's Rust Belt. In effect, globalization was a definite and planned wealth transfer from one place to another that has gone largely unreported.

Any national security professional will tell you the economy is a major part of the national arsenal. POTUS has shown the world how to weaponize our GDP for the national interest.

There is another side of the not-so-glossy globalization coin: increased domestic inequality and exacerbated social division. Both are threats to the stability of our country.

The benefits and monetary flows sold to the unknowing public turned out to be all one-sided and went exclusively to the very highly skilled, to employers, to cities, to cosmopolitans and elites—*not* to ordinary working people. The United States and Europe have been ravaged by financial crises and decades without a raise in pay or the standard of living for the masses and by the effects of austerity while the few got richer. Globalization gutted the existing social contract and ushered in a stigma of unfairness in what Trump calls "a rigged system."

The playing field is hardly level. The winners took all, and Goldman Sachs bankers always seemed to come out on top whether they were selling distressed mortgage debt or shorting it (sometimes simultaneously). In the end, the political economy of globalization and globalist agency is, we have discovered, not politically sustainable.

Economic integration (in the European Union or globally) has definite and unacceptable real costs that people cannot and will not bear. This explains the rise of economic and political populism. Economic populism and its cousin political populism are an antidote to and a reality check on excessive globalization and globalist values and institutions. This represents the nation reasserting its interest and place at the table as a factor to take into account.

You spell that Trump: *Geo Deus.*

Looking back, 2016 was a watershed historic year. The Clinton globalists did not want to lose to the Trump nationalists. They did not want their world or their ambitions for globalism disrupted. They have been by one Donald J. Trump.

Who Is Trump's Speechwriter?

A true patriot will defend his country from its government.

Who will govern the governors? There is only one force in the nation that can be depended upon to keep the government pure and the governors honest, and that is the people themselves. They alone, if well informed, are capable of preventing the corruption of power, and of restoring the nation to its rightful course if it should go astray. They alone are the safest depositories of the ultimate powers of government.

Were we directed from Washington when to sow and when to reap, we should soon want bread.

I think myself that we have more machinery of government than is necessary, too many parasites living on the labor of the industrious. Government big enough to supply everything you need, is big enough to take everything you have. . . . The course of history shows that as a government grows, liberty decreases. The two enemies of the people are criminals and government, so let us tie the second down with the chains of the constitution so the second will not become the legalized version of the first.

Nothing can now be believed which is seen in a newspaper. Truth itself becomes suspicious by being put into that polluted vehicle. The real extent of this state of misinformation is known only to those who are in situations to confront facts within their knowledge with the lies of the day.

> A wise and frugal Government, which shall restrain men from injuring one another, which shall leave them otherwise free to regulate their own pursuits of industry and improvement, and shall not take from the mouth of labor the bread it has earned. This is the sum of good government, and this is necessary to close the circle of our felicities.

> The man who reads nothing at all is better educated than the man who reads nothing but newspapers.

All these quotations come directly from the pen of our third president (1801–1809), an author of the Declaration of Independence and a Founding Father, Thomas Jefferson.

Does anyone, Democrat or Republican, question his patriotism?

Each quote sounds identical to things Donald Trump has said on crony capitalism, military security, guns, overregulation, government oversight, democracy, elites, bureaucracy, media misinformation, fake news, and limiting government in our lives during his presidency.

As patriotic an American as Jefferson, Trump speaks as the real populist American voice, not for the elite globalist views of his immediate predecessors. His views are embodiments of the sentiments of American citizens and a sovereign nation.

Listen to Thomas Jefferson even if you can't stand Trump. Then realize that they are one and the same. Trump is a new voice but one that resounds with American history from its founding to Lincoln and Teddy Roosevelt.

Anti-Americanism: Why Europe Hates Trump

Let me take you back to the year 2012, when President Obama was running against the presidential nominee for the Republican Party, Governor Mitt Romney.

During the second debate, which focused on foreign policy, the sitting president delivered (twice) a line that would live in infamy: He mocked Romney's aggressive stance on Russia, which the Republican candidate described as being America's "greatest geopolitical foe."

As it turned out (unlike the Russia-mad Dems today), the Democratic National Committee (DNC) knew that Romney would bash Moscow and had crafted a Twitter-ready retort. It read: "The 1980s are now calling to ask for their foreign policy back."

Democrats all over America all laughed, and the rest of the world, especially in Europe, chuckled right along with them.

Why did they laugh? It wasn't a particularly funny joke. The delivery wasn't exceptionally well executed either. Were they laughing at Putin? Perhaps at a stiff Governor Romney? Or at America itself? Were they all disciples of Francis Fukuyama, laughing at Romney for thinking that history is still plugging along, that it had not in some Hegelian fashion ended?

Of course, it wouldn't be long before Romney was proved absolutely right. As the Georgians already knew from their brief war in 2008, President Putin was indeed a geopolitical threat to the West. The Ukrainians have found out the hard way again and again. The Eastern and Central European parties, to their credit, weren't as shortsighted as most of their Western European counterparts, which triumphantly celebrated America's leftward lurch under President Obama.

The European Union in particular showed its true anti-American stance and embraced Obama with a zeal rarely seen in modern politics. They nearly anointed him. But why?

Yes, the Cold War had ended some decades earlier, but the Cold War wasn't solely about Russia versus the United States. It was about capitalism versus communism.

Indeed, the Western, capitalist countries spent much of the Cold War fighting with one hand tied behind their backs. The so-called mixed economies of postwar Europe and the United States hadn't (and still haven't, really) given way to consistently capitalist social organizational and market structures.

Europe in particular is permanently tilted toward socialism, and the left still holds sway over most of the Continent. There is energy on the European left.

America's Reagan revolution and Britain's Thatcherite ascendancy completely upended postwar politics in both of those countries. Not so for Europe. Britain, in which wartime rationing was largely still in place (a particularly wasteful kind of centrally planned command economics), was suffering intermittent power shortages—brownouts—like some sort of developing economy. London was often paralyzed by unionized labor going on strike and had received an International Monetary Fund (IMF) bailout for a balance of payments crisis in government finances. America was suffering from Jimmy Carter's malaise—stagnant growth, price inflation, and an oil shortage—which was dealt with by (you guessed it) government rationing of gasoline.

Within the space of Margaret Thatcher's three splendid terms (1979–1990), the United Kingdom again became an economic powerhouse and has remained so ever since. Post-Brexit "Global Britain" has plans to throw off the shackles of EU regulation and become the free trading global powerhouse it once was, if allowed.

Ronald Reagan's 1980 election would see Republican control of the White House for twelve years, free market policies, and a reformed Democratic Party that would have felt at home in Presidents Nixon's and Ford's White Houses, though Democrats would never say it.

The transformation of the domestic economy produced such a boom that the great question of the last 200 years had its answer: Capitalism produced such immense riches that minor forms of socialism became a small price to pay for the advancement of humanity. Democratic capitalism not only in America but also around the world raised living standards as never before, cured diseases, led to greater longevity, and allowed people to prosper.

Countries, such as Cuba, North Korea, and Venezuela, that remained mired in pre-1980s social organization could never hope to give their people such standards of living.

This story is familiar to most people on the right of the political spectrum.

What often escapes notice, however, is that most other countries in the developed West did not experience similar revolutions in their politics. In 2018 France and Germany both largely fell into this category.

Indeed, whereas America and the United Kindgom experienced paradigm shifts to the economic right of the political spectrum, France experienced the exact opposite in 1968.

Whereas unionized labor was never again a major political force in America and Britain, French unions are still capable of paralyzing the country at will, and German unions remain some of the most powerful political entities in the world. France has a majority of its workforce employed by the government and has tax rates you wouldn't believe. In truth, socialism is what's wrong with today's Europe and its EU project. It also underscores why Europe is anti-American to the core.

Present at the creation of all major European institutions were politicians who bore allegiance to political stripes that have since been proved to be subpar, inferior alternatives as social models and ideals. Conservatives and Christian Democrats have outperformed European liberal and socialist parties in Western European countries every time, especially the founding signatories of the Treaty of Rome.

France, a political universe unto itself, left an exceptionally deep mark on European superstructures as the most powerful and influential European country until it was supplanted by the unified (and more capitalist) Germany. France's dirigiste centralized power structure is the lay of the land to this day in the European Commission. To make matters worse, the trend in America was, until Trump's election, going in the same wrong direction.

Forty percent of the American public, it was found, preferred socialism to capitalism. A poll of millennials revealed that a third of them think George W. Bush killed more people than did Joseph Stalin. So much for facts and a solid civics education.

At the same time, the trend on the left has turned: Multiculturalism has become a more powerful force than labor solidarity. Whereas unions across the West opposed liberalizing immigration rules in the 1970s—migrants were seen as competition to unionized labor—the broader left has now decided that fully "open borders" is the only just state for immigration laws and illegal sanctuary cities are to be blessed, not cursed.

Tellingly, the unions never budged on their protectionist position, and many of their members, it appears, ended up backing Donald Trump for president in 2016. This, as is the case with many other positions of the Trump administration, has been horrendously misinterpreted.

The Trumpian insight is that globalization can be free market and fair only if devoid of government intervention everywhere, not just in America. Europe hates hearing that message.

Currency manipulation, insuperable nontariff barriers, and outright national preferences will always be facts of life in countries that still have communist parties in power. Europe insists on acting as if this position were unacceptable. Yet the European Commission has imposed steep antidumping tariffs on Chinese steel at various times.

Similarly, the media made it sound like a flip-flop when President Trump said he supports NATO, which is not entirely obsolete. Seemingly, they must have forgotten that the "NATO is obsolete" rhetoric was replaced with "they're now dealing with terrorism because of my criticisms" months before the election.

Trump mentioned that during nearly every campaign rally after NATO began implementing an antiterrorism agenda, and it was one of his major talking points.

But Trump never gets the credit.

Nor does his insistence on Europeans sharing the burdensome cost of their own defense and security. Socialists like "free" things. The culprit here is not only shortsighted European politicians with anti-American sentiments; it is the press, which refuses to come out of its bearish inclination to bash and hate the U.S. president. The media lead the Trump resistance forces.

Must he continuously pay lip service to NATO after it significantly changed its position to reflect his views of current security priorities? After more countries are finally paying up?

The double standard is in plain view: Lest we forget, Obama's State Department was literally recorded saying "F*ck the EU" and didn't suffer the pile-on that the Trump administration has received from the press and so many European politicians. This is despite Europe's agreement with his new actions, whether in Syria or on NATO or on economic policy (not climate change).

Press alarmism is still in a bear mode when it should be bullish, and the politicians (Democrats in the United States included) who are naturally inclined toward anti-Americanism are champing at the bit to keep criticizing this "failed" presidency.

The American press must realize that they are playing into the hands of a latent anti-American strain in the European Union and that the old rule that politics stops at the water's edge should count for Republicans as well as Democrats.

Most important, we cannot normalize this behavior among European politicians. Loathing the American president is unacceptable. Looking down on Americans as fascist is ahistorical and without evidence or merit. It should never be accepted as the legitimate norm.

Right now, it seems it is acceptable to be anti-American in Europe as long as a Republican is in the White House. We hear it all the time in European capitals: "When can we get Obama back?"

This administration's priority in Europe should from this day be twofold: Make better friends and let everyone know that alliances aren't dependent on political parties. You're either a friend of the United States and pay your fair share of the burden or you are anti-American no matter which party holds the presidency.

One other person understood this well.

Thatcher and Trump: Twins in Politics

Margaret Thatcher was a most divisive prime minister. She transformed British history and saved her country. She put the "Great" back into Great Britain.

Everywhere she went, she sowed division: in her party, in UK politics, and in world affairs. To this day, her legacy is bitterly debated. But she was unique as the first woman to be prime minister and as a true conservative.

She was extremely successful in carrying out her agenda. If she had not succeeded, her country would have gone from crippled to doomed.

Today we call it Thatcherism. Her ultimate successor (Tony Blair) had to redefine a (new) Labour Party to look more like Thatcher's Tories to get elected. Divisiveness is the result of bringing into the open an underlying, festering, fundamental disagreement that few wish to acknowledge but that needs to be resolved.

Trump is the perfect analogue. He is divisive in his party, in U.S. politics, and especially in foreign affairs. But in the end, we will all be Trumpians.

He is unique as a nonpolitician and a total outsider. His ambition is to disrupt politics as we know it, and he is doing just that, and rather masterfully.

He seems, against all odds, to be succeeding in his "America first" agenda.

Hence, there will be policy and career winners and losers and therefore much resentment about his achievements. The underlying disagreement is between those who seek to preserve the United States as a specific historical entity, a democratic republic, and a constitutional nation-state and those who seek to redefine the nation as an elitist and globalist abstraction.

This tension already existed in both parties and was shown in the inability of the United States to deal with a host of domestic issues (terrorism, immigration, outsourcing, stagnation in the middle class) and in world affairs (with the European Union, on migrants, on radical Islam, etc.). It is predictable that Trump will be reelected in 2020 and the Democrats eventually will win a national election by redefining themselves, as the British Labour Party did after the reign of Margaret Thatcher ended.

Hollywood could eventually make a film about Trump in his declining years starring Alec Baldwin as Trump. It will be a favorable treatment this time.

But like Lady Margaret Thatcher, who eventually was elevated, Trump may never be fully loved by the powers that be. Yet without him, America would still be crippled, locked into no growth, and moving toward creeping socialism.

Thank God for Thatcher and her twin, Donald Trump.

Forget Left and Right: The New Fault Line for Trump Is Patriots versus Globalists

The European Union said there was nothing else available, and so this is the deal that is right for the United Kingdom in the Brexit withdrawal negotiations. That was the gist of Theresa May's argument for the deal she negotiated. Does this sound like the leader of a proud and productive nation, the fifth biggest economy in the world, and the very founder of modern democracy? A country trusted to wield nuclear weapons and bearing a veto on world affairs?

Peddling the withdrawal agreement on a flight to the G20 meeting, she displayed the supplicant attitude that her government took throughout the protracted Brexit negotiations. Where was the bulldog spirit? Where was the "Great" in Great Britain?

Sadly, May's stance is typical of political establishments across the Western world. Since World War II, most liberal politicians, including those in the United States, have been hoodwinking their citizens and herding them toward postnational globalism. The patriotism of common people is derided, if not excoriated.

We see this all the time in attacks on President Trump by the media, by Never Trumpers, by globalists, and by academics.

Mass immigration has dramatically changed the demography of the UK and other European countries as well as the United States, shifting the electoral balance in major cities. But the culprits for the demise of national identity in society are not the incomers but a middle class so ashamed of its country that any expression of national sentiment is perceived as far right, xenophobic, or racist. This pejorative use of the label "right" is a convenient means of vilifying opposition to the prevailing set of liberal opinions, now literally policed as "hate crime."

Students are more likely to see themselves on the left of the political spectrum, but scratch below the surface and you will find that the fault line is not really socialism versus capitalism. They won't get their smartphones or skinny lattes from nationalized industry. Unlike the radical campus activists of the late 1960s, today's students are in fact very proestablishment.

David Goodhart perhaps best conceptualized the social divide, which in the United States is openly discussed as a culture war, in his book *The Road to Somewhere.*

On one side are Anywheres, the graduate class who populate the upper echelons of our political and cultural institutions and dominate professions such as teaching. Upwardly mobile, they have little sense of belonging to their hometown or country. These rootless citizens of the world contrast starkly with Somewheres, who value their families, community bonds, and nationhood and see the impact of globalization as a threat to their culture. You are more likely to find Somewheres in the pub and Anywheres in an expensive, trendy ethnic urban restaurant.

The Somewheres are more numerous; they are the ordinary people. Are they left or right? Ask them about public services and unscrupulous business practices and they will espouse state provision and regulation. But ask them about queen and country or the extremes of identity politics (such as transgenderism) and they will appear more conservative than progressive. Indeed, Somewheres are a mixture of working-class Labour voters and "Middle England" Tories.

Brexit has exposed the redundancy of the old left-versus-right dichotomy, as has Trump.

The same transcending of the spectrum is happening across Europe, as illustrated by Marine Le Pen's National Rally in France and by the marriage of the Five Star and Lega political groups in Italy (previously positioned as left and right, respectively).

Steve Bannon's "The Movement" is building links between such parties, following the success of Donald Trump in luring blue-collar workers from their habitual attachment to the Democratic Party.

The established social democratic and center-right parties are in serious decline throughout Europe. Belatedly, the people have realized that their representatives take votes for granted while pursuing policies that are gradually destroying Western civilization: using identity politics to divide and rule; practicing moral relativism to subvert the Enlightenment triad of democracy, freedom of speech, and equality before the law; creating by stealth an Orwellian surveillance system; making unholy alliances with global corporations; and sending hard-earned taxpayers' money to dastardly regimes.

The terms "left" and "right" originally appeared during the French Revolution of 1789 when members of the National Assembly divided into supporters of the king to the president's right and supporters of the revolution to his left.

That is all very outdated. As the *gilets jaunes* riots in France indicate, the New World Order is stoking the ire of the masses. "Extremists" are setting fire to cars and pelting the police with road furniture. The *Guardian* suggests that they are right-wing; the *Telegraph* suspects leftists. The protesters don't care how they are labeled. They have lost faith in politicians and their media lackeys.

Each country will have its own flavor of antiestablishment agitation, but the phenomenon is basically the same. A people's revolt is brewing, and right against left is not the frame.

Patriots versus globalists is a more apt description of the new ideological divide, which will shape the politics, economics, and culture of the next decades.

Trump has redefined the ideological spectrum and realigned U.S. and now global politics.

What's at Stake?

America has created institutions of government, economy, and law that provide unprecedented freedom for its people and a body of natural scientific knowledge and technological achievement that makes possible a level of health and material prosperity undreamed of in earlier times and unknown outside the West and the areas it has influenced.

Do we fully appreciate this?

This is what is at stake right now. Elections matter! Forces on the left seek to destroy the very roots of our culture and the foundation of the rule of law and market economies. We should not let them.

The late novelist V. S. Naipaul, born in Trinidad of Indian parents, is right to speak of the modern world as "our universal civilization" shaped chiefly by the West and its exemplar, America.

Most people around the world who know of them want to benefit from the achievements of our science, medicine, and technology. Increasingly, they also want to participate in our political freedom and enjoy our economic prosperity.

The evidence suggests, moreover, that a society cannot achieve the full benefits of this technology or freedom without a commitment to reason and objectivity as essential to knowledge and to the political freedom that sustains it and helps it move forward.

The primacy of reason and the pursuit of objectivity, therefore, both characteristic of the American experience, seem to be essential for the achievement of the desired political and economic goals anywhere in the world but best exemplified in American exceptionalism.

The civilization of the West as embodied by America, however, was not the result of some inevitable process through which other cultures will automatically pass. It emerged from a unique history in which chance and providence often played a vital part.

The institutions and ideas that provide for our freedom and improvement in the material conditions of life cannot take root and flourish without an understanding of how they came about (our founding) and what challenges they have had to surmount. Non-Western people who wish to share in the things that characterize modernity need to study the ideas and history of Western civilization to achieve what they want, and Westerners, particularly Americans, who wish to preserve them must do the same thing.

The many civilizations developed by the human race shared basic characteristics. Most tended toward cultural uniformity and stability. Reason, though employed for all sorts of practical purposes in some cultures, lacked independence from religion and the high social status to challenge the most basic received ideas. The standard form of government was monarchy; outside the West, republics were unknown. Rulers were thought to be divine or the appointed spokesmen for divinity, and religious and political institutions and beliefs were thoroughly intertwined in a mutually supportive unified structure. Government was not subject to secular, reasoned analysis; it rested on religious authority and power, and the concept of individual freedom had little or no importance.

The first and sharpest break with this common human experience came in ancient Greece. The Greek city-states were republics, not democracies. Differences in wealth among their citizens were relatively small. There were no kings with the wealth to hire mercenary soldiers, and so the citizens did their own fighting.

As independent defenders of the common safety and interest, they demanded a role in the most important political decisions. In this way, for the first time, political life came to be shared by a large proportion of the people, and participation in political life was highly valued.

Such states needed no bureaucracy, for there were no vast royal or state holdings that needed management and not much economic surplus to support a bureaucratic-political class.

There was no separate caste of priests and little concern with existence after death. In this varied, dynamic, secular, and remarkably free context there arose for the first time a speculative natural philosophy that was based on observation and reason, the root of modern natural science and of philosophy, free to investigate or ignore other authority.

What most sets the Greeks apart is their view of the world. Where other peoples have seen sameness and continuity, the Greeks and the heirs of their way of thinking (us) have tended to notice disjunctions and to make distinctions.

The Greek way of looking at things requires a change from the use of blind faith, poetry, and intuition to a reliance on reason. It permits a continuing rational inquiry into the nature of reality. Unlike mystical insights, scientific theories cannot be arrived at by meditation alone but require accurate observations of the world and reasoning of a kind that other human beings can criticize, analyze, modify, and correct.

That was the beginning of the liberation and enthronement of reason, to whose searching examination the Greeks thereafter exposed everything they perceived: natural, human, and divine.

From the time they formed their republics until they were conquered by alien empires, the Greeks also rejected monarchy of any kind. They thought that a human being functioning in his full capacity must live as a free person in an autonomous polis ruled by laws that were the product of the political community, not of an arbitrary fiat from a man or god.

These are ideas about law and justice that have not flourished outside the Western tradition. The Greeks, however, combined a unique sense of humankind's high place in the natural order and the possibilities it provided with a painful understanding of its limitations. Those views were merged with Christianity in the centuries that followed.

This is the tragic vision of the human condition that characterized classical civilization. To cope with it, they urged human beings to restrain their overarching ambitions. Inscribed at Apollo's temple at Delphi were the slogans "Know thyself" and "Nothing in excess," meaning "Know your own limitations as a fallible mortal and exercise moderation."

Beyond these exhortations, they relied on a good but limited political regime to enable human beings to fulfill the capacities that were part of their nature, to train them in virtue and restrain them from vice. Aristotle made the point neatly:

> As man is the best of the animals when perfected, so he is the worst when separated from law and justice. For injustice is most dangerous when it is armed, and man, armed by nature with good sense and virtue, may use them for entirely opposite ends. Therefore, when he is without virtue man is the most unscrupulous and savage of the animals.

The justice needed to control this dark side of human nature can be found only in a well-ordered society of free people who govern themselves.

This brings us to the urgent need today: commonsense principles that are critical to limited government, support for a free market, and the building of great enterprising companies in a prosperous and growing economy.

All this is at stake as America, indeed most of the West, bends to the siren song of creeping socialism and cultural Marxism and closes off its cherished patrimony: the Greco-Roman–Judeo-Christian inheritance.

We cannot let this pass. We need to defend our heritage, uphold it. This is the role of conservatism: tradition, custom, and faith—the very things the left despises.

Their hatred for America is clear to see. Do not let them steal power. The consequences loom large.

Indeed, much is at stake, and Trump realizes this.

Déjà Vu All Over Again!

Yes, the present is starting to look a lot like the recent past. Yogi Berra was right.

In 2018, the Republicans did not hold their majority and keep control of the House, but the loss was less than many expected. All the pollsters and TV talking heads said this was impossible. They said that Trump would be put in his place. They said Beto and Antifa and all those loonies would come to power.

How could they get it so wrong? Again.

When you control the media, you control the news. And when you control the news—the flow of history, both past and present—you have the power to control the way the world thinks.

The American ideal is, after all, equality. Like sheep being led to the slaughterhouse, too naive to see the knife hidden behind the shepherd's back, there is great danger in this race toward conformity in thinking. It seems as though equality is the gravest threat to our civil liberties and free will.

Americans aren't buying it. The media get it all wrong.

Behind America's mainstream media is a fluid collective of top intelligence agencies—including the CIA, FBI, and NSA—which we've come to know as the deep state.

These agencies work in tandem to promote an agenda that they disguise as democracy and equality. The public thinks they were part of this decision, as though they exercised their own free will and judgment, when really, they've been told not just what to think but how to think through calculated manipulation. In this new prescriptive age of democracy, determinism is disguised as free will.

In today's world of rapidly advancing technology and instant-gratification news—where by the time the newspaper hits your front porch, it's old news—an unverified bit of information can be established as truth and then plastered across social media platforms. Just like that, the opinions and agendas of the few become the ethos for the masses.

The most glaring example of manipulation in recent history was the 2016 election, in which the deep state crafted a myth, a one-size-fits-all narrative for immediate American consumption.

Yet the best-laid plans of mice and men often go awry. Left behind was a trail of crumbs riddled with inconsistencies. Using advanced technologies, dissident intelligence practitioners from Veteran Intelligence Professionals for Sanity (VIPS) were able to sift through the troves of electronic data, accessing e-mails and text messages, and reveal a deeply buried truth: It wasn't the Russians who attempted to hack the election; it was done from within (look it up).

As we know now, the deep state, working covertly and closely with the Democratic National Committee and Hillary Clinton, orchestrated a plot to subvert the 2016 presidential run of Donald Trump.

Yet the unthinkable happened: Clinton lost. After Trump's victory, these intelligence agencies and Clinton herself (and much of America) were shocked. In a volatile mix of embarrassment and revenge, they continued to perpetuate the myth of collusion to delegitimize Trump's presidency, slander his name, and weaken his reputation.

A majority of Americans—the ones sucking at the teat of the mainstream media, the carnal consumers of CNN—wanted answers: How could this happen? Clinton and the deep state concocted a prescription to remedy their devastating loss, a fabricated panacea for all those wounded Americans. Clinton herself wrote a 512-page book to address the simple question "What happened?"

Instead of playing by the rules, she tried to buy votes and rig the election, calling in favors from her deep state cohorts, and she was still bested by Trump.

That's what happened. End of story. But no one wants to read that book. Instead, what they got was a never-ending story of all the ways in which the world conspired against her, most notably those pesky Russians. But it's pulp fiction, as phony as the dossier at the center of this ornate lie that begins with Christopher Steele, the master fabricator himself.

Using the mainstream media as its voice, the deep state is waging a slow relentless war on reality. Democrats, like sheep too distracted to notice the knife in the deep state's hand, were force-fed a narrative that confirmed what they wanted to hear.

Every headline, Tweet, and blog post acted as another turn of the screw, tightening their foregone conclusion: The Russians did it.

What the mainstream media wants us so desperately to believe is that Hillary Clinton lost the 2016 presidential election to Donald Trump because of the Russians. That a select group of Internet hackers were able to influence the results so heavily in Trump's favor that we need to exact revenge through endless circular investigations that drain the taxpayer's wallet and undoubtedly will lead nowhere, since after all, there was no collusion between Trump and Russia, as the Mueller report admitted.

Yet the media and the deep state didn't stop there: They want us to believe that Trump and his campaign have had long connections to the Kremlin and that Vladimir Putin, channeling Nostradamus, had the overarching foresight to plant a seed back in 2013 and set up Trump as a Manchurian candidate, so to speak, and sowed that seed and relationship to undermine America, using Trump like a puppet, his very own Moscow stooge.

Their aim is clear: Control humanity by convincing the world that what they say is true. Democracies do not have permanent ruling classes, but Clinton and the deep state don't want to relinquish their hold on the most powerful country in the world. With the wool pulled over our eyes, we could rapidly descend into the most oppressive tyranny ever seen.

Through oppression rises revolt. As in any successful revolution, we must band together, arming ourselves with voices that oppose the sheeplike mentality, in search of the truth.

Alone, our voices are lost like echoes down a water well. But together, our voice will be louder than the sum of its parts, breaking through these political echo chambers. In time, we will have the power to forge a new path forward, exposing the truth about the deep state's manipulation.

In doing so, we must look beyond the prescribed notions so deeply ingrained in the water supply, such as who is our natural sworn enemy. Yet these are the notions we need to challenge most. These are the ones that deserve the most critical thinking. Oddly, these are the ones the majority of America think require no further examination because we accept them as truths when they are in fact fabrications and manipulations by the deep state.

The recent elections rebuked the deep state and the Democrats (now increasingly socialists) and reenergized our commander in chief: Geo Deus.

They wanted a referendum on Trump. They got it. In 2020 we have another chance to prove it. The world awaits the outcome.

The Collapse of Free Societies

Starting in the 1960s, intellectuals, including most journalists, began accepting the view that all perception is interpretation and that everything is a matter of interpretation (postmodernism, deconstruction).

It was pointless or obtuse to ask if that view was true. There is no way to avoid some framework. We were told that there is always bias, that even the idea of being balanced reflects an interpretive bias.

In itself, this is a profound but relatively harmless insight. All it requires is that we be aware of our presuppositions. We can challenge our framework, amend our framework, even surrender our framework, but what we cannot do is pretend that we do not have a framework.

We can envisage a society in which there is a plurality of substantive frameworks but in which each and every one of those extant frameworks has within it the resources to agree to the procedural norm of being tolerant of other frameworks.

This shared procedural norm is reflected in the way religious toleration was possible (articulated by John Milton and John Locke and later by John Stuart Mill).

That is the society we thought we had in the Anglo-American world (civil association). There was a host of other supplementary procedural norms for conversing in such a society.

All this changed with the cultural triumph of scientism. In the scientistic framework, there is only one correct or objective framework. There is also, therefore, a scientific explanation for other prescientific frameworks and why people cling to them.

At first glance, this might not appear threatening. Once we all agree on the scientific facts, there will be intellectual and social harmony. It is the responsibility of universities to discover and teach those facts and the responsibility of journalists to bring them to the attention of the larger public.

Unfortunately, it did not work out that way. Some of the professors and even some of the journalists (otherwise bright and articulate) did not go along. Clearly, some people resisted "education."

Social scientists then explained why even some intellectuals and journalists could not be educated: They had a deformed previous framework (racist, homophobic, etc.). Education and debate did not work with those recalcitrant individuals. They were not only wrong, they were spreading mischief, specifically the wrong public policy positions.

Changing a framework was akin to a religious experience or revelation. Debating with them is counterproductive because it gives the false impression that there might be something legitimate about their thinking.

Education had to be indoctrination; anyone who disagreed had to be silenced for the public good. Imagine the self-righteousness needed to believe this.

What should such university-trained journalists do? First, they should all speak with one voice (the one they heard from the professors). Second, it is their duty to warn the public that advocates of certain policies are both wrong and dangerous. They could not do this by debating and refuting the arguments. Refutation works only when we share the same framework, and debate gives the appearance of legitimacy to the wholly misguided.

What happens when the deplorable part of the public (the part that does not take the *New Yorker* magazine as gospel) elects people who advocate the wrong policies? What if they are named Trump?

Again, there cannot be debate or refutation. First, they attack the policies by showing the underlying motives of those who advocate those policies (French intellectuals and journalists think reading Marx and Freud is good practice for this). They do not debate the merits or reasons; rather, they identify and attack the motives.

What if even this does not work? Then one must fabricate a Platonic-type myth about why the deplorably elected advocates are part of a vast conspiracy. The public lives in the "cave." It is the responsibility of the elite to fabricate a myth for the supposed public good.

All this, believe it or not, is based intellectually on the framework of scientism. It showed up first in sociological positivism, then in legal positivism, then in legislative positivism, and finally in educational positivism.

What we are witnessing today, particularly in the current Paris disorders, is the collapse of free societies. Free societies depend on a long cultural and intellectual history but are subject to both external and internal threats. In the United Kingdom and in France (and to some degree in the United States) what we are witnessing is (1) the loss of institutional memory, (2) the substitution of theory and technocracy for knowledge of historical practice, and (3) the indifference and blindness of financial/political/cultural elites to economic malfunction.

This all can be traced back to the prevailing educational predicament outlined above, which now infests teaching, journalism, the professions, and the culture.

Free societies need to exercise a judicious policy toward the great disparities of wealth and the question of truth. If they do not, they eventually will fail.

The New Dark Age of European Progressivism

I readily admit to being a Europhile. My family roots in Scotland and Holland and my education, faith, and upbringing, though quintessentially American, are deeply rooted in the European experience. My faith was founded in the Protestant Reformation that shook Europe 500 years ago.

I spent my formative summers teaching and touring throughout Europe while I was in graduate school and as a young professor. I still recall with enthusiasm my first trip to Europe in 1972 at age nineteen.

I studied and took degrees and have lectured at European universities. I was a Deutsches Austauschdienst at Kiel University and was made an honorary member of the Christian Democratic Party of the Netherlands in 1979. More recently I was a visiting professor at Tübingen University in Germany. I was president of one of the four ancient Scottish university trusts in the United States. I wrote a doctoral dissertation largely about European ideas in politics, philosophy, and economics.

I spent four years in Geneva, Switzerland, in an ambassadorial post in the United Nations from the late 1980s until 1992, when European history shifted and the Cold War ended. I had a front row seat as a deputy executive secretary of the UN Economic Commission for Europe.

I was an executive board member of the World Economic Forum, which started as the European Management Forum.

I was present at the Berlin Wall just days after it came down. My friends in Eastern Europe, the radical economists, all became leading figures—ministers, central bankers, and prime ministers—in their respective countries after the fall of the Soviet Union.

I was an adviser to the Polish government during its shock therapy and privatization. I speak several European languages; regularly read European books, magazines, and newspapers; and have been a firm supporter of the so-called Atlantic alliance my entire life.

More recently I have lived in the United Kingdom and taught at Oxford University and visited and spoken on the Continent regularly. To steal a line from President Kennedy, *Ich bin ein Europaisch.*

Thus, it is with a deep sense of disappointment and true sadness that I have to say what I am about to say: *Europe is dying.*

A new Dark Age is coming. Europe's churches are empty. A recent mass in one of the largest cathedrals was virtually unattended. The cathedral was not just sparsely filled; it was, except for a handful of tourists, vacant. Mass was being conducted in a side chapel large enough for the couple of dozen worshippers, all older women, who showed up for it.

Europe is adrift without a soul and is moving rapidly away from its moorings. Most of Europe's churches are unused these days, reduced to monuments for tourists and artists to admire.

There is a reason for this neglect.

In his brilliant book *The Cube and the Cathedral,* George Weigel describes a progressive European culture that has become not only increasingly secular but in many cases downright hostile to Christianity.

The cathedral in his title is Notre Dame, now overshadowed in cultural importance by the Arche de la Defense, the ultramodernist "cube" that dominates an office complex outside Paris. "European man has convinced himself that in order to be modern and free, he must be radically secular," Weigel writes. "That conviction and its public consequences are at the root of Europe's contemporary crisis of civilizational morale."

You will remind me that throngs of believers descended on Rome to bid farewell to Pope John Paul II. Yet even as Catholics mourned that pope's passing, socialists and greens in France decried the French government's decision to fly the flag at half-mast in his honor. Officials were reduced to claiming in response that the honor was afforded to John Paul in his capacity as a head of state, not as a religious leader.

The incident that forms the centerpiece of my critique is the debate over whether Christianity should be explicitly acknowledged in the European Union's constitutional treaty. By the time the constitution was completed, a grudging reference to "the cultural, religious, and humanist inheritance of Europe" had been shoehorned into the preamble's first clause. That's all. This was about as much religion as Europe could stomach in a constitution of some 70,000 words.

Practicing Christianity in Europe today enjoys a status not dissimilar to that of smoking marijuana or engaging in unorthodox sexual activities: Few people mind if you do it in private, but you are expected not to talk about it much or ask others whether they do it too.

Christianity is considered at best retrograde and atavistic in a self-described "progressive" society devoted to obtaining lifelong holidays, short work hours, and generous government benefits.

What is the deeper source of European antipathy to religion? For Weigel, the problem goes all the way back to the fourteenth century, when scholastics such as William of Ockham argued for "nominalism." According to their philosophy, universals—concepts such as "justice" and "freedom" and qualities such as "good"—do not exist in the abstract but are merely words that denote instances of what they describe. A current of thought was set into motion, Weigel among others believes that that pulled Europeans away from transcendent truths.

One casualty was any fixed idea of human nature. If there is no such thing as human nature, there are no universal moral principles that can be read from human nature. If there is no universal moral truth, a religion positing them is merely a form of oppression or myth, one from which Europe's elites see themselves as liberated.

These people look down on their American and third world cousins who continue to believe in such irrational flights of fancy.

As Richard Weaver said a half century ago in *Ideas Have Consequences*, "The issue ultimately involved is whether there is a course of truth higher than, and independent of, man, and the answer to the question is decisive for one's view of the nature and destiny of humankind."

I think the critics are on firm ground when they analyze the current condition of Europe, with its low birthrates, heavy government debts, worries about Muslim immigration, and tendency to carp from the sidelines when the fate of nations is at stake.

This is European progressivism, and it is coming to America.

In what is certainly the most attention-grabbing passage in an engagingly written book, Weigel sketches the worst-case scenario—the "bitter end"—for a Europe that is religiously bereft, demographically moribund, and morally without a compass: "The muezzin summons the faithful to prayer from the central loggia of St. Peter's in Rome, while Notre-Dame has been transformed into Hagia Sophia on the Seine—a great Christian church become an Islamic museum."

One need not find this scenario altogether plausible to feel persuaded by measured arguments about Europe's atheistic

progressive humanism and European Union–generated globalism, a cosmopolitanism severed from Europe's past.

Without a religious dimension, a commitment to human freedom is likely to be attenuated, too weak for people to make sacrifices in its name.

Europe's political elites especially, but its citizens as well,
believe in freedom and democracy, of course, but they are reluctant to put the "good life" on hold and put their lives on the line
when freedom is in need of a champion in the Balkans, Darfur, or
the Middle East.

The good of human freedom, by European lights, must be
weighed against the risk and cost of actually fighting for it. It is
no longer transcendent, absolute. In such a world, governed by
a narrow utilitarian calculus, sacrifice is rare, churches go unattended, and over time the spiritual capital that brought forth all
that we know as the West is at risk of being lost.

Here are five things that might turn the tables and perhaps
even begin to revive Europe:

1. Coming to grips with its unique place in world history and
   acknowledging the importance and source of those original
   ideals.
2. Realizing that culture matters and that Europe's culture has
   been the most formative for Western Christian civilization,
   or what used to be termed Christendom.
3. Accepting the social, political, economic, and especially military responsibility of a great continent, now more and more
   united.
4. Realizing the evident demographic realities and Islamization
   and stepping up to reverse them to avoid an eventual Eurabia.
5. Most critically, sparking the second great Reformation such
   that there is a wider recognition of transcendence and a moving of the spirit of God across the whole Continent from the
   westernmost shores of Portugal, Ireland, and Britain to the
   easternmost steppes of Russia.

I pray every day for such transformation and reawakening.

Weigel suggests that Europe is a society adrift, untied from the source of its greatness. The very cultural foundation that provided the values that made Europe great is disintegrating, leaving Europe (and soon the entire West, including America) on sinking sand.

More specifically, as the past is erased, rewritten, or ignored, the rich Judeo-Christian history of Europe is being left behind. At what cost? Why is European productivity dwindling to an all-time low? Why is European politics rife with senselessness? Why does Sweden have a increasingly higher level of its population living below the poverty line? Why is Europe undergoing what Niall Ferguson has called the "greatest sustained reduction in European population since the Black Death of the fourteenth century"? Why are "open borders" changing the very definition of Europe?

Could the recent woes of Europe be tied to the ever-decreasing Christian minority on this now decidedly post-Christian "progressive" continent?

I am reminded of Orwell's quote, "We have now sunk to a depth at which restatement of the obvious is the first duty of intelligent men." We should restate the obvious: "Culture determines civilization."

Without its distinctly Christian history, Europe would not be what it is. Or perhaps Europe would not have been what it was. However, from the perspective of our American pilgrim tradition there is more to lament than the secondary effects of a decline in European productivity, living standards, and art.

That is, merely reviving spirituality as an end in itself is not what Europe needs.

It demands rather a call back to its first love, to the God who blesses and rewards those who diligently seek and serve Him. Trump knows and embodies this.

2

Trump's World Economic Model

America will never be a socialist country.
—PRESIDENT DONALD TRUMP

Defending Capitalism

Capitalism is as American as apple pie. Among the Western countries, only the seafaring mercantile powers—Britain and the Netherlands—can lay claim to the horn of plenty. President Trump knows that, and he embodies its very spirit.

His economic czar, Larry Kudlow, defends the market better than almost anyone.

Capitalism is under attack everywhere from the House of Representatives to the socialists penetrating our culture, media, universities, big tech, and economic system itself.

You could make the claim that common sense is patient and capitalism needs to be so too if it is to succeed in the long term. Capitalism must succeed or we are all doomed.

If you chart all of history, the last 200 years will show that we have gone from sick and poor to healthy and rich. But what exactly made this dramatic and remarkable result possible? The market and the technological progress it has fostered.

Patience might sound antithetical to success in business. Believe it or not, when we talk about patience in business, we shoot for the same "bigger, stronger, faster" that the impatient flash-in-the-pan businesses are shooting for. We're after the same worldwide impact and influence. We just want it for the long haul, not only this fiscal quarter. Day trading does not an economy make.

We want our impact to contribute to the betterment not only of the company but of every group the company touches, including the workers. Stakeholder capitalism got the West to where it is now, and shareholder capitalism has shown its limits.

"Patient capital" investing has an eye on long-term stability and strength. It also bridges the gap between the efficiency and scale of market-based approaches and the social impact of pure philanthropy, which is another great American tradition rooted in generosity.

Patient capital has a high tolerance for risk, masters the long-term horizon, flexes to meet the needs of entrepreneurs, and refuses to sacrifice the needs of end customers for the sake of shareholders.

At the same time, patient capital ultimately demands accountability in the form of a healthy return: proof that the underlying enterprise can grow sustainably in the long run.

There are boom and bust cycles in any economy, and the shape of economic charts shows that companies invest in order to survive. Common sense tells us that such investment requires patient capital, which has a longer-term horizon.

Patient capital isn't just good for people; it's good for profits. A palpable impatience is infecting much of our decision making about investments today, and a decapitalization of business is accompanying it. It's happening in every sector and across industries. As a result, our standard of living as a nation has stagnated despite an increase of more than 50 percent in economic output since 1970. Real average wages in that period dropped until 2017, with wage growth picking up during the Trump administration.

There has been an increase in productivity (in the 2 percent range), but it is not keeping pace with historical averages and shows signs of leveling off. Declining prices and swelling competition leave nothing over for wage increases in American business. People who feel that their wages are going down in real terms are correct. In recent years, equity has actually flowed out of the corporate world. A large chunk of it has been invested in Ozymandian Chinese projects that can only crash. Destruction of capital on a scale never before seen is happening in Asia, and manipulation of the market is to blame. The crash will be spectacular.

Dividend payments have increased to half of current income, up from less than a quarter two decades ago. U.S. firms constantly announce stock repurchases, meaning that less money is spent on compensating every share.

The figures are astounding, a product of the mistaken belief that greater profits can be found outside the United States, and American companies continue to relocate overseas because of lower taxes, transfer pricing, or special tax relief packages called "holidays" offered by distant regimes.

Asian and European companies that follow systems defined by dedicated and patient capital are outperforming U.S. businesses in general. Those businesses invest in both tangible and intangible assets at a noticeably higher rate. Business owners in those locales consider themselves principals rather than agents, and so they seek long-term appreciation for shares, which generally are held by buyers for long periods. The wider role of family-owned firms is a double-edged sword in this regard.

U.S. publicly traded companies, by contrast, increasingly chase the approval of the transitory owner. The stockholders are indoctrinated to buy low and sell high—quickly. It's part of the rush of "playing" the market.

To feed the needs of the impatient stockholder, firms favor consumption and debt over earnings and capital formation—whatever will post the right numbers. Spending a fiscal quarter investing in assets would result in a knee-jerk reaction by stockholders to the resulting short-term decline in profits.

Thus, despite growth in many sectors, shareholders are not benefiting. If you compare U.S. shareholder earnings over the last thirty years with those of their Asian and European counterparts (and adjust for currency fluctuations and purchasing power), the U.S. shareholder has not done so well.

Europeans may have a serious stagnation problem in terms of jobs and employment, but they are still building plants, training their workforces, and developing new products. As for Asian companies, they are expanding in every possible way.

Why are firms in the United States behaving differently? There are four things to consider.

First, over the last fifty years, U.S. companies have concentrated on the need to improve their return on investment (ROI) and earnings per share (EPS). This was easy to do by decreasing the size of the denominator: Cut the asset's size down and keep the earnings the same. This results in an increased ROI. Then, if you buy your stock back, you further increase your earnings per share.

Like most of America, managements are influenced by their own compensation, which is based on current accounting profits or by unrestricted stock options that heighten stock price sensitivity.

Business schools have done a very good job of turning out bright people who have figured out how to do this "denominator magic" and do it efficiently: Underinvest in intangible assets and improve ROI. That's why net investment in fixed assets has fallen from twenty-five years ago.

Important intangible assets such as research, workforce development, and the establishment of brand names, new products, new markets, and first-rate distribution systems are all underfunded.

Second, U.S. industry continues to spend on mergers and acquisitions.

Much of the "investment" in acquisitions is only a change in ownership. It does not create anything new. Most of these mergers fail. If you build a steel mill in Arizona, for instance, you take a big hit. The start-up costs can kill you. Acquiring a mill, in contrast, means smoother sailing for now, though it also means less innovation, job creation, and improvement from the ground up.

U.S. companies also demand higher hurdle rates than do their foreign competitors; we won't invest unless we can expect a return of over 12 percent. That's the "cost of money" in our minds.

If you look at the ROIs of Asian, European, and U.S. companies, you will see U.S. companies outperforming the other two by about 5 percentage points. However, the higher hurdle rate in the United States gives Asian and European companies a performance umbrella to work under while dissuading U.S. firms from making a whole range of important investments.

Third, the real owners of U.S. business today are retirement funds. Fifty years ago, 70 percent of stock ownership was in private hands. Today more than 70 percent is in the hands of pension and mutual funds.

We have passed the responsibility for managing onto an agent, and this is essentially incompatible with capitalism. Lying back and cashing in dividends is not a recipe for creative destruction. Capitalism in the long run relies on people and their interaction with businesses.

When we lose that because our economy is based mostly on institutional and not individual investors, we lose core strength.

Individuals think about long-term gain. Most agents trade not only quarterly but nowadays by the nanosecond.

In an ideal world, the process of capital investment in a nation would align itself with the returns of private investors and those of society overall, but our brokers are making all the decisions for us, and their goals are chiefly to keep their clients happy by fattening their portfolios.

Although the U.S. capital system is still the most effective, that is not because it creates a divergence of interests between shareholders and corporations; it is in spite of that. The U.S. capitalist system in fact impedes the flow of capital to those corporate investments with the greatest social and private payoffs over the long term.

Fourth, the current governance system of U.S. companies does not serve the companies well. Bankers, customers, and suppliers can't serve as members of a company's board of directors. However, the Asians and Europeans don't have the same laws and take full advantage of their insight.

Further, we have laws that keep shareholding in the United States fragmented rather than concentrated. The power of group influence to inform companies for the better is therefore diluted. Management has to interpret signals from somewhere, and its views are frequently colored by the latest televised sound bite.

Corporate boards have become dominated by outside directors with no other links to the company, and they exert only a limited influence on corporate decision making anyway.

What's more, the agent who now does the investing for us does not face a tax consequence when he or she makes a trade. Therefore, pension funds will sell a company out on a whim or a rumor and will manipulate the last decimal point any time day or night. The rest of us have a 40 percent cost on selling stock.

In light of these challenges, how can Americans still practice patient capital and invest with common sense?

First, we must not fear failure in the short term even though stockholders may balk. This is easier said than done; we are a society that punishes failure. But making some investments that fail is essential to a dynamic plan of learning and growth. An institutional structure that overpenalizes failed investments may undermine the competitive capacity of a firm over time.

Some investments generate no profit but create capabilities that benefit future development. A company can increase profits by cutting out certain things, such as research and development (R&D), employee training, and customer relations. However, you would also "save" yourself the trouble of invaluable social returns such as watching candidates compete to work for you, seeing worker skills grow, and improving the quality of your product or service. You also wouldn't have to worry about happy customers and cutting-edge breakthroughs that raise your firm's leadership in the field.

Governance in most U.S. publicly traded companies is not for perpetuation or long-term investment and strategy. To curtail this trend and stop decapitalization, we should tax pension funds so that they have a transaction cost.

If they hold a stock for less than one year, those funds should be taxed at 40 percent, with the rate decreasing annually so that in year 5 there will be no tax on trades. Only then will pension funds look at companies that have some kind of long-term future.

This kind of proposal would have many advantages: It would increase government revenues, correct the tax inequity between individuals and institutions, punish short-term stock speculation, and focus ownership on long-term performance. It also would give management the courage to stop playing the game of denominator management.

It is likely that transaction costs would drop, because there would be less churning, thereby increasing investment in the U.S. economy. This could improve the savings rate, increase job numbers, and help get the capital gains tax down for transactions within a family or a closely held unit.

We also should relax some restrictions and allow banks to hold stock in companies and bank directors to sit on boards. They are allowed to do so in Germany and Japan.

These changes would start to align the firm with the purpose of society. That is a profound task in front of business everywhere.

We need to invest in those intangible items—training the labor force, new distribution systems, and research and development—for the future of business and capitalism as well as the American worker. If we fail to do so, we are going to end up in the near future seeing the last public company in the United States disappear. May the last stock buyback turn off the lights on the stock exchange before they ring the closing bell.

We can't let that happen, so Trump agrees that we must start defending stakeholder capitalism again here and worldwide.

Donald Trump Thinks Like a Modern-Day Adam Smith

Donald Trump is not an economic theoretician. He is an active business actor and political leader. However, like Adam Smith, he knows that there are three explanations of the origins of prosperity. First, prosperity is viewed as the product of magic. Second, prosperity is the product of conquest. Third, prosperity is rooted in human creative capacity. The first two views assume that wealth is preexisting; the third posits that prosperity can be created by human effort.

Trump's notion of capital reflects the third view. The kind of knowledge and effort involved, however, cannot be wholly captured by the liberal neoclassical economic assumption of a completely rational, utility-maximizing, fully informed homo economicus.

In the past, attention was focused on financial capital and physical capital as static, limited assets to be accumulated and managed. The source of economic prosperity was always taken for granted, largely as an existing condition to be exploited. In this context, economics was modeled on resource management in large systems, with growth and development resulting largely from management of costs and with little government intervention

For Trump, economic growth is not reducible to a mechanical model that can be planned at the macro level or directed by the state. It requires freedom, it requires inspired effort, and it requires commitment to a larger "spiritual vision," a sense of American greatness.

Economic development is also, as Peter Berger reminded us in *Pyramids of Sacrifice*, a "religious category." Economic development is clearly a vision of redemptive transformation. President Trump spelled this out convincingly in his State of the Union address in January 2018.

This sense of capital is founded on an understanding that all resources are entrusted to people. It posits that individual persons, families, and groups are called to preserve and develop a wealth of resources for which they are accountable now and later and which must be managed and deployed wisely. Thus, spiritual capital is about this stewardly entrustment of responsibility and a care for the creation it exhibits.

Trump knows this intuitively.

Within the Judeo-Christian inheritance, creative obedience or norms in economic activities are a primary way for adherents to acknowledge and demonstrate faith.

Such capital is reflected economically in three ways. First, phenomenal economic growth has been associated with the technological project that cannot be explained in traditional ways. Second, some people are more productive and entrepreneurial and work harder than their counterparts in other developed or undeveloped national economies. Third, some people are more philanthropic than other people, more than any in the history of the world.

How is Judeo-Christian spiritual capital related to economics and particularly to the democratic capitalism featured in Trump's America? Part of the answer depends on how one understands economics. Economics as a discipline is often very helpful, and individual economists often present important insights. However, understood as a pure social science, economics has not generally been useful for two reasons.

First, there are no timeless truths in any of the social sciences, only occasionally useful, highly qualified generalizations. Second, economic institutions and practices interact with other noneconomic ones. We can neither understand economic phenomena independently of history and other social institutions nor reduce our understanding of other social institutions to economics.

Trump knows that markets and trade, including international trade, have existed from time immemorial. He also knows, as did Adam Smith, that to be mutually beneficial they must be free, fair, and reciprocal.

It is of course the presence of technological innovation that accounts for the extraordinary importance of market economies in the modern world and in the American experiment.

David Hume (an empiricist and historian among many things) and his friend Adam Smith (a moral philosopher and the first economist who held a Scottish Enlightenment view of historical stages) were the first to appreciate the connection between technological innovation and free market economies.

The connection between economic phenomena and other social phenomena is reflected in Smith's two most important works: *The Wealth of Nations* and the earlier *The Theory of Moral Sentiments*.

The head and heart are tied together and produce the kinds of unprecedented economic results we are experiencing in the Trump era. President Trump has made this connection, and his policies are aimed at economic growth for all citizens, not for a few, an elite, Wall Street, or any subgroup. Everyone is participating for the good.

If you want to comprehend Trump, think like Adam Smith and praise the results.

Trump's Populist Economics

Davos Man is dead, and we need a new kind of economics to replace globalist multinational corporations. The place to look for this may be micro, small, and medium-sized enterprises (SMEs).

Trump knows this, and his world economic model revolves around the place where innovation takes place, companies are started and grow, and most jobs are created. Ninety-nine percent of American jobs are in SMEs, and it gets easier every day for normal people to run small, profitable projects over the Internet.

You don't hear anything about these companies at Davos, probably because the eye-watering $1 million entrance fee is meant to keep riffraff like them out.

Forty-odd years ago a kindly German economist living in Britain named E. F. Schumacher delivered a sanguine argument in his telling book *Small Is Beautiful*. Its equally weighty subtitle was *Economics as If People Mattered*. It was ranked among the 100 most influential books written since World War II by the *Times Literary Supplement*.

Schumacher's argument assaulted the meaning of "progress" in the liberal economic lexicon. He asked what had gone wrong when a few live in almost obscene wealth while large parts of the world and portions of our own nations barely get by. The book was a call to arms, an attempt to understand things we all seemed to have forgotten: What is value? What actually matters in life? Do the means always justify the ends? What is work for? Is big always better?

The major question asked, which remains most relevant for Trump, is: Who put all these elites and experts in charge?

This was the original tract of "populist economics." These are questions that reverberate even more demonstrably today as we witness nearly total frustration with globalization and the uneven economics and the havoc it has wrought. The globalist Davos crowd has delivered wealth and a livelihood for themselves, but what about the rest of us?

Trump thinks that message should not be lost on leaders around the world, captains of industry, or governments these days. It could be rephrased as follows: Small and medium-sized enterprises are the lifeblood of our economies. Listen up, prime ministers and presidents everywhere.

SMEs are the places where jobs are created, the location where economies truly prosper and innovations take place. In our current age we should realize that SMEs are beautiful—the place of economic action. We need to cultivate them as good places and places for good.

Look at some telling statistics: Small and medium-sized businesses accounted for 99.3 percent of all UK private sector businesses at the start of 2018. Total employment in SMEs was 15.7 million, accounting for 60 percent of all private sector employment in the United Kingdom. Three times more new jobs were created by SMEs than by companies in the FTSE 100 in the last five years. This is where the current economy is centered, where people live and work. The same thing is true in the United States and elsewhere, but the elites despise and look down on SMEs the way they despise and look down on the common person.

SMEs are important in terms of employment and gross value added (GVA), especially in smaller countries. However, they are also significant in Germany, where they account for a high percentage of GVA. The German *Mittelstand* is well known for its characteristics and world-class companies.

This is also true in the United States, where 30 million SMEs accounted for two-thirds of net new private sector jobs in the last several decades. According to international statistics, SMEs, provide more than two-thirds of all jobs in Africa, Asia, and Latin America and 80 percent in low-income countries.

Trump believes that we should celebrate these engines of growth and ask how they can do even more. What we need is a new way to foster SMEs, and that revolves around capital itself.

One way to foster SMEs is to favor flat tax regimes that put money back into the hands of the populace. Tied to that is what is called purchase order financing. That is a new way of getting funding to suppliers when they most need it. It has the potential to attract and boost smaller suppliers, enabling them to handle bigger contracts more reliably, creating a more resilient supply chain, and lowering input costs while helping contractors deliver on time and on budget.

What exactly is SME capital? Is it possibly the very core of an emergent populist economics? It is a completely new way of financing small and medium-sized businesses that are supplying into large supply chains, based on the buyer's creditworthiness but without any advanced payment by the buyer or impact on the buyer's balance sheet. And it can be insured for risks.

Cash is advanced to suppliers at the time when it's most needed—when the purchase order is issued—up to 50 percent of the value of the purchase order.

This process involves the buyer as a critical participant, but at zero cost to the buyer and with no impact on the buyer's balance sheet. The supplier pays a finance charge with no need for security or any director's guarantee. For the supplier this amounts to unsecured borrowing that is available earlier and more flexibly than other forms of funding. It is cheaper than invoice-based finance and certainly cheaper than debt on the balance sheet.

Such a form of capital could be made available to construction and other industry suppliers, providing access to finance that traditional providers, such as large banks, struggle to advance, especially in light of the lack of need for security or collateral.

Such supplier resilience reduces the risk of supplier failure and enables smaller suppliers to take on bigger contracts than would be possible otherwise. This grows small, local companies into medium-sized ones and in the process adds many jobs and fosters economic growth.

Supply chain resilience means that not only do suppliers and buyers benefit, but suppliers are attracted to work with buyers that take the needs of their suppliers seriously. There is also a significant cost savings as more viable suppliers means keener competition, lower prices (potentially with big savings for buyers), and more incentive for suppliers to innovate.

The social benefits of this kind of collaborative approach provide a unique selling proposition for contractors tendering for public sector construction projects and for companies looking for new suppliers anywhere. It would provide spending procurement budgets locally and allow for a Brexit-driven infrastructure push in the United Kingdom. In the United States and across deindustrialized Europe, it would put jobs back in down-and-out places that badly need them. In the developing world it would encourage market-based development and take businesses from start-up phases onto the next rung on the ladder.

This kind of financing favors smaller, more local suppliers, who are often more cost-efficient but have been unable to access finance. It strengthens local communities with the social and economic benefits of a multiplier effect by keeping spending and employment local, efficient, and sustainable.

This new and better scheme of financing would complement prompt payment codes and transparency and fits around stage payments and approval processes, helping to reduce cash flow volatility. Time is money, and this fixes that problem. We need a market-oriented populist economics that benefits real people and the firms they create.

SMEs often struggle because they can't fund growth and don't have the financial ability to face off against giant companies. This process of greater flexibility to fund anything, including additional equipment, software, materials, manpower, or services such as training, puts them back in the game and makes them truly competitive. It is a lifeline.

Trump and his Small Business Administration, at one time headed by his friend Linda McMahon, say that SMEs need a sustainable way to do business collaboratively. By helping small and medium-sized suppliers compete and grow, we all benefit. We achieve what we all want—economic growth at a more robust and sustainable rate of development—while creating better, well-paid jobs, jobs, jobs for hardworking, talented everyday people. This would alter and renew our entire economic culture.

This is Trumpian economics. Combined with fairer taxation and deregulation, it can transform economic growth and performance wherever it is practiced.

Thirty-Five Trumpian Propositions to Renew America

We all have our own lists: to-do lists, action lists, shopping lists, lists for this and lists for that. Whether it is Ten Commandments, seven habits, or nine suggestions, people have been making lists to keep score or form culture since time immemorial. Some lists nailed to cathedral doors in the form of Luther's Ninety-Five Theses actually changed history.

What's on Trump's list?

In the mid-1980s Peter Berger, the renowned sociologist, took on the Marxists and provided a tough-minded, provocative analysis of how capitalism, as the great engine of change, has revolutionized modern life. His empirical findings laid a basis for a powerful and testable new idea that was shaping what he termed "economic culture." The core idea was simply that the modern market economy we call capitalism transforms every other aspect of society.

In his final analysis, Berger postulated *Fifty Propositions* about prosperity, equality, and liberty. Marxism was proved wrong. The purpose of the stated propositions was "to take a look at these propositions as a whole and then to ask what practical uses emergent theory may have."

In a similar vein but not nearly as theoretically, Trump is forging a large argument, a case about the need to renew American culture while keeping very much to the framers' intention regarding the "pursuit of happiness." This is a firm rebuke of socialism in economics and also a case for the working person embedded in a larger economic culture.

Here are thirty-five propositions that taken together sum up nothing less than what Trumpian economics seeks to bring about for the renewal of American culture and its economy.

1. The pursuit of happiness is a uniquely American dynamic and outlook that continues to shape our destiny and also affects people around the world.
2. This transcendent right is not derived from any government, institution, or individual and is inalienable.
3. The Founders' bold proposition that the purpose of society is to support each individual's definitive right to live freely and happily is the most monumental experiment in history.
4. It follows that the central purpose of government, culture, and work is to put power in the service of human flourishing.
5. The rapid interlinked dynamics of technology, the growth of knowledge, and globalization have created a perfect storm of change—all unleashed by the American experiment.
6. Trade in ideas and products and the movement of people are leading to a more global and integrated yet complex technological civilization. The world's operating system is in effect being rewritten.
7. In this global economic transition, a new Schumpeterian cycle of creative destruction and intense entrepreneurial competition and repositioning is sweeping through like a tornado.
8. The prospects for civility are grounded in notions of human flourishing and conditioned on the premise that the private,

public, and social sectors all have something unique to provide the future.

9. The humanities are being rethought to become the keystone that holds together the converging forces of globalization, technology, and the explosion of knowledge as well as the interaction of different cultures and religions.

10. As moral animals, humans are inescapably interested in and guided by normative cultural orders that specify what is good, right, true, beautiful, worthy, noble, and just in life and what is not.

11. Human beings, in distinction from physical, biotic, and psychical entities, function as active agents in the entire range of fundamental dimensions: They think, they speak, and they believe.

12. As liberty, leadership, and happiness all depend on a well-developed self-regulating system of character, creative intellectual and artistic work requires self-delineation.

13. The world is now akin to a series of local area networks that form a cybernetic wide area network that is accessible through the World Wide Web. To be outside the loop is to be cut off from the forces shaping the future.

14. Humanity needs to befriend technological change and tame its darker side, since technology advances the prospects for human flourishing, empowers individual learning and innovation, and places learning at the core of economics. The humanities comprehend and record that fact, including the all-important human dimensions.

15. The traditional gulf between the spiritual and the economic can be bridged, as there is a spiritual basis for economic activity, a "spiritual form of capital" that is linked to human and social capital.

16. Genuine economic growth consists in creative management of endowed resources by stewards acting on their commitments, guided by normative laws, character, principled habits, and practices.

17. Markets influence and are influenced by the moral character of culture. Put simply, markets matter.

18. The state alone is no longer able or willing to fund the arts and humanities. Publics, as customers, are being asked to pay for services and goods on a contributory basis or in competitive real markets.

19. The humanities must be reengaged with intellectual renewal and with science, the arts, and religion in a constructive effort to envision and articulate a positive vision of a future of human prosperity and flourishing.

20. In a robust knowledge economy driven by innovation, the not-for-profit sector needs to be rethought and the humanities should play a critical role in helping to define both purpose and strategies.

21. Leaders in the private sector must articulate the larger humanistic goals of commerce, and leaders in the social sector and the humanities must come to understand the practical methods and rationales of knowledge-based economics.

22. If personal happiness consists of well-fitted energies of individual character, social happiness or justice consists of well-fitted arrangements of a differentiated society and the skills and actions made possible through the humanistic mechanisms of finance and money.

23. The integrated knowledge economy of global proportions is freeing us from the conflicts and shackles of the past. It is becoming more and more boundaryless.

24. As global dynamics in economics, knowledge, and culture become increasingly powerful, a complementary power develops for localities that understand their role in the global order. Ironically, globalization results in an enlarged value for the local.

25. Humanities-rich communities that succeed in linking leadership, education, and cultural assets are more competitive and offer the prospect of a greater state of well-being and wellness for their citizens.

26. Cultivating the potential for enlightened and responsible leadership appropriate to the new context of action means envisioning and designing a curriculum for a diverse leadership.
27. Victimhood as a model of social and political analysis is a variation on the same idea of "conscious detachment" that created rationalism and romanticism and, like them, is an intellectual dead end. Victimhood as a universal model paralyzes action toward and hope for some future good.
28. In the last decade a plethora of new laws, rules, and practices have made all organizations more accountable. The spread of higher standards for governance is laudable worldwide.
29. The future of democracy and civil society depends on the success of corporations as key structures through which people freely associate and work together in a highly diversified and productive society. Corporate organization in the for-profit and nonprofit sectors is the primary organizational structure for creating free and diverse societies.
30. The public humanities are a critical source of social capital. The adage that societies with an abundance of social capital are healthier, more democratic, and more prosperous has been proved.
31. As the wellspring of civic mindedness, the humanities will achieve their intended purpose when they help build more and longer lasting social capital.
32. If the humanities are to flourish and regain their rightful place in public life, thereby influencing public discourse for the good, they must be based in the philosophy of the good.
33. There is an urgent cry for humaneness, civility, and a restored sense that human persons and the cultures they form and interact in should be rooted in a theory of development anchored not just in ever-growing material wealth, necessary as that may be, but also in a philosophy of human flourishing.
34. Practical people may disagree about virtue or which virtues to exalt, but religion is the keeper of wisdom and personal

narrative that allow and encourage such dialogue and contain it in the public sphere.

35. More than ever in a complex and technological setting and on a lonely planet, we seek wisdom, a dialogue grounded in the good. Only then we can renew our culture.

This is the Trumpian worldview.

Car Wars

"The European Union doesn't take a lot of what we have, and yet they send Mercedes in to us, they send BMWs in to us, by the millions," President Trump lamented. "It's very unfair, and it's very unfair to our workers and I'm going to straighten it out."

The U.S. Commerce Department under a Section 232 investigation issued a report that would result in the unleashing of steep tariffs on imported cars and auto parts.

This is all about unfair trade. It poses a national security risk to the United States.

Is Trump right? Are there too many German cars in America? Here are some facts.

In 2017, the German auto industry sold 1.35 million vehicles to U.S. buyers. That was 8 percent of all our car sales.

The large German carmakers are Mercedes, BMW, and the VW Group, which includes Audi and Porsche as well as Volkswagens. Among all those German cars, some are actually produced in the United States. That total is about 800,000, of which half are exported elsewhere.

BMW has a huge factory in Spartanburg, South Carolina. Mercedes products are made in Alabama, and VWs are manufactured largely in Tennessee and Pennsylvania.

Make no mistake; Germany is most at risk in the entire European Union from any car war. The French and Italians do not send many units to America.

New U.S. tariffs would move up to 25 percent. They are currently at just 2.5 percent. EU tariffs on all auto imports are currently 10.5 percent. You can see the structural imbalance and lack of reciprocity.

New U.S. tariffs would add approximately $11,500 to the sticker price of the average German car sold in this country, according to industry estimates. The effect probably would be a 50 percent drop in those exports, according to one German economic forecast.

In other words, the $226 billion trade surplus Germany enjoys could quickly vanish.

"Look, we are proud of our cars," Angela Merkel, chancellor of Deutschland said. "We are allowed to be. And these cars are built in the United States of America. If these cars, which are no less a threat than those built in Bavaria, are suddenly a national security threat to the U.S., then that's a shock to us,"

Yet President Trump seems adamant.

Germany still refuses to pay its 2 percent of GDP to the NATO budget, and so Americans pick up their defense tab.

Trump's response was, "I love tariffs, but I also love them to negotiate."

Watch for the coming car wars at a dealership near you. Common sense dictates reciprocity—at a minimum.

A Dose of Fiscal Conservatism

Our national debt has reached $22 trillion. This is unsustainable.

We pay nearly $400 billion a year in interest. Citizens for a sound economy need to do something about it and get Congress to act. "Fiscal conservatism"—the public face of thrift—is a term used to refer to an economic and political policy that advocates restraint of government taxation, government expenditures and deficits, and government debt.

In an earlier era, this tendency was known as public thrift, because thrift was said to have both a public and a private side.

A major tenet of the American Revolution was "no taxation without representation." Americans insisted that their historic rights as Britons entitled them to a voice in setting tax policies, which the government in Britain denied. The issue was not the tax itself or its size but the fact that it was imposed without the consent of those it affected.

The Democratic-Republican Party of Thomas Jefferson supported a weak central government and a more laissez-faire approach than that of Alexander Hamilton's rival party, the Federalists. They opposed Hamilton's plan for the federal government to pay off debts owed by the states for the expense of the American Revolution because some of the debt was held by financiers and speculators (who did not deserve payment) rather than the original holders. Hamilton got his legislation passed and imposed taxes to pay the debts.

Jefferson strongly opposed having any national debt, although he relented when the opportunity came in 1803 to purchase the territory of Louisiana: Put it on the credit card, Napoleon.

The Democratic-Republican Party elected James Madison, James Monroe, and John Quincy Adams, but after the fiscal disasters of the War of 1812, it came to support most of the Federalist position, realizing that the nation needed a central bank and a steady income flow from tariffs.

In the mid-1800s, a new fiscal conservative political party emerged: the Republican Party. Unlike some of their contemporary counterparts, those fiscal conservatives were supporters of protectionism and tariffs.

In the early 1900s, fiscal conservatives were often at odds with the progressive President Theodore Roosevelt, particularly for his support of antitrust laws.

During the 1920s, President Calvin Coolidge's probusiness economic policies were credited for the successful period of economic growth known as the Roaring Twenties. After the great crash of 1929, however, Coolidge's policies and then Hoover's took the blame.

Coolidge not only lowered taxes but also reduced the national debt from World War I. His actions, however, may have been due more to a sense of federalism than to fiscal conservatism.

Many noted that as governor of Massachusetts, Coolidge supported wages and hours legislation, opposed child labor, imposed economic controls during World War I, and favored safety measures in factories and even worker representation on corporate boards. If he did not support those measures while president, it was because in the 1920s such matters were considered the responsibility of state and local governments.

During the 1930s many conservatives opposed Franklin Roosevelt's New Deal because it greatly expanded the scope of the federal government and regulated the economy. It wasn't so much that the government was doing this, that, or the other but that the federal government was doing it instead of state and local governments.

In general, Roosevelt did not raise taxes above the high levels Hoover had set. But he spent liberally to move the country out of its deep economic travail.

Roosevelt's treasury secretary, Henry Morgenthau, believed in balanced budgets, a stable currency, reduction of the national debt, and the need for more private investment. He accepted Roosevelt's double budget as legitimate, that is, a balanced regular budget and an "emergency" budget for agencies such as the WPA (Works Progress Administration), the PWA (Public Works Administration), and the CCC (Civilian Conservation Corps) that would be temporary, in force only until full recovery was at hand. He fought against the veterans' bonus until Congress finally overrode Roosevelt's veto and gave out $2 billion in 1936.

Morgenthau's most notable, though controversial, achievement was the new social security program: He managed to reverse the proposals to fund it from general revenue and insisted that it be funded by new taxes on employees.

In World War II there was broad agreement in favor of heavy taxes, with conservatives insisting that the income tax base be broadened to include the great majority rather than the 10 percent who paid all income taxes before 1942. America was at war, and we had to foot the bill.

Fiscal conservatism was most loudly and rhetorically promoted during the presidency of Ronald Reagan from 1981 to 1989. During his tenure, Reagan touted economic policies that became known as Reaganomics.

Based on supply-side economics, Reagan's policies cut income taxes, raised social security taxes, deregulated the economy, and instituted a tight monetary policy to stop inflation. Reagan favored reducing the size and scope of government, sought a limited government, and proposed a balanced federal budget. Despite this, the ramping up of the arms race in both nuclear and naval matchups ate through a lot of the gains in the bottom line.

Conservatism of the fiscal sort has had its supporters and detractors throughout just about all of American history. Unfortunately, some of the Republicans who ran on its premises did more to grow the bureaucracy and big government than even their opponents once they were in office.

Except for Margaret Thatcher's Britain, few countries have had an ongoing public debate in political circles about public thrift, the size and cost of government, or balanced budgets, let alone the rivalry between the individual and the all-powerful state.

On a communal and personal level Americans seem predisposed to policies of thrift in their personal as well as their civic lives. America has a net savings rate of zero, which means that a lot of people are leveraged and a lot of people are extremely wealthy. Both conditions are in a sense long term positions on America's future: one poor, the other rich. Behaviorally, however, they often act, spend, and vote quite differently.

When things are going gangbusters, all the focus is on spending and consumerism, not thrift. But when recession strikes, out from under the floor resurfaces that odd virtue, thrift, as in "I should have saved more and consumed less."

What is it about thrift, public or private, that makes it so hard to achieve? Does it necessarily contradict or oppose economic growth? Is it really a lost and forgotten virtue? Is that necessarily a bad thing? A paradox?

Democrats love free things and higher taxes. Republicans need to fight creeping socialism and spell out the cost of excessive debt over generations. Conservatism's central plank on fiscal matters is balanced books.

"Venture Politics": Referendums, Participatory Democracy, and the New Parties

A new wind is blowing in Western democracies. New parties, some no more than a few weeks old, have defeated established movements with far-reaching structures and much greater campaign funding. The disruption has reached the party-political sphere, with deep and lasting consequences for the West.

The first hint of the direction we are heading in came from Europe. The Eurocrat establishment had just finished negotiating what it hoped would be a constitution for the European superstate. The prospect that democratic governments would vote against their agenda was unconscionable, not worthy of consideration.

That is, until the referendums returned a negative in France, the linchpin of European integration. Ireland, Denmark, the United Kingdom, and Greece all delivered results that were not meant to happen. Some countries were forced to vote again and again until the "correct" result was achieved, a strategy currently being pushed by the Remain camp in the United Kingdom. In other cases, such as the various Greek referendums against EU-imposed austerity measures, it sufficed to ignore the result.

The great Nigel Farage got his start in a referendum to decide whether to join the euro or keep the pound sterling as the United Kingdom's currency. Having saved sterling, the United Kingdom dodged a bullet by avoiding the diktats of the neoliberal elite on that particular matter. To the extent that Brexiting from the European Union is possible, the lack of British participation in the common currency laid the groundwork for 2016.

No less liberal a place than California, where referendums are enshrined in the state constitution, returned a negative verdict on gay marriage in the mid-2000s. Switzerland, whose 800-year democratic culture has included referendums since the days before the separation of church and state, also buttresses the deeply conservative impulse of the population at large when faced with major changes to its system: It kept the one-family, one-vote system until 1974, when universal suffrage was introduced decades after the entire civilized world had given women the vote.

Direct democracy is clearly the way forward on many issues. The limitations of representational republicanism, parliamentary democracy, and other forms of indirect representation are myriad. They are systems for the pre-Internet age, in some cases even preceding the printing press. The class of legislators who claim to represent the interests of their constituents is rebuked by the approval ratings of the American Congress, which are now at single digits.

Pioneering a new model of representation, the Five-Star Movement (M5S) in Italy has found a way to square this circle. The membership is consulted on the political issues facing the party, and that is why M5S is so hard to categorize on the left–right spectrum. Governing in coalition with a right-wing party, M5S takes left-wing positions on a number of issues, such as foreign aid and refugee flows, because that's what its members voted for. Internal campaigns are heated but friendly, and the membership accepts the system as legitimating the party's stances regardless of the result. Such healthy democratic norms should be celebrated even when the result goes against one's preferences.

Nigel Farage's new party—the Brexit Party—copied this model successfully and rode to a first-place finish in its most recent electoral contest. The Dutch Forum voor Democratie (FvD) started out as a Facebook group in which citizens debated and voted on the issues of the day. Thierry Baudet, the thirty-something founder of FvD, is now in the Dutch parliament and had a first-place finish in the recent election to the upper house.

These new parties, which offer a disruptive alternative to the stale orthodoxy of the political establishment, are routinely called "populist" for giving people what they want.

President Trump did something similar in 2016. By bringing millions of new voters to the Republican Party and registering them so they could vote for his candidacy in the state primaries, he performed a hostile takeover of the old orthodoxy and rode to the White House on the back of millions of people who hadn't voted since the early 1990s, presumably because they felt that neither major party represented their views.

Participatory democracy has become a much more viable prospect. Even now, the establishment is moving to block it. The ultra-liberal Berggruen Institute, funded by the Wall Street billionaire Nicolas Berggruen, wants to temper this trend by establishing intermediating institutions. In his recent opus *Renovating Democracy*, Berggruen and his pet academics called for "citizen assemblies" instead of referendums to decide these issues.

It is unclear where these "juries" would get their political legitimacy. Unelected, randomly picked, and bombarded with propaganda from the establishment for months before they cast their opinion, they would be part of a transparently rigged system. French President Macron is a big fan of the citizen assembly, especially after the Irish referendum on lifting a ban on abortion returned the result the establishment wanted. Citizen assemblies are the establishment's answer to political disruption, and this is a shame considering that Macron himself seemingly brought much-needed disruption to the French political system.

The relevant comparison is to the start-up world in business. Just as venture capital has funded bootstrapped projects that changed the world, venture politics should be regarded as its political equivalent: New parties with new positions will bring a new balance to the West.

It remains to be seen if the neoliberal establishment actually believes in competition at the source of their own power or if it will fall into the protectionist reflex that it so decries in economic matters. Trump as disrupter should continue to ride this wave and stoke it everywhere in the world as a viable and democratic alternative to popular sovereignty and a way to tear down old regimes, cliques, and patterns.

Viva la populism.

Populist Rebellion

The motif of the era we are living through has emerged as one of rebellion against the establishment and the oligarchy that perpetuates it: Davos globalists and the deep state. It is evident everywhere from Brexit, to Trump, to Italy, to Brazil, to the yellow vests.

The larger question is whether a politically amorphous dissident army can upend the status quo.

The establishment's horror at the prospect of a successful rebellion contrasts with the history of a nation that was founded in such a rebellion. Remember 1776 and the shot heard round the world.

The ghost of rebellion that haunted the English psyche for centuries and that the authorities were determined to crush in 1776 was named Jack Cade. Have you ever heard of him?

In 1450, Cade led a makeshift rebel army against the forces of King Henry VI. He was almost certainly a peasant, but other than that, very little is known about him. That enabled him to shape shift like a specter of discontent.

According to some, Cade was plotting with Richard of York under the name "John Mortimer." According to others, he was Dr. Alymere, son-in-law of a Surrey squire, and still others believed he was a practitioner of witchcraft.

Jack Cade's real name is unknown to this day, as is his history before 1450. He appeared, it seems, out of nowhere in the human form of Jack Cade or whoever to haunt the kingdom into chaos.

What is known about Jack Cade is that he led a threateningly large group of peasants, small landowners, some clergy, and even some property-owning men to the gates of London, mostly in rebellion against taxation from the Hundred Years' War and pervasive government corruption. This group of minor gentry and rural laborers did not seek sweeping social change as much as basic government reform, mostly in the form of lower taxes.

Upon first hearing of the peasant rebellion, the king sent his troops to Sevenoaks, about eighteen miles southeast of London, to strike down the ragtag reformers. The king's troops were promptly defeated. Cade's impromptu army marched to London, where they were treated as victors. Londoners generally agreed that taxes and corruption were pressing problems.

Cade's army became enamored with its success and proceeded to storm the Tower of London and behead a few government officials, including Sir James Fiennes, the king's treasurer, and Sir James's son-in-law, William Crowmer.

The bodiless heads of Fiennes and Crowmer were placed atop stakes and paraded through town kissing each other. For good measure, Cade's men also killed the sheriff of Kent, who, needless to say, had intended to arrest Cade. The king's men regrouped and fought again but could gain no ground on Cade's army of malcontents, at which point Cade presented his list of demands to royal officials, who agreed to the demands and to granting pardons to the rebellion's participants.

The demands can be summarized as "run a decent government." With an agreement on the demands, the rebel army largely dispersed. King Henry, though, had no intention of meeting the rebel army's demands either to run a decent government or to pardon Cade and his men. The new sheriff of Kent chased Cade for forty miles until he finally stopped him with a fatal blow of a sword.

To further punctuate his rejection of the agreement he'd supposedly accepted, King Henry subjected Cade's dead body to a show trial. Upon being found guilty, Cade's corpse was hanged and then cut into pieces that were distributed throughout Kent as a reminder of the king's disposition on peasant rebellions. Finally, Henry had Cade's head staked on a pole on London Bridge, kissing no one.

The specter of Cade's peasant rebellion has haunted English historians and poets ever since: "For our enemies shall fall before us, inspired with the spirit of putting down kings and princes" (*Henry VI, Part 2*).

Peter Oliver, the loyalist chief justice of the Massachusetts court, wrote in his 1781 *The Origin & Progress of the American Rebellion*, "The Hydra was roused. Every factious Mouth vomited out Curses against Great Britain, & the Press rung its changes upon Slavery. . . . A Mr. Delany a principal Lawyer of Virginia, wrote the first Pamphlet of Note upon the Subject; which, as soon as it reached Boston young Mr. Otis, the then Jack Cade of the Rebellion . . . ."

More frightening to the oligarchs than the specter of Jack Cade was the idea of Jack Cade with a printing press marshaling a literate rebellion. Sending the sheriff of Kent to arrest Cade with a blow of a sword would do no good, because as John Milton had observed a century earlier, "Books are not absolutely dead things, but doe contain a potencie of life in them to be as active as that soule was whose progeny they are."

If knowledge had become untethered from a world of fixed relationships and its value increasingly lay not in the degree to which it supported and completed a stable and fixed edifice of knowledge and if books were not dead things, how was the sheriff of Kent to respond? He could hardly chase down an idea and put it to the sword.

Peter Oliver's evocation of Jack Cade as "The Hydra" demonstrates that in the new media world of the eighteenth century, the press could create many-headed ideas that could not be terminated by a sheriff's swift sword.

However, the foundation of colonial education was in fact the Bible, and Oliver undoubtedly was referencing the hydra in the Book of Revelation and fully intended his readers to think of the Judgment Day beast.

Only an oligarch would apply that metaphor to the many printing presses fueling the media war and not to the empire that wished to return to the days when rebellion could be quelled by putting a single man to death.

In the end, Oliver's interpretation lost, and the rebels' version of the hydra was memorialized in the American founding document: the Declaration of Independence ("He has erected a multitude of New Offices, and sent hither swarms of Officers to harass our people, and eat out their substance.").

The colonial oligarchs of the 1700s had feared that the press would transform the specter of Jack Cade into an irresistible force of history. When the prime minister requested that King George charge James Otis—the "Jack Cade of the Rebellion"—with treason (a crime cured only by execution), the king demurred.

It was too late. Though the king still harbored hopes of regaining control of colonial Boston, easy access to the press had transformed Otis's rebellion far beyond anything readily solvable with a sword.

In the end, Jack Cade vanquished the hydra with the consequential help of new media.

If Otis had had Twitter, the king's hopes for regaining control might have been dashed well before 1776. The distinction between the failure of Cade's rebellion and the success of the American Revolution is before our eyes today.

Trump, however, is a leader of a different kind of populist rebellion, one that understands that to be effective the rebellion must leverage media to become a movement that lives in ideas rather than through any individual.

Ironically, this makes Trump not a dictator (where the power resides in the person) but rather a true child of the American Revolution (where the power resides in ideas promoted through the media). Trump's power is generated by his persistent refusal to come to agreements with the oligarchy and the established elites because unlike Jack Cade, Trump's peasants won't get fooled again.

That's why populism today is not going to be vanquished any more than Trump will be destroyed. It is "We the People."

Trump's Wall

THE PROBLEM

The U.S.–Mexican border stretches for more than 2,000 miles across some very rugged terrain. It has become a symbol of insecurity and a complete failure of control.

It also has become the pivotal political issue between the two countries and the hot button issue in the presidency of Donald Trump. It is the issue that got him elected.

Trump closed down the government over new funding for his wall and acquitted himself well in the ensuing arm wrestling. Illegal trafficking in drugs, guns, and persons remains a reality that no amount of compassion can solve. Internment facilities leave much to be desired.

It is the economic opportunities that encourage a nearly constant flow of migrants into the United States. About 20 million illegal immigrants now reside in the United States, or over 5 percent of the nation's population. Mexicans account for half of the unauthorized immigrants, according to a recent Pew survey. Most of the other immigrants come from Central America. The trend is more caravans of illegals organized by NGOs coming from Honduras, Guatemala, and El Salvador.

Six states account for 60 percent of the illegals (California, Texas, Florida, New York, New Jersey, and Illinois).

Nevada has the largest share at 8 percent of its population. About 27 percent of all K–12 students now have at least one unauthorized immigrant parent. Although there is a valid economic argument for letting them stay, the institutional and political costs are extremely high. The problem continues unabated.

The source of the problem is the underdevelopment of the immigrants' countries of origin, which certainly don't benefit from the loss of risk-loving citizens: Anyone crazy enough to walk from Honduras to Texas has a lot of potential upside doing jobs Americans would like to do. Nobody ever got wealthy picking strawberries.

The escape valve that migration provides to dictatorial regimes such as Cuba and Venezuela should not be underestimated either. Three million people, about 10 percent of Venezuela's population, have walked away from that country. There are around 6 million Syrians who are "internally displaced" or have left the country altogether. It is up to them to fix their homelands, and they cannot do it from America or Europe.

As Donald Trump succinctly put it: "A nation without borders is not a nation."

A nation without patriots is not a nation either.

Trump Knows That the Business of America Is Business

In 1925, then U.S. president Calvin Coolidge boasted in a now familiar line, "After all, the chief business of the American people is business. They are profoundly concerned with producing, buying, selling, investing and prospering in the world."

Ronald Reagan said much the same thing in the 1980s but with far more charisma, and Donald Trump is reiterating that message as the core of his domestic agenda.

He went to an army tank plant in Lima, Ohio, while all the Democrats were trying to rip down the institutions of America from the voting age to the Electoral College, from the Supreme Court to immigration.

His plea was strongly worded. Trump blamed Democratic union leaders for General Motors's decision to shutter a plant in Lordstown, Ohio, eliminating about 1,700 jobs.

Such common sense isn't only for business. As a kind of practical wisdom grounded in the virtue of prudence, common sense is for all of life, everywhere, and at all times.

We live in a turbulent and uncertain age of constant betterment brought about by specialization, collaboration, and a sustained upsurge in the discovery of new and useful knowledge and technologies.

Yet even before Adam Smith penned *The Wealth of Nation* in 1776, he wrote a much more important book, *The Theory of Moral Sentiments*, in which he argued for such common sense.

That notion of benevolence and sympathy was rooted in a moral philosophy in which economic activity combined the best head with the best heart. Mind and soul were seen not as separated but united as a whole. Reason and faith were two sides of the same coin.

The operative tide was a "commercial republic," a society of liberty fashioned through trade and commerce to advance individual well-being—materially, intellectually, aesthetically, and morally. Commerce and governance were the twin pillars of the common good.

Although commercial activity was paramount, the common-sense mentality had implications for all the mediating institutions of the society in which life is lived and experienced: families, churches, voluntary associations, schools, and universities—indeed, all of civil society.

The dominant cultural values include endeavor, self-governance, collaboration, subsidiarity, and patriotism.

Such a collaborative and democratic state provides liberty for all; freedom of speech, thought, and religion; and property protected by the rule of law, all informed by the commonsense learn-by-doing virtues of self-governed persons.

The overwhelming processes of modernization, globalization, and digitization are putting to test our experiment in self-governance. The affiliated organizations so critical to its success have too frequently been abandoned or ignored.

Business, however, remains the first among equals in our materialistic and acquisitive societies. It is necessary therefore to bring common sense back not just in the realm of business but also in every corner of society and for the common good.

Common sense and the common good are in fact joined together. You can't have one without the other. You can't sustain one without the other.

The notion that business practitioners should play a significant role in the development of the country can be attributed to the common sense and fortitude of the many businessmen and businesswomen in the nation's very founding, notably Benjamin Franklin, George Mason, Samuel Adams, John Hancock, Betsy Ross, Robert Morris, and George Washington himself.

Those revolutionaries understood full well the necessary sequence of business success and the spirit needed to achieve national well-being. Their practical insights and wisdom, combined with the scholarship of more youthful collaborators such as Thomas Jefferson and John Jay, led to a national celebration of individual autonomy, inclusion, and free markets. That collaborative endeavor positioned business and its practitioners as valued actors in the process of building a nation and forging a just society.

The subsequent engagement of businesspersons from all industries and every part of the nation, beyond wealth creation and invention, in national governance and in philanthropy has arguably been exceptional in all of recorded history.

The growth, wealth, and prosperity of America came about because of such common sense. It continues to this day, but it is under threat, and Trump says so.

It should be no surprise that the United States is characterized in terms of business: as a business civilization, as a business-centric society, and as a commercial republic.

Business imparts its values to the rest of society and assures the success of our institutions and our culture in all of society and now increasingly around the globe.

As Thomas Paine suggested in his original and timely tract Common Sense, we need American independence and the health of a society founded in the business of common sense. We cannot let our forms and organs of governance drift toward an administrative or authoritarian state. This departure from the nation's traditional scheme of governance in a collaborative democratic republic would spell our demise.

Therefore, with Paine we are proud to end in restatement: "Society is produced by our wants, and government by wickedness; the former promotes our happiness positively by uniting our affections, the latter negatively by restraining our vices. The one encourages intercourse, the other creates distinctions. The first is a patron, the last a punisher."

Tradition tells of a chime that changed the entire world when it rang on July 8, 1776. It was the sound from the tower of Independence Hall summoning the citizens of Philadelphia to hear the first public reading of the Declaration of Independence by Colonel John Nixon.

The Pennsylvania Assembly had ordered the bell in 1751 to commemorate the fiftieth anniversary of William Penn's 1701 Charter of Privileges, Pennsylvania's original constitution. It spoke of the rights and freedoms valued by people the world over. Particularly insightful were Penn's ideas on religious freedom, his stance on American rights, and his inclusion of citizens in enacting laws.

The Liberty Bell gained iconic importance when abolitionists, in their efforts to put an end to slavery throughout America, adopted it as a symbol.

As the bell was created to commemorate the golden anniversary of Penn's charter, the quotation: "Proclaim Liberty throughout all the land unto all the inhabitants thereof," taken from Leviticus 25:10, seemed particularly apt.

Like Trump, we all need to ring that bell again, to defend and rearticulate our common sense.

3

Trump's Political Philosophy

When someone attacks me, I always attack back . . . except 100X more.

—President Donald Trump

The State of Our World

America is a center-right polity and the modern exemplar of the Judeo-Christian heritage of spiritual capital. There is an animating political philosophy here that undergirds Trump's actions, linking him to this deep reservoir of civilizational inheritance. It is necessary to unearth it.

The reelection battle of 2020 will be a critical and historic crossroads. The world desperately needs strong leadership. Trump realizes this truth.

Let us present two theses in this regard and demonstrate what they mean for this president's leadership and political philosophy so that we can comprehend his view of government and its place in our lives.

The first thesis concerns the logic of modernity. What distinguishes modernity is the technological project, the transformation of nature for human betterment as opposed to fatalistic conformity.

The technological project requires inner-directed individuals—entrepreneurs—and free market economies that maximize competition and innovation. Through this simple process, technological advances are generated, sometimes at astonishing speed.

Trump professes this, too.

Free market economies operate best with limited government (Montesquieu's commercial republic and Madison's Federalist Number 10). Limited government can be maintained only under the rule of law, which restricts the exercise of power and provides for predictable outcomes.

The rule of law can be sustained only if there is a larger cultural context that celebrates responsible individual autonomy, with no exceptions.

Finally, responsible individual autonomy presupposes a larger ontological claim about human freedom or free will that requires a theological argument. Say what you will about faith, it is invulnerable to the sort of self-doubt currently wracking the secular impulse in the West.

Moreover, personal autonomy avoids self-destruction and adds a spiritual content to the technological project. When responsible use of freedom helps fulfill God's plan by eliminating suffering and promoting freedom, a spark of the divine imbues the project and allows it to do good. Consequentialists and deontologists should both be happy.

Recognizing, pursuing, and sustaining autonomy are the spiritual quests of modernity and the technological project. This is best evidenced in the American experiment. Emancipation flows through the barrel of an iPhone.

The ultimate rationale for the technological project is not just material comfort or consumer satisfaction but the production of the means of accomplishment. Money and productivity cannot be the end in themselves: Fulfillment is humanity's ultimate goal. To discover that our greatest sense of fulfillment comes from freely imposing order on ourselves to impose a creative order on the world is perhaps the closest way of coming to know God.

Three considerations lead us to maintain that responsible personal autonomy requires deep support.

First, personal autonomy presupposes free will. This amounts to saying that there is no naturalistic (and scientific) explanation of the ultimate truths. Any paradox involving your faith and your freedom of action is a mystery that cannot be solved through introspection or philosophizing.

Second, we understand ourselves as historical beings, but history does not form a self-explanatory system. Our interpretation of the whole human drama depends on an intimately personal decision about the part we mean to play in it. In the end, this is a religious decision, not a scientific or scholarly one.

Third, sustaining our autonomy under trying circumstances requires spiritual stamina. Since naturalism and scientism fail so often, spirituality emerges as the only discipline capable of carrying humanity through this journey.

The second thesis is the documented history of how settlers, pioneers, and immigrants to the United States brought precisely this larger view to the nation, nourished it, and sustained it. Trump relishes this uniquely American philosophy.

The most important historical development in the last 400 years has been the rise of the technological project (TP). Building a better mousetrap is a quintessential part of American capitalism, and every mousetrap helps bring humanity closer to a life free of drudgery and filled with creative pursuits and general fulfillment.

The TP, not the market, is the starting point for our American narrative because although there have always been markets, it is only since the seventeenth century that markets have come to play such a dominant role in our lives. It is the presence of the TP that explains the centrality of markets.

The TP is the control of nature for human benefit. The first man to saddle a horse gave himself an edge over the rest of humanity. The world's largest empire to date—Mongolia—was built on the back of a removable seat.

These days, we invent our own horses. The TP radically changed the way people in the West viewed the world and their relationship to it and led to fundamental changes in the major institutions of the West (economic, political, legal, and social). This in turn led to the expansion of the West and its domination of the non-Western world and finally to globalization: the internationalization of Western institutions.

The following claims with regard to the TP can be made:

1. It is an irreversible historical process. Luddite protesters are forced to use technology to mount a protest against it.
2. Abandonment of the TP would have catastrophic consequences for humanity and threaten its very existence.
3. To the extent that the TP creates environmental and other kinds of problems, we are irrevocably committed to using future developments in the TP to address and, one hopes, solve those problems.

Cultures that have embraced the TP (including military technology) most fully have come to dominate the world and to spread the TP. America's scientific might is arguably the most important factor in its primacy. The spread has not been a matter of the powerful imposing on the weak; the weak have largely come to embrace the project on their own and are arguably the greatest beneficiaries of it.

This leads to the following tension and paradox: Domestically, the government is to maintain a low profile and assume a fairly passive supporting role for commerce, but in the international context, the government is to promote actively the entire panoply of the technological project, free market economics, limited government, and the rule of law.

It is incumbent upon free governments to intervene in foreign affairs to bring about this result. It is no use pretending that the implications could be otherwise: Every brain currently enslaved in a North Korean coal mine could contain the moon-shot technology that lets humanity burst forward to the next plateau.

This "optimization imperative"—leave no brain behind—is limited and guided by a political philosophy. It is not essentially interventionist as is the neocon outlook that Trump has abandoned. Freedom is always asked for, never imposed. The package must be accepted wholesale or not at all: The post-1991 relationship with China is the biggest warning yet against those who say one can have elements of markets without limited government or the rule of law.

Our American president abides by and acts within the established heritage of America's long-established spiritual capital; bringing freedom to the oppressed is a godly pursuit. As President Madison declared in 1821, America is the "well-wisher to the freedom and independence of all," though he did caveat with an isolationist, noninterventionist streak that America jettisoned sometime between the Louisiana purchase and the Civil War.

This is the same America that enshrined the "self-determination of peoples" in the UN Charter after fighting a two-front war on three different continents. Defeating imperial Japan and the fascist European powers was a matter of winning. America went abroad and found a monster to destroy. When the United States was handed the chance to remake the world in its image, two ideologies born of the liberal enlightenment—Marxism and Madisonian democracy—contrived to liberate (decolonize, in UN-speak) vast swaths of humankind from the opposite of self-determination: imperialism.

Marx and Madison competed in what can be seen as a fascinating natural experiment. Dozens of African, Caribbean, Pacific, and Asian countries, with all the mixed variables you can come up with, were being thrown into modernity. Winning that argument kept America busy for a while.

This is America's project. President Trump knows that he cannot deny it, reject it, or pretend it away.

The democratic ideal of "interventionist socialism" the West has toyed with in recent years must come to an end, as it is totally at odds with the essence of America's spiritual capital, which is built on localism and self-government. Insofar as the United States has gone down the road to serfdom, it is imperative that it double back. There will always be a socialist experiment somewhere other than America. There is no need to do it here.

President Trump fully articulates America's spiritual capital in all the senses described here. Every day, his unstated political philosophy becomes clearer. No rally is complete now without Trump saying that America will never be a socialist country. He understands the technological project, the free economy of markets, the rule of law, and the limits to government. He is making America greater on the basis of a definitive political outlook: Trumpism.

Speak loudly and swing your big stick around, especially where the old order won't grow back.

Scripture and Economics

One cannot derive specific contemporary economic policies from the Old Testament. The Bronze Age economy was largely limited to mining and agriculture. Economic reflection was necessarily limited to the family and the household, at least outside the monarch's palaces.

What we do find are important general moral admonitions. To begin with, there are the Ten Commandments. Most relevanrt to commerce are the commands that tell us not to lie, cheat, or steal. Covetousness, however, is encouraged these days.

It is hard to imagine any market-based society or institution that does not embrace these norms. Square dealing is essential to making the trains run on time without coercion. In addition, we are urged to work hard, take care of the poor, promote just institutions, and be good stewards of God's creation. Economic gain was not the ultimate purpose of life (wealth then consisted of land, perishable agricultural products, and jewelry), nor should it be today.

The same thing can be said of the New Testament. Despite a long-standing tendency among some Christian writers to derive antimarket policy implications from the New Testament, scholars have made it clear that this is a distortion of the Gospels. For example, Martin Hengel has pointed out that Jesus saw the root cause of evil in individual hearts, not in economic exploitation or political domination.

All these norms continue to have importance, but their meaning in specific sets of circumstances evolves over time. We shall, however, identify these moral principles as (1) basic norms, (2) personal responsibility, (3) social responsibility, (4) dealing with poverty, (5) the environment, and (6) ultimate purpose.

Matthew's parable of the talents is not about equality but about contractual responsibility and merit. Luke, especially in the Acts of the Apostles, where he states famously "from each according to his ability and to each according to his need," has been used by Marxists, progressives, and Christian socialists to justify some kind of egalitarianism. But scholars now agree that what Luke was discussing and advocating was a sort of communitarianism of the Christian community within the Roman Empire and not universal and timeless public policy. "Christian" socialism is an ahistorical figment of nineteenth- and twentieth-century imaginations with no biblical basis.

What is more relevant and interesting in this regard are the reflections of prominent medieval thinkers on economic issues and their ideas in response to evolving political and economic conditions. Among such insights is Saint Augustine's claim that the price reflects the buyer as well as the seller; this is Economics 101.

Thomas Aquinas acknowledged that profit is legitimate, and Albertus Magnus asserted (in agreement with Aquinas) that "goods are worth according to the estimation of the market at time of sale." In 1323 Pope John XXII declared as heretical the radical Franciscan positions that everything was owned in common and that poverty was essential to Christianity.

Of special interest is the debate over usury. In the Old Testament, specifically in Deuteronomy, Jews were admonished not to charge interest when dealing with other Jews, but it was permissible in commercial dealings outside the Jewish community. Turning to the New Testament, in Luke 6:34-35, Jesus urged us to "love your enemies, do good, and lend, expecting nothing in return." In response to evolving economic conditions, Christians recognized that it was legitimate to compensate a lender for lost opportunities and permissible to charge interest for purchases made on credit. A conceptual distinction was made, as it is today, between interest, which was considered legitimate because it contributed to the long-term economic well-being of all, and usury, which was not legitimate because it promoted exploitation and did not promote everyone's economic well-being.

Implicit in late medieval and early modern thinking is the notion of economic growth. No doubt the discovery of the New World and sea routes to Asia, which was aided by the use of the newly developed compass, played a part. However, the central issue is that the classical and medieval world viewed the economy as fixed or potentially shrinking. In such a world, poverty is natural and the norm. There is no problem of poverty because poverty is an unalterable fact of life. In fact, during the medieval Christian period the poor were sacralized, viewed as special manifestations of God and objects of concern to the Church. In such a world, anyone seeking a bigger piece of the pie must necessarily take a piece from someone else.

Those who sought to improve their economic lives were viewed as greedy, as taking something at someone else's expense. Starting around the time Europe discovered the New World, the Continent's economies began a sustained burgeoning of wealth, unique in history, that continues to this day. During this period, human accomplishment in the arts and sciences flourished to a degree unique in history. A connection seems inescapable.

Locke took economics out of the private household, where it was placed in the thought of the ancients, and moved it to the public or political realm. This is the origin of political economy. There is something about the issues generated by political economy that is different from the quarrels of the ancients. That world argued about virtue and vice, courage and cowardice, excellence and ignorance, innocence and sin, whereas the modern world has as the subject of its argument something new: liberty versus equality.

In the classical and medieval world, the economy was largely agricultural and trade was confined mostly to agricultural products; populations as well as economies were static. Reflection on such issues revolved around a perspective in which the world was seen as finite, cyclical, and teleological and therefore non-evolutionary and self-contained; this was a finite and no-growth universe. Theoretical economics focused on questions of the just price and the charging of interest.

With modernity the world came to be viewed much differently. Both René Descartes and Francis Bacon promoted the idea that wisdom consists not in conforming to nature but in manipulating it; this was the seed of the technological project. The voyages of Christopher Columbus, Vasco da Gama, and Ferdinand Magellan contributed to the notions of growth, trade, and expansion. Suddenly, nations were engaged in economic growth and the quest to compete and win. It was at this point that economies came to be viewed as operating nationally. Reflection was focused on the wealth of nations, not on households.

Once the economy is seen as expanding, everything changes. To pursue economic growth is not only to help oneself but to help others precisely because the pursuit of growth expands the entire pie: Everyone gets a larger piece. The economy is no longer zero-sum. Whereas begging had been institutionalized in the Middle Ages, in the modern period, as reflected in the writings of Martin Luther and John Calvin, it came to be viewed as an abuse of public trust and a form of exploiting the more industrious members of society.

The technological project within a free market economy became the greatest engine of economic growth in the history of the world, as the statistics amply prove. This growth requires and demands changes in all other institutions: government, law, the family, and even religion. Even what constitutes virtue gets redefined.

Contemporary scholars have been especially helpful here in explaining the evolution of the virtues. For example, Jane Jacobs contrasts the virtues of a feudal agrarian society with the virtues of a modern commercial society:

> Perhaps the most important factor in the economic development of the West has been the extent to which the Judeo-Christian heritage promotes autonomy. "Progress in science in the West has been fostered by enthusiastic, nonstop, competitive argument in which the goal is to come out on top. East Asia did not have the cultural wherewithal to support enthusiastic, nonstop, competitive arguments.

The Judeo-Christian heritage is also the origin of the concept of equality, with Christianity specifically proclaiming the equal moral worth of all persons in the eyes of God. Drawing both on Stoic doctrine and on Genesis, we find that all human beings "male and female" were created in the "image of God." This doctrine of equality was expressed by Paul (Galatians 3.26-29): "There is neither Jew nor Greek, there is neither bond nor free, there is neither male nor female: for ye are all one in Christ Jesus."

Early Christians had no direct interest in political participation or political rights such as equality before the law. Even slaves can be Christians. Within the Church, Christians still maintained the classical hierarchical conception, such as the distinction between clergy and laypeople. For a person to achieve salvation, the sacraments had to be administered by someone in a theologically superior position. Christians were all equally entitled to receive the sacraments, but they were not equally entitled to administer them. Equality in medieval Christendom led not to identical treatment but to vastly differential treatment.

With the advent of the Protestant Reformation, Luther challenged the notion of hierarchy within the Church. Calvin went further in asserting that all authority derives from voluntary agreement among equals to submit to it. This is first confined to the organization of the Church and then extended to the entire political sphere. Anabaptists, most notably Thomas Müntzer, went further and asserted a position from which both Luther and Calvin dissented: that complete social equality could be achieved by violence if necessary.

The Protestant work ethic promoted the notions of the inner-directed individual, an emphasis on work or achievement, equality before the law, and differentiation based on achievement or merit. Protestants were willing to accept an arrangement in which the political realm was not subordinate to the religious realm as long as the political realm respected the traditional spiritual realm of Christianity. Here we see the beginning of the tension between liberty and equality.

For Protestants, the spiritual realm was now understood to mean the opportunity to do God's work by transforming the world economically and all of its attendant circumstances. Equality before the law came to mean that there should be no legal barriers to economic activity that did not apply equally to everyone. To place legal barriers to equal participation in the economic realm was to thwart God's plan. One consequence of this conception of equality was meritocracy. In its Protestant form, meritocracy was a reflection not just of personal merit but of divine preordination. After all, it was God who inspired us and accounted for the differences in achievement. At the same time, higher status was accompanied with a sense of greater responsibility, not self-indulgence. To whom much is given, much will be required.

Equality before the law was an expression of Christian liberty. This Calvinist notion of political and legal equality influenced the Dutch, British, and American revolutions. The Calvinist influence in the English Civil War is reflected in a group known as the Levellers. The Levellers consisted of the rising middle classes, small property owners, tradesmen, artisans, and apprentices. In one pamphlet, John Lilburne asserted that there is no authority without consent. In the famous debate held at Putney in 1647, speaking on behalf of the Levellers, Colonel Rainsborough asserted that "the poorest he that is in England hath a life to live as the greatest he"; no one is obliged to obey a government "he hath not had a voice to put himself under." At the same time, the Levellers wanted to deny the franchise to all those whom they considered lacking in moral independence, such as alms takers and house servants.

A more radical group was called the Diggers. Their spokesperson, Gerrard Winstanley, rejected private property as a reflection of original sin. His claim was that "one man hath as much rights to the earth as another." He went on to attribute the existence of poverty to exploitation by the rich and advocated a form of primitive agrarian communism.

The difference between the Levellers and the Diggers heralds the ongoing dialectic in the development of modern notions of equality. What we see here is the difference between equality of opportunity and equality of result. Equality of opportunity is the position that a practice is unjust if it fosters inequality of treatment on the basis of irrelevant differences. Equality of result is the advocacy of a total equality that entails a collective conception of the good in which the individual good is subsumed.

The Levellers challenged the political power structure but not the economic and social system. This was a consistent expression of Calvinism and the commitment to doing God's work in an increasingly market-oriented society. The Levellers adhered to the Platonic-Augustinian view that we live in two cities so that as a result of original sin, this world will always be an imperfect reflection of the City of God. Poverty was a consequence of a lack of moral independence that itself reflected original sin. In contrast, the Diggers reflected the medieval Anabaptist call for complete equality within a feudal agrarian economy that was still committed to the notion of a collective good. The Diggers believed that a sort of social utopia was possible here on earth.

Writing a century later, David Hume made the following critique of radical equality and fairness. First, there was no agreement on what those concepts meant. That is, they seemed to be a rhetorical flourish rather than a serious position. Second, distributing resources to those who could use them best required a kind of knowledge that humans did not possess (this anticipated Hayek). Third, if resources were redistributed equally, this would soon lead to a new inequality once people began employing (or wasting) those resources. Fourth, to maintain the original equal redistribution, we would need a new form of absolute tyranny.

To be a fit participant in a modern market society, it is necessary to be a certain kind of person in a certain kind of culture. This is equivalent to "commercial moralism" or a related concept.

We now turn to the kind of person who internalizes its values and makes it work. It is no accident that Max Weber identified Benjamin Franklin as the epitome of the Protestant work ethic. Nor is it an accident that America is the most philanthropic country in the world. Franklin was the quintessential American, an entrepreneur in every sense of the word and a proponent of both thrift as a virtue and generosity as a practice.

Franklin and his intellectual heirs may well abolish scarcity one day. If technology ever provides so abundant a context that scarcity is defeated, the ideas of equality will find new winds to fill their sails. One can even identify a cycle: Abundance produces material equality, but the system eventually balances back to unequal optimalities, selecting for the productivity levels that can push forth to the next context of major abundance—the mythical rising tide that lifts all boats.

This is the heritage of the Judeo-Christian West. It is Trump's mantra.

Trump: The New Roosevelt

President Donald Trump is best viewed as the twenty-first-century Teddy Roosevelt.

The two leaders have much in common, from style and swagger to substance and outlook. Teddy was the ultimate poster boy for the Protestant work ethic; born weak, he made himself strong.

The last century would not have bent along the American arc if it had not been for our unexpected president, and this century might not go our way without the likes of a Trump. There would be no Panama Canal, no national parks, and no trust-busting without Roosevelt. There will be no changes in Washington without the likes of a Trump.

On a hot summer August day early in the twentieth century, Theodore Roosevelt gave his famous "New Nationalism" speech in Kansas. He sounded much like the enthusiastic and charismatic candidate Donald Trump sounds like today. The speech centered on the uplift of humanity and our country, "this great republic," and its ultimate triumph. Such bold rhetoric was thought not audacious but inspiring. Trump's claim "to make America great again" is nothing less.

For Roosevelt the history of America had become the central feature of world history. He said that "each of us, head erect, should be proud that we belong, not to a dozen little squabbling contemptible commonwealths, but to the mightiest nation upon which the sun shines." He decried all factionalism and division. Trump is doing the same thing, calling all Americans, regardless of their station in life, to greatness.

It is the combination of all our individual talents that makes this country great.

Echoing Lincoln, Roosevelt talked at length about the value of capital and labor. His words included "wise kindness and charity" but not "to weaken our arm or numb our hearts." Trump has said more or less the same thing in the language of our times. He is a democratic capitalist and wants everyone to benefit from the nation's riches. He, like Roosevelt, extols the strenuous life, a work ethic, and the virtues of spiritual capital.

By restoring America's main objectives in human betterment, measured in equality of opportunity, Roosevelt wanted America to strive again, to find its full glory. Trump realizes what we have lost in the Obama nation and calls it the abomination that it is. The country wants to find its rightful place again, and this is why Trump resonates not just with Republicans but also with Reagan Democrats and even the trade unions. He resonates with every aspiring soul who wants the freedom to be what America always was: a beacon of hope and a land of opportunity.

Based on a fair chance "to make of himself all that in him lies," Roosevelt's urge was one of true capacity building, both personal and national. It was one that included a clause stating that every citizen should offer the commonwealth his or her highest service. Trump knows this from his successful business career and all his commercial dealings and globetrotting. He also realizes that we have to stand up to our adversaries and contain the new evils that threaten our way of life.

Such a "Square Deal" freed all persons from "sinister influence or control of special interests." Calling for corporate responsibility, Roosevelt put forth a strong, effective policy of American nationalism. He said, "No man should receive a dollar unless that dollar has been fairly earned." He wanted a sound financial system and an efficient army and navy large enough to ensure our security and guarantee the peace. Trump is saying the same thing.

Roosevelt sought a form of conservation in the original meaning of the term for both natural resources and the country's moral foundations. Trump desires nothing less than to make America strong again in word and deed. He too is a conservationist. They both confronted our enemies and in the "art of the deal" sought to reform trade and investment to favor America.

This spirit of "broad and far-reaching" nationalism meant for Roosevelt that we "work for our people as a whole." Defending property as well as human welfare, Roosevelt sought material progress, technological advancement, and a nation of prosperity. All these things lead to "the moral and national welfare of all good citizens." He saw America's place as the leader of the twentieth century. He witnessed no class divide. Neither did he parse citizens by gender, race, or national origin. For him, there were no hyphenated Americans. The same rhetoric has appeared in the words of Trump in debates and on the campaign trail. He could unite America like no other president because although he is an outsider politically, he is a national figure who actually believes in America. His legal form of immigration would find support from Roosevelt. So too would his defense of our borders—the very borders Roosevelt fought for in the first place.

When Roosevelt spoke, he stressed "good character"—character that makes a good person: a good spouse, a good worker, and a good neighbor. He ended his speech with a clarion call (as was his entire two-term presidency) for good government rooted in good citizenship. Trump will do precisely the same thing. He will clean house, get rid of overregulation, and fix both the tax code and the spirit of America. He will continue to carry a big stick and will make Congress work for the people, not for special interests. He will end cronyism, as Roosevelt did first in the New York State Assembly and then in the civil service.

Trump is indeed the new Roosevelt. For America to survive and flourish we need his action and determinism, his enthusiasm and will to succeed.

President Roosevelt was also the first U.S. president to win the Nobel Peace Prize for brokering peace between imperial Japan and the Russian Empire. Donald Trump may well find yet another point of similarity with Teddy: peacemaking in Asia. They may even share the category of Nobel Prize–winning presidents with a few of their liberal predecessors: Woodrow Wilson, Jimmy Carter, and Barack Obama.

Von der Leyen: The Last Gasp of European Federalism

Eight votes. That was the margin by which Ursula von der Leyen (VDL), most recently the unsuccessful defense minister of Germany, became the president-elect of the European Commission, the executive arm of the European Union's two-headed administration. She will act as the head of government for the aspirational nonstate that the European Union currently embodies. The head of state will be Charles Michel, an almost unknown member of parliament from Belgium.

Palace intrigue dominated the undemocratic selection process. Macron wanted Francophones. Merkel wanted one of her own. The Brussels aristocracy wanted to impose a presidential candidate selected by the European Parliament's political parties during the election in May 2019. Falling into line, the European socialists came to the aid of the center right's U-turn on their own presidential candidate, Manfred Weber, another German who took one for the team. The centrist liberals, led by own forces, also voted in lockstep as expected.

This was par for the course. It is the European Union, after all.

More surprising was the support of the Greens, who traditionally oppose the centrist establishment. The strong Green performance in the election surprised everyone. That they would turn their backs so quickly on their historical environmental stances confirms the suspicions of many Eurosceptics: Supposedly left, supposedly environmentalist, they voted in a center-right figure with no bona fides on either count and don't seem to have gotten so much as a thank-you for it. Lacking a Green head of state in the European Council, they were, as the old saw goes, not at the table and therefore on the menu.

Among all the votes that put VDL in power, none were more unexpected than those of the European Conservatives and Reformists. The ECR, formed by British PM David Cameron after the 2014 edition of this electoral contest, was composed mainly of the heavily Eurosceptic Polish PiS Party and the British Conservatives, along with a number of other similar parties. The Tory wipeout in 2019 (losing all but four seats, including that of the ECR leader) was probably a factor in the decision to enthrone VDL. That the ECR would swing the election for the European People's Party (EPP), the party they all left in 2014, is disgraceful.

Blocking VDL would have been a victory for Eurosceptics of all stripes. Enforcing the much-maligned *spitzenkandidat* process also would have made the European Union a little more democratic, which it desperately needs to be. It was, after all, the idea of one of the great European federalists (the opposite of a Eurosceptic), Martin Schulz, himself a *spitzenkandidat* for the socialists in 2014.

The prospect of an alliance of Eurosceptics and federalists was quashed with the lashings of parliamentary whips and patronage, the smokiest of smoke-filled back rooms. ECR had put forward its own presidential candidate, Jan Zahradil, a Czech. Like Weber, Zahradil had no executive experience, but then, VDL hasn't been chancellor of Germany. ECR shied away from coalescing with the political parties to its right. If it had had more courage, it would have assembled a group large enough to surpass the center-right EPP, becoming the largest group, with first dibs on the presidency of the European Commission.

Instead, Nigel Farage's massive victory in the United Kingdom in which his party became the largest in the European

Parliament was wasted on the nonaligned independent group, a mishmash of rejects that don't fit into any of the serious parties.

The notion that the Eurosceptics could have forced the 500-odd other members of the European Parliament (MEPs) to vote for Zahradil is pure fantasy. But if they had played by the rules of the centrists, the railroading through of VDL would have been a much costlier operation. Already tying themselves in knots to double back from their *spitzenkandidats*, the center's self-serving hypocritical nature would have been bared for all to see.

Actually, blocking VDL (again, eight votes!) would have thrown a spanner in the works and forced the center to reconsider much of its received wisdom. As things stand, the center has taken the result of the election as a green light to continue with business as usual.

One can only imagine the seething rage that Manfred Weber, having dodged these many bullets—second place in Germany, the prospect of a Eurosceptic party larger than his—felt after not getting the spot he campaigned for. One might almost invite him to the Eurosceptic parties.

So what can we expect from VDL? She's allowed a dyed-in-the-wool socialist, Josep Borrell, to run the EU's foreign policy. As Borrell is an old-school, anti-imperialist, anti-Israel, pro-Chavista lefty, one is almost reassured by the fact that the embryonic European foreign policy establishment has yet to show any teeth. The presidency of the EU parliament, another of the great plum posts, will go to an Italian socialist even though his own country doesn't want him, with the attendant consequences for European legislation.

Having been Germany's weak defense minister since 2014, with the responsibility to implement the NATO commitment from Wales extracted by President Obama and more strongly supported by President Trump that NATO allies would spend 2 percent of their GDP on defense, VDL has shown very little mettle in delivering on those priorities. German defense spending remains at 1.2 percent of GDP, where it was when VDL assumed leadership of the armed forces of the Bundesrepublik. Her predilections appear to be more for a redundant EU army than for the survival of NATO.

In other words, she wasn't a head of state, she wasn't a candidate, and her record isn't any indication of competence, skill, or courage.

Shed a tear for Europe. Nobody has his act together: not the center, not the Eurosceptics, not even the much-celebrated Greens.

With a political class like this, is it any surprise that the place is coming apart at the seams? Is it any surprise that Trump has completely dismissed them?

Next Crisis: The Balkans Again?

NATO announced that it plans to build its first air base in the western Balkans, according to the prime minister of Albania, Edi Rama. Why?

The word "Balkan" comes from the Turkish *balken,* or "chain of woods," sometimes translated simply as "swampy forest." Of course, after the dissolution of Yugoslavia in June 1991, the term gained a rather negative meaning even in casual usage in the form of the verb "to balkanize" and all that term has come to imply.

In part, as a result of the historical and political connotation of the term arising from various military conflicts of the 1990s, the new term "Southeastern Europe" has begun to be employed, but it doesn't cover up the realities. It only papers them over.

The peninsula surrounded by the Adriatic Sea to the west, the Mediterranean Sea to the south, the Black Sea to the east, and the Danube River to the north is a landmass roughly the size of Spain and has a population of over 60 million people. It has known chaos and discord for some time. Europe's next crisis again will be in the Balkans.

Historically known as the crossroads of cultures, it has been a juncture between the Latin and Greek traditions of the Roman

Empire, the destination of an influx of pagan Bulgars and Slavs, and an area where Orthodox and Catholic Christianity met as well as a melding point of Christianity and Islam. That has made life difficult with many crosscurrents, ethnicities, and cultural affinities. It is the seam in the "clash of civilizations."

Since the Middle Ages the Balkans have been the stage for a series of nearly endless wars between empires. Most of the Balkan states as we know them today emerged in the nineteenth and early twentieth centuries as they gained independence from the Ottoman and Austro-Hungarian empires. In 1912, the world witnessed the First Balkan War. World War I was sparked in the Balkans in 1914.

With the start of the World War II, all the Balkan countries with the exception of Greece were allies of Nazi Germany. At the close of that devastating war, the Soviets entered Romania and Bulgaria, forcing the Germans out. What was left was largely an area of ruin and wartime exploitation.

The thrust of the long Cold War meant that most of the Balkan countries had communist governments and were within the Soviet sphere of influence. Greece and Turkey, the exceptions, were and still are part of NATO.

The post–Cold War period has not been easy for the Balkans as they have found independence and the move to democracy and market-based economies difficult.

The long-lasting wars after the dissolution of Yugoslavia led to a UN operation and the use of NATO ground and air forces to bring about a tumultuous peace.

This history serves as a cursory sketch of the backdrop we face today. The question for this troubled region is: Will the area be the place of the next crisis? One might realistically ask if the region has ever stepped out of crisis mode.

At a recent closed think-tank meeting, a well-informed German official was asked what problem in Europe caused him the most worry. His answer came without hesitation: the western

Balkans, where a new crisis was brewing as Turkey and Russia stirred the pot.

In his worst-case scenario, Russia and Turkey would encourage their proxies in the Balkans—Serbia and Albania—to redraw the region's borders.

The Serbian government, with Russian support, could annex large portions of Bosnia populated by ethnic Serbs. Turkish support could help Albania pull off a similar maneuver not only in heavily Albanian Kosovo but also in Macedonia, where much of the large Albanian minority would like to reunite with the motherland.

As the historian Walter Russell Mead said, this course of events might seem unlikely. Since some of the territory claimed by greater Albania partisans is in Serbia, it would be difficult for the two countries to agree on a new map. However, it's not an impossible outcome, as he said, if the idea would inspire a James Bond villain rather than a foreign minister. And increasing numbers of wannabe Bond villains seem to be popping up in world politics these days.

There is a grave reality underlying these concerns. The Balkans are unraveling, and the West now must worry about more than overt Russian meddling. Despite deep Turkish suspicions of Russia, President Recep Tayyip Erdogan is cooperating more closely with President Vladimir Putin. The West, it appears, is pushing him into willing and open arms.

Their opposition to Germany and the European Union has brought Turkey and Russia together. Russians don't just hate NATO; they see the European Union as a barrier against Russia's historical great-power role in European affairs. Turkey also has turned against the European Union and is looking for leverage against Germany. For Russia and Turkey, the chance to cause Europe troubles in the Balkans with relatively little risk and cost may be too good to pass up.

The prospect of EU membership for countries such as Serbia, Macedonia, Montenegro, Kosovo, and Bosnia has done more than anything to keep the fragile peace in the western Balkans. Every Balkan country would rather be part of the European Union than be allied to Russia. But will the European Union have them?

Hopes of near-term EU membership are fading. Europe has lost Britain and has had a hard time managing relations with more nationalist members such as Hungary and Poland. The twenty-eight—soon to be twenty-seven—EU members have little desire to take in five obstreperous new Balkan states that would make the union even more ungovernable and would expect financial aid at a time when the post-Brexit EU budget will already be stretched.

Serbs and Albanians are both signaling that if the West walks away, they will have to look eastward, and that will mean shifting to a nationalist agenda with Russian and perhaps with Turkish help.

For the European Union, a new round of Balkan chaos would be a near disaster: refugees, crime, and radicalization among Balkan Muslims and greater opportunities for hostile powers to gain influence at Europe's expense. However, the European Union doesn't think it can manage the Balkans on its own. The United States will have to be part of the solution, Germans say. But will it under President Trump, who has said, Why give American lives for Montenegro?

Will the United States play ball? Engaging in distant Balkan quarrels to make Germany's life easier isn't exactly Donald Trump's idea of smart foreign policy. Even as Atlanticist a president as Bill Clinton struggled for two years to keep the United States out of the post-Yugoslav wars.

Mr. Trump is more skeptical of intervention and treats the possibility of a new round of Balkan wars with the chilly aloofness that Barack Obama displayed in Syria.

Although the quarrels in the Balkans may be trivial compared with larger problems elsewhere, such as on the Korean peninsula, what happens in the Balkans doesn't always stay in the Balkans, and NATO as well as the EU countries could be shaken to the core by the prospect of another round of Balkan bloodletting. The crisis even has the potential to redefine U.S.–European relations for decades to come.

Europeans argue that relatively small, short-term American investments—active diplomacy, nation building, and building up U.S. forces in Kosovo—could go a long way, but we have a president who does not find that argument convincing. An America first stance dissuades him from overinvolvement in Europe's battles.

Trump's core foreign policy conviction seems to be that the United States has let its allies enjoy a decades-long free ride. Europeans who worry about Balkan peace need to think about how they can persuade a skeptical White House to engage. The old appeals to NATO solidarity, defense of freedom, and fear of Russia may not and probably will not be enough.

The next crisis in the Balkans is very much going to be a European affair, but dragging in NATO amplifies the issue. According to *Foreign Affairs*, much of the region is in danger of becoming a "new grey zone": "an area beyond the European Union's reach, vulnerable to Moscow's influence, and at risk of domestic breakdown."

To prevent the western Balkans from deteriorating further, Europe should reinvigorate its efforts to integrate the region, encouraging its leaders to fight corruption and demonstrating to ordinary citizens the benefits of reform and closer ties with Western Europe. But the European Union recently balked at this proposition.

Will Europe act before it is too late? That is the looming question. Is Europe too preoccupied with its own demise, cultural relativity, and inability to muster action militarily, politically, or economically to see the next crisis on the horizon?

4

Trump's Spirit

That's the whole ball game. Where the spirit of the Lord is, right?
Where the spirit of the Lord is, there is liberty.
—President Donald Trump

Trump's Uncommon Common Sense

Donald Trump said at one of his rallies in Montana, "I'm not really an ideologue. I think I'm a person of common sense." What was Trump appealing to, and why is it inherently both American and conservative to do so?

Here's the answer: Early on the freezing cold morning of January 10, 1776, in Philadelphia, a forty-seven-page booklet was published that would change American and indeed world history. It was the watershed moment in the American Revolution.

The publication was called *Common Sense,* and its author was Thomas Paine. The arguments contained in the petite volume galvanized opposition to the Crown and catalyzed the political movement to independence.

Paine had been born in Britain and had immigrated to America only in 1774 at the suggestion of Benjamin Franklin. Writing for the *Pennsylvania Magazine* under the pseudonyms of Atlanticus, Aesop, and Vox Populi, he lashed out at the folly and wrongs of British rule. His commonsense opus, written in language every person could understand, had an instant and dramatic effect.

Striking a chord with colonists' conscience, it was rapidly translated into many languages, reprinted thousands of times, and circulated widely. It did nothing less than convince Americans who were undecided on the issue of independence that they should unite and separate.

Paine considered the content of his pamphlet to be a plain truth (that was at first his working title), clear to all right-thinking, rational persons. He had borrowed the phrase from its earlier use in England (as early as the fourteenth century), in which it was considered a sense very much like our other senses. They were called the "five wits," and the "common" sense united them into a useful whole.

Like that powerful expression of the American consciousness, today we need another jolt of common sense, and Donald Trump is providing it. We need it to restore faith in the market and wealth generation and also to give common people, regular men and women in America and around the world, a prudent voice for creating a better future, putting America first. The president knows this and based his campaign and presidency on it.

Unfortunately, it is often said that common sense is not as common as it ought to be. One of the best spokesmen for common sense was President Ronald Reagan. In his farewell address, the fortieth president defined his time in office as "a rediscovery of our values and our common sense." Actually, from the very start of his career, Reagan dedicated his tenure to the idea that society "could be operated efficiently by using the same common sense practiced in our everyday life, in our homes, in business and private affairs."

Decades later, responsible, purposeful leaders are taking up his mantle and laying claim to the phrase "commonsense business." What exactly does this mean, and how does it work? What truths do we hold as self-evident in a commonsense framework, and what are the benefits to leaders, employees, shareholders, communities, and, most critically, companies and all of America?

In the field of economics, commonsense behavior has been seen as saving more money when one is faced with an uncertain future; it's part of "risk aversion." The so-called precautionary saving motive is one of many faulty principles of this dismal science. In accounting, economics' cousin, prudence, is a fundamental concept. It determines the time at which revenue can be recognized, which is not an unimportant or inconsequential event. Lawyers also still abide by the "prudent man rule," a nearly 200-year-old judgment method appealing to common sense. Some governments have even established prudential conduct authorities that are intended to guide fiscal choices in a better direction after the financial crisis.

Arguably the most dominant organization on the planet, the Catholic Church, has insisted on maintaining the virtue of prudence in all ventures, making it part of its standard for belief and practice, the Catechism: "Prudence is the virtue that disposes practical reason to discern your true good in every circumstance and to choose the right means of achieving it." It goes on to conclude with some sound advice: "The prudent man looks where he is going."

If prudent behavior is right reason in action—or, as we define it, the natural intelligence that is available to all rational people—why has it been mostly abandoned, forfeited in more recent times, and nearly totally forgotten by our postmodern culture and governments?

That is, except for Reagan and now President Trump. Contrast the experience-based performance of the economy under Trump with the socialist rationale and abstract lack of achievement of his predecessor. Trump's commerce department and treasury have spent almost three years cutting regulations by the dozen; a rule requiring that two old regulations be suspended for every new one implemented has been oversubscribed by a factor greater than 10.

Which does American business prefer? Not woke, bloated megacorporations like Starbucks but middling enterprises that don't have lobbyists to fight for them in Washington. They prefer Trump and common sense. Trump is their lobbyist, fighting for the little guys by making the government burden on them lighter every day he remains in office.

The State of Our Union

Remember when President Trump was supposed to go to Congress and deliver his annual State of the Union speech?

House Speaker Nancy Pelosi tried to cancel it, but he would have none of that, so she disinvited him until the shutdown was over. Now it is over, but the speech has not yet been scheduled.

Why?

He should have played her for what she is—a loser and a petty person—and given the address on his time and at a place of his choosing.

It would have behooved him to give that constitutionally described and mandated address in the U.S. Senate chambers or in another state capital. Why let Pelosi and the radical Dems control and box him in?

In that address he could outline where we have come and where we will go under his leadership in the coming year. That is precisely what all presidents are called to do.

He should take a bow for what has been accomplished and also signal how much more he hopes to achieve in the year ahead.

Few presidents have been so productive.

With the election, 2020 is a critical and historic crossroad, and we desperately need his strong leadership. We need it on a range of policies and also in spirit.

America is a center-right polity and the modern exemplar of the Judeo-Christian heritage of spiritual capital. Trump realizes this truth. He should say so loudly and clearly.

The democratic ideal of "interventionist socialism" we have toyed with in recent years, now front and center in the Democratic Party, surely must come to an end, as it is totally at odds with the essence of America's spiritual capital.

President Trump needs to articulate America's spiritual capital in all the senses described here. In our opinion, Trump is the leader we need not only to endorse but to pray for. All of us, not just conservatives, need to rally behind him *now*.

He alone has the business acumen; he alone has the executive experience; he alone articulates all the necessary ingredients spelled out here.

He understands the technological project, the free economy of markets, the rule of law, and the limits to government. He is making America greater and putting it first.

We desperately need a leader in America's best spiritual tradition to get us through the current malaise and economic chaos.

But make no mistake; he is under attack, and so is America. We should support our president and use the framework laid out here to inform that support for a stronger union. In so doing we will enhance the legacy of America's spiritual capital and renew its spirit.

Is Trump Churchillian?

After appearing in the award-winning movie *The Darkest Hour*, Gary Oldman rightly won the Oscar for best actor for his portrayal of Winston Churchill; that was after he won the BAFTAs.

The story depicts the utter failure of the Neville Chamberlain government and the coming to power of Prime Minister Winston

Churchill. It is May 1940, and the Nazis are sweeping through Western Europe. Chamberlain has lost because he proved unprepared for the historical moment and tried to placate Hitler.

Churchill alludes to a single purpose: *the national interest.* The question asked in Parliament is, "Where's Winston?" The nation needed a leader.

It was the same question asked in 2016 when Donald Trump assumed the presidency of the United States of America. What is America's interest after failed policies?

The British establishment was interested in just one thing: appeasement, throwing in the towel in defeat. Similarly, in the United States, even the Republican Party opposed Trump. Both Trump and Churchill are best seen as antiestablishment figures, unexpectedly coming to power in times of crisis even though both were aristocrats in their respective countries.

Only one man, Winston Churchill, could win the day. Just like Trump, it took a man of uncommon courage to turn the ship of state—to "drain the swamp," to use Trump's metaphor.

Although there are many differences in the specifics of time and place, if you take an airliner view of this, you can see that their essence is the same.

While Neville Chamberlain had been practicing strategic patience, the Nazis were taking Europe. The leadership assumed that Britain would always exist, as if it had been granted that right by God. Churchill saw the evil forces in the world that were bent on the destruction of Western civilization and vowed to fight for the existence of his country, the only way to ensure its survival.

Compare that to Trump. As soon as he took office, Trump dropped the MOAB (Massive Ordnance Air Blast) on ISIS, then surrounded them and killed them, not leaving them to fight another day. With North Korea, the thought of a million Americans perishing at the hands of an evil dictator did not sit well. He will end this threat instead of appeasing and letting "Little Rocket Man" grow stronger. It takes the same fortitude that Churchill had to go to this uncomfortable place. Pundits claim that Trump will kill us all in a nuclear war. Actually, it's just the opposite: Fight now or die later. For the survival of Churchill's Britain and Trump's United States, this direction needed and needs to be taken.

Upon entering office, Churchill inherited a nation with a deteriorating military, unprepared for war. He immediately ramped that up, just as Trump has done. Why has the United States dithered for so long on missile defense? Taking care of the troops? He is ready to defeat evil in any form.

Further, Churchill had to implore Europe to fight back against the Nazis, not just surrender and leave it to England. This is exactly what Trump is doing as he forces the NATO nations to pay their fair share for defense.

And in return for this policy? For promoting the national interest and the survival of the sovereign nation, both men were despised by their governments and the press. And both were threatened with removal from office on day 1!

But these men understood that freedom isn't free, and so they fought on. They had an inner spiritual strength that propelled them.

True, Churchill loved his gin and tonic, Pol Roger champagne, cigars, and a full English breakfast. Wearing his smoking jacket, he was seen as "an awful brute." He was called unkind, rough, and rude. Trump has his own vices, *sans* alcohol, and is universally viewed as a bully. Yet both Trump and Churchill spoke truth to power—and it is a powerful truth.

Neither political figure cared about the chattering, focusing only on results. With his backward V, his opponents called Churchill abusive and even a tad crazy. Has Trump been called anything less—deranged, unstable, and every other name in the book?

Churchill took his strength from the everyday people—the average man—just as Trump represents the forgotten man, a silent majority, so-called Middle America.

The enormous task for both was, as Churchill stated, "to not bugger it up."

In his war cabinet of rivals, Churchill found all the forces aligned against him. Trump faces similar discord in Congress and with appointed colleagues and unruly staff. Churchill exclaimed that it would take, "blood, toil, tears, and sweat" to prevail. Trump may use saltier language, but it all comes down to the same sentiment. Nothing will come easy.

For Britain in 1940 the policy was to "wage war against a monstrous tyranny." Its aim was just one word: "victory."

Churchill's team tried to remove him from office in his first year on a no-confidence vote. In response to them, he paraphrased Cicero on fortune, where them with a spirit of feeling thy do not yet have. Trump may have lesser rhetorical skills, but he summoned the same spirit in his inaugural address when he empowered all the people to take their country back.

The power not to surrender to servitude and shame motivated Churchill to find a way forward. Trump saw what he termed a "crippled America" and likewise sought to "make it great again."

For Britain the terror was coming (in the form of the Luftwaffe and the Wehrmacht), and there was only one telling: It was called the unmitigated truth. Churchill asked the nation to "fight on." Trump is asking the American people to do the same thing in the face of danger, calamity, ISIS, China, economic demise, and rogue nuclear powers. Trump cares only about winning!

Churchill's party wanted compromise with and appeasement of Herr Hitler. They were ready to capitulate. Winston would have none of it. Trump's foes don't want to take on the enemies at home or overseas and are willing to fold their hands, shut down the government, or engage in more strategic dithering.

An assembly of civilian boats to evacuate the 300,000 British troops from Dunkirk saved the day. Operation Dynamo was a historic watershed, as has been the first years the Trump administration. With its allies and Trump's morale-boosting rules of engagement, the United States has defeated ISIS, U.S. companies are moving manufacturing back home, the New York Stock Exchange is at record highs, and unemployment among black males is at an all-time low.

Churchill was unwanted. Even the king told him he "scared people." He lamented, "No one knows what will come out of your mouth next." Sound familiar? Trump's less than diplomatic tweets have set the world on fire and unsettled many at home and abroad. But they have a purpose: to circumvent the biased news media and appeal directly to the populace. Just as Churchill mobilized the English language, Trump has mobilized social media.

Churchill asked in the movie, *The Darkest Hour*, "When will the lesson be learned? You cannot reason with a tiger when your head is in its mouth." Trump said in his 2018 UN speech, "In foreign affairs, we are renewing this founding principle of sovereignty. Our government's first duty is to its people, to our citizens, to serve their needs, to ensure their safety, to preserve their rights, and to defend their values."

It all boils down to courage, a virtue shared by Churchill and Trump. "No one puts words together like you," Churchill's able secretary said when he mumbled. Trump articulates the heart and soul of America in the vernacular of ordinary people. He speaks their language.

Churchill and Trump doubtless felt the weight of the world on their shoulders. Both sought the recognition of the people and told them an unvarnished version of the truth. Churchill asked the British people, What is your mood? Their resounding answer was "Fight!" One exclaimed, "They'll never take Piccadilly." No peace with Hitler and fascism. Trump has drawn his own line in the sand with North Korea, Iran, and the globalists.

In the movie, as Prime Minister Churchill gets off the Underground at Westminster to give the speech of a lifetime to Parliament, he concludes that the swastika will never fly over

Buckingham Palace. Trump defends the American flag and national anthem with the same vigor and zeal.

Churchill put the nation first. Trump has a strategy of America first. Churchill sought to defend his island home. Trump defends America's borders and its economy and jobs.

The grip of the Gestapo will not come to England, Churchill said: "We shall not fail—we shall go on to the end. We shall fight on the beaches; we will fight them on the landing grounds . . . we shall never surrender." Trump has the same fortitude and will not lie down or give in. He is indefatigable.

Churchill saw that in good time the New World (America) would step to the side of the Old. Trump would be lucky if the Europeans paid their way and shared the burden they promised to share.

Churchill sent his nation into battle. Five long, hard years later, a bloodied Britain and its allies, essentially America, finally declared victory.

In eight years' time, one hopes, Trump can do precisely the same thing. Fighting evil is the real inconvenient truth.

After all, perhaps Trump is another Churchill.

Returning Hong Kong

Riots in the streets of Hong Kong have reached a fever pitch. What began as an extradition case involving one man has become the symbol of the oppression of all Hong Kongers.

Hong Kong needs to return and stay on the side of democracy and freedom—the values it was built on—and Trump and the free world need to say so.

Would you want to live under the Chinese Communist Party? Given extra points on your social credit score for memorizing Xi Jinping's "thought"? If by fortune or hard work you happened to be a resident of Hong Kong, one of the freest places and most open economies in the world, would you willingly give Beijing the right to extract you from the city and judge you in a communist tribunal somewhere unfamiliar and foreign?

Three million or so Hong Kongers have answered with a resounding "no." Protests on workdays, with violent clashes with police forces and the looming threat of another Tiananmen Square, hang over the situation. The Communist People's Liberation Army is ready to march in. Then what?

The faction that won the power struggle after Tiananmen Square remains in power in Mainland China and has the same attitude toward protesters that it had back then. The year 1997 rolled along, and Britain honored its commitment made a century earlier between the empire and a Chinese royal house that no longer existed. Hong Kongers weren't consulted on the matter in an early demonstration of the hubris of the 1990s.

Military force isn't supposed to impede the self-determination of peoples. Is there any doubt that Hong Kongers would rather be independent?

Beijing would never let them. The latent threat of violence—of which Tiananmen was only the most recent episode—is the only thing keeping China together. Actual violence is currently being employed against the Muslim Uighurs in Xinjiang province to deafening silence from the international Islamic community.

The question of Taiwan also remains a vexing one for both Beijing and the West. To the extent that China's claims in the South China Sea are debatable (which they certainly are), the cards fall very differently for America's allies if the one-China policy is recognized. Since that policy has been abandoned by all but the smallest countries in the world, Taiwan's independence should be considered seriously. A security guarantee would be necessary for its survival, as Beijing has promised to invade if it ever tries to separate from the mainland.

The world is on a collision course. An aggressive and adversarial China, a communist polity with a state-run economy, is a contradiction in terms with the capitalist front they present to the rest of the world. Inevitably at some point and probably during a Trump administration, it will have to be confronted before it is too late.

Trump realizes this and is getting ready for the coming onslaught.

Latin America: Malign Neglect

When Trump assumed the presidency, he encountered generations of failed policy toward Latin America and the Caribbean. Trump had his work cut out for him: Undoing the past was impossible, and creating a better future would take hard work, good luck, and new thinking. He has made strides with Mexico, Guatemala, El Salvador, and Honduras and to some extent has stemmed the flow of illegal aliens. Brazil turned in his favor with a new "Trump of the Tropics," and Colombia finally was stabilized. But Cuba remains a thorn in our side, and Venezuela is the locus of most consternation as a result of radical Marxist ambitions run amok.

The history of the greater Caribbean has deep connections with the march of universal history through interactions, sometimes unlikely, with other remote regions caused by the struggles of the great powers. The configuration and location of the nations in the larger region define the interests that guide their actions on the international scene.

Geopolitics has been defined as "the geographical consciousness of the states," and as Robert Kaplan demonstrates in *The Revenge of Geography*, the ideas and visions about domains and use vary with scientific and technological advances.

THE CARIBBEAN ANTILLES IN THE AMERICAS

Trump has begun by remembering that it was in the Caribbean Antilles where the phase of great expansion of the European powers that constitutes the basis of Western civilization began.

Columbus was looking for an alternative route, shorter than the historic Silk Road, for trade with China and India. The discovery of what came to be called "America" was an event of universal significance, heralding the advent of what we know as the modern world.

It also established a new civilization: the Latin American subsidiary, a part of the Western world, with which it shares the Judeo-Christian–Greco-Latin traditions. In this respect, if the new administration traces the genesis of modern international law, especially the valuable developments in human rights and freedom, it will find it in the early struggles for the dignity of indigenous peoples and the campaigns initially waged on the island of Hispaniola.

From the late fifteenth century to the third decade of the nineteenth century, the Caribbean was a formidable battlefield, an imperial frontier in which the European powers clashed incessantly in a projection of their struggles and wars in the old continent. This is the context for present policy; there is simply no escaping it.

It has been rightly said that in the Caribbean, empires are made and unmade. Trump wants to rearrange and disrupt the current stalemate, but it is taking longer than he imagined. Some history explains why this is so.

The Caribbean islands played an important role in the process of independence of the nations of the southern continent: After the defeat of the Second Republic of Venezuela, Simón Bolívar took refuge in Jamaica and there published his *Answer of a Southern American to a Knight of This Island*, which has become been known as the Charter of Jamaica and in which he invites England and the other European powers to support the independence of all the American nations.

For security reasons, Bolívar moved to Alexandre Petion's Haiti, where he gathered support in the form of ships, weapons, supplies, and other resources before returning first to Margarita and then to the Continent to resume the emancipation struggle after promising his protector that he would suppress slavery. The governors of Haiti did not notice that the priority of José Revenga was to achieve recognition from the United States and France, just as it was Bolívar's intention to deepen special ties with England. None of those nations recognized Haiti.

In the ninth instruction given by the Liberator to the delegates to the Congress of Panama on the elimination of the slave trade, it was indicated that "America would no longer fear that tremendous monster that has devoured the island of Santo Domingo."

In fact, the heads of South American independence, including Bolívar and Santander, had serious reservations about the suitability of supporting the independence of Haiti, which was achieved in a violent and atrocious struggle, for fear that that it would stimulate "the war of colors," or races, on the entire continent.

Both episodes, along with others no less relevant, contributed to the formulation of the Monroe Doctrine and the transcendental program of the Panama Congress, which would inspire and guide relations between the American nations as well as their links with the European powers.

Bear in mind that the leaders of the American Revolution had formulated in 1796 what would be known in time as the Washington Doctrine, from Washington's farewell address. Trump is the latest embodiment of that doctrine.

This indicated that the "main rule of conduct in relation to foreign countries was to try to broaden our commercial relations and have as few political ties with them as possible" and proposed to the Europeans that "it will not be prudent to mix ourselves by means of artificial ties."

However, the United States never concealed its interest in seizing the islands that it considered necessary to protect its security and its trade. Thomas Jefferson proclaimed in relation to Cuba: "I frankly confess that I always looked upon Cuba as the most attractive addition that could be made to our system of States."

The impact of this geopolitical gravitation on the backwardness and fragility of the independence processes of the states of the region is undeniable. These were tendencies that would be accentuated when, during the construction of the Panama Canal, their security requirements were increased and the area received the transforming effect of the investments of American companies.

At the end of the nineteenth century, the United States renounced its neutrality on Cuba. In a fulminating war, America undid what remained of the Spanish empire in the Caribbean and the Pacific. Puerto Rico came under U.S. control. The Platt Amendment would mediate the sovereignty of Cuba.

In 1903 President Theodore Roosevelt obtained the authorization of Congress to acquire for $40 million the rights of the broken French company of the Panama Canal in order to restart its construction, which would conclude in 1914. After the traumatic secession of Panama from Colombia, Latin American foreign policy would be guided in the future by the "North Star"—America.

All these actions were aimed at reducing the presence of European interests in the Caribbean region. The geopolitical vision of the canal was fully enshrined with Admiral Alfred Thayer Mahan's doctrine of naval power and conceptualized that imposing seaway as the extension and integration of its continental coasts. The secretary of the navy would go beyond the formulations of Mahan in terms of the need to control more territories in the region to ensure the strategic defense of the canal.

America's role in the region was slow to develop, always in reaction to the machinations of European powers. In 1902 the first international crisis occurred on the coasts of Venezuela. A powerful squadron of German, British, Italian, and Dutch ships blocked and bombed La Guaira and Puerto Cabello, demanding that the government of General Cipriano Castro pay the debts contracted by his subjects.

Venezuela, which was not yet an oil exporter, was plunged into a state of chaos and civil war that prevented it from fulfilling its obligations. The United States saw in that action a clear challenge to its security, especially because the emerging European power Germany was beginning to deploy its own naval forces.

The threat of mobilization of the U.S. fleet and its energetic diplomatic action contributed to containing the aggression. The matter was brought before the International Court of Justice in The Hague, which ended up validating the European naval action.

In 1901, U.S. Secretary of State John Hay protested strongly against the Kaiser, demanding that he remove the German fleet that was marauding Isla Margarita. Plans to expand German naval power included the acquisition of a base in the Caribbean and another on the Pacific coast of Mexico. At the end of the blockade crisis, it was the Dutch who obtained for their claims to Venezuela the surrender of the islands of Aruba, Curaçao, and Bonaire.

The naval blockade of the Venezuelan ports of 1902–1903, the international judicial decision, and the role of mediator that led to the signing of the Washington Protocols brought about a substantial change in the Monroe Doctrine with the formulation of the famous Roosevelt Corollary. By virtue of it, the United States reserved "the right to exercise international police power" in unstable countries affected by civil wars or conflicts that prevented them from guaranteeing American interests. The United States proclaimed its obligation to preserve civilization against "acts of malfeasance" and would guarantee the collection of the accretions or compensations as the most reliable liquidator.

The Dominican Republic was the first country in the region where the Roosevelt Corollary was applied in the form of the imposition of a political-financial protectorate. In January 1903, a protocol was signed with the government of the United States of America by virtue of which the amounts owed—a value of $4.5 million—would be paid to the Santo Domingo Improvement Company (SDIC), an emblematic company of the North American interests. Those debts would be addressed as a priority, with the revenues generated by the Dominican customs, which was being run by America.

A little-known episode deeply frames the history of the continent and the world: the Zimmermann telegram. The British historian Barbara Tuchman explained it in a formidable work of investigation named after this secret document that changed the course of World War I.

The German foreign minister, Arthur Zimmermann, secretly proposed to Mexican President Venustiano Carranza an alliance against the United States while transmitting to the Wilson administration his interest in negotiating peace with the Triple Alliance. Zimmermann, as a member of a cabinet devoted to unrestricted underwater warfare, feared that the United States would become involved in the war against him. To prepare that scenario, he understood that Mexico, with its historical grudges against the United States, could be a valuable ally.

The strategic objective was to open a fighting front in Mexico to force the United States to deploy a war effort on its southern border. The secret telegram was intercepted by British naval intelligence, and its disclosure to the Wilson government determined that the United States, upholding the Washington Doctrine, would declare war on Germany and its allies.

The enormous power of the United States decided the contest in short order and cemented its great-power status. The subsequent withdrawal, which was nothing more than a return to the Washington Doctrine, after the League of Nations was established is considered one of the factors that led to World War II.

The German war maneuver corresponded to another, no less audacious gambit with enormous repercussions: the Machiavellian decision of the German military high command to facilitate the seizure of power in Russia by the Bolsheviks to get that nation out of the war.

Another defining episode that would take place in the greater Caribbean was the most serious of the entire Cold War, exposing humanity to destruction by nuclear conflagration: the Cuban missile crisis. Cuba is the seed of American despair in the region, and Trump knows this; nothing has much changed over six decades.

The continent in general had closed ranks with the allies against the Nazis and adopted in 1945 the Act of Chapultepec. This established the concept of collective defense against extra-continental aggression, which would be reflected in the Treaty of Reciprocal Assistance (TIAR), or Rio Pact, in 1947.

The violent events in Bogotá in 1948 and in Guatemala in 1954 were denounced by the United States as attacks of communist subversion. This was in line with the Monroe and Washington doctrines to keep European influence from the hemisphere.

Even the overthrow of President Jacobo Árbenz in Guatemala was preceded by a formal American complaint about an arms shipment from communist Czechoslovakia. There would be an atmosphere of mistrust about the real magnitude of that threat and about the purposes of the actions to combat it: In an area with deep social injustices, American corporate interests were the most favored.

The triumph in 1959 of the so-called Cuban Revolution led by Fidel Castro, who established a communist dictatorship that has lasted until this day, benefited from these ambiguities in U.S. policy. Because of the Kennedy-Khrushchev pact, Cuba would exert great and undue influence throughout the continent and has been a factor in every crisis in the hemisphere since then.

The Bay of Pigs fiasco generated a crisis in the power centers of the United States and sent a signal to the Soviet leadership of a weak, inexperienced President Kennedy. The repercussions were enormous. This was evident in the tense meeting of the two leaders in Vienna, in which the young president looked intimidated by Khrushchev, a seasoned Soviet apparatchik who had climbed the greasy Stalinist pole at its greasiest. Rigging Texas for the Democrats was child's play in comparison.

It was clear that the powers had played a very dangerous game and that the weak nations could pay a very high price if they were caught in the cross fire. The whole continent and the world shuddered for a long time after that unprecedented clash, which led to a hardening of the American posture in the region. Senator J. William Fulbright would say of the 1965 invasion of the Dominican Republic: It was decided with punitive design to demonstrate that the United States would not allow "another Cuba."

President Reagan, shortly after inaugurating his government in 1981, asked Alexandre de Maranches, the head of the French intelligence services, what the greatest threat to the national security of the United States was. Maranches told him that it was the conflict in Central America not because those small countries would represent a danger by themselves but because that conflict could spread to Mexico, where similar social and economic conditions prevailed. The eventual emergence of a radical and hostile regime in Mexico would pose a high risk to the national security of the United States.

This was compounded by the fact that the Mexican migrant population was quickly growing and that the United States would have serious difficulties continuing the integration and amalgamation processes without compromising its historical identity and border. Undoubtedly, Maranches had in mind the vision of Kaiser William II and Zimmermann defining Mexico as the "underbelly" of the American republic. Reagan would be made aware of the connection of both conflicts, not least because of Soviet agitation.

With the fall of the USSR in a bloodless and surprising way, U.S. leaders were seduced by the neoliberal utopia of a global order under American hegemony, an end of history that had already been announced and outlined with the grand coalition formed to recover Kuwait after it was invaded by Saddam Hussein in 1990.

Back then, globalization and Americanization were the same thing. Insofar as that is no longer the case, President Trump has justifiably reduced American support for globalization. But Latin America remains a particularly difficult predicament.

In the 1990s America built a "globalist" ideological discourse that spread the universalist belief that markets, liberal democracy, technologies, and multilateralism would progressively erase borders and national identities and thus dilute backward cultures and religions. That grand strategy and the globalist ideology supporting it have failed. Trump realized this.

Faced with a debacle he saw coming, years ago our perennial nemesis Fidel Castro conceived the astute strategy of preserving his regime and relaunching socialism in Latin America. For these purposes, he formed the São Paulo Forum in 1990 with Brazil's Luiz Inácio Lula da Silva and the Workers' Party of Brazil. When the Venezuelan political crisis generated the populist phenomenon of democratic Caesarism on the part of Colonel Hugo Chávez, Castro managed to capture it and put it at the service of his cause. Lula's rise to power in Brazil in 2003 allowed him to align all the "progressive" leftist currents of the continent and rudely reject the proposal of a free trade agreement (FTA) for the Americas by President Bush in 2005.

This strategy, which was a crass and costly mistake inspired by a dogmatic, failed, destructive ideological vision, was reinforced by a fiery anti-imperialist discourse. Something similar happened with the pilgrim project to share the vast oil reserves of Venezuela with the rivals of the West as a way to fight and defeat the supposed plans of imperialism to seize them.

The global economic crisis of 2008 stimulated an even bolder and more challenging strategy: to encourage the constitution of the BRIC nations (Brazil, Russia, India, and China) and its new institutions. Brazil, which strengthened its influence through its large companies and banks and generous lashings of oil money, would be the continental articulator that would change the balance of world power and thus accelerate the often announced decline of the West.

While the United States concentrated on free trade agreements with the Pacific region and Europe and on bilateral FTAs with some countries, China advanced on the continent with huge investments and control of strategic assets. The influence of Russia and Iran in the background was felt in Venezuela, Paraguay, Argentina, and Brazil.

Cuba, after promoting the peace process in Colombia, apparently had achieved, along with its continental leftist allies, the isolation of the United States, as was evident during the CELAC Summit in Havana in January 2014.

The Obama administration, wanting to put an end to the conflict of the Cold War with Cuba, accepted the formula of a transition similar to that in Vietnam, that is, under the dictatorship of the Communist Party and the armed forces, absurdly and unjustifiably excluding the Cuban diaspora that legitimately aspired to a Cuba reconciled with democracy.

This was necessary to justify Obama's Nobel Peace Prize without noticing that from the point of view of democratic principles and values, validating one of the oldest communist dictatorships in the world was tantamount to reinforcing autocracy throughout the continent. It was a tacit suspension of the Inter-American Democratic Charter of Lima, which ironically first was invoked in 2002 during the attempted overthrow of President Hugo Chávez.

This brings us to the present day. Much of what is happening in Venezuela, Bolivia, and Nicaragua and what can happen in other countries, including ours, is directly related to the ideological vision of the Latin American left that those who make the socialist revolution or propose major changes that qualify as progressive have the right and legitimacy to do what they must to consolidate power indefinitely.

This has aggravated the biggest problem in Latin America, which stems from its deep-rooted authoritarian political culture: failure to put limits on presidential power and assume the values of a moderate government in which the opposition counts and has reasonable prospects of forming a government. This ancestral problem has to do in the end with the most arduous question: In Latin America and in many parts of the world, "there is only one thing more difficult than reaching the government, it is getting *out* of government." Lula, currently in a Brazilian jail, surely has choice thoughts on the matter.

All this would change substantially with the election of Donald Trump, whose agenda for the role of the United States in the world, validated by the broad support of the American people, is prodemocratic.

It is evident that Trump represents a stream of ordered withdrawal by the United States from many conflicting scenarios in the international order. No longer, he has thundered, will America be the world's boy scout, cleaning up after irresponsible actors the world over. Nor will we pay the bills.

Similarly, the tendency that we have analyzed in this section would reappear: Remote conflicts originated by the struggles in the South China Sea caused by the Chinese maritime policy of the nine-dash line and the secessionist tendencies in Hong Kong and Taiwan would have a powerful replica in the Caribbean Sea and Basin.

Trump sees that China is trying to demonstrate with its compensatory power—checkbook diplomacy for governments in economic distress—its brand-new relations with Panama, El Salvador, and the Dominican Republic. America is being challenged in its own backyard. American diplomacy reacted angrily to the 2018 Dominican decision to end relations with Taiwan and establish them with Beijing, warning that the decision does not contribute to regional stability.

The response of the Trump administration and its hard-line team has been to make it a priority to topple the main regimes allied with China, Russia, and Iran: Venezuela, Cuba, and Nicaragua.

This is the hard core of the Forum of São Paulo, which has developed a web of relationships and interests involving groups of narco-guerrillas and terrorists, such as the ELN, the FARC, and Hezbollah. The economically statist model that they promote has imploded the economy of Venezuela, which has been destroyed by unprecedented hyperinflation and generated an exodus of millions of people.

Trump's national security adviser, John Bolton, has his priorities mixed up. It is Cuba that must be the focus of American policy. Both Nicaragua and Venezuela are puppet states of Havana. Take out the Cuban Communist Party and the situations in the other two countries will resolve themselves quickly. One shudders to recall the Angolan war, in which tiny Cuba, on the other side of the world, fought a proxy war against American-backed regimes and emerged victorious. Havana should not be underestimated and should be dealt with before any other issues.

In what seems like a new version of the Cold War, Trump's nationalist United States of America goes on the offensive to regain its influence in the region, provoking a continental ideological political realignment reinforced by Brazil and Colombia. Both states are today pillars of hemispheric security. It is in this context that Colombia has become NATO's first global partner, and Brazil, headed by Jair Bolsonaro, swept away Lula's party and jailed him for the unabashed influence buying and corruption that Odebrecht performed on behalf of international socialism.

It is necessary to record that these changes that have reversed the hegemony of the "progressive" leftist governments are largely the result of new forms of competition and war: both the impact of the fracking revolution in energy, which lowered the prices of gas and oil, and that of lawfare and information wars.

Europe, understanding the implications and scope of this contradiction in the greater Caribbean, also adds to this current. That is why it is supporting, albeit with some reluctance, interim Venezuelan President Juan Guaidó. But as Trump and our democratic allies have discovered, mere support is not enough. Recognition does not suffice. Military intervention is undoable with thousands of Cuban militiamen backing up Maduro's criminal regime. Russian military hardware and advisers are also present. Trump needs to play hardball with the linchpin: Cuba.

There remain great unknowns: Can the dictatorships of the left fall without triggering major conflicts in the region? Will Russia, China, and Iran bet on violating the Monroe doctrine in an effort to bait American action?

What will be the impact of Mexico's position in the continental scenario? Will it be a moderator or mediator, or will it end up aligning itself by ideological affinity? Mexico's unwillingness to recognize Juan Guaidó brings an echo of Zimmermann with it. What role will be played by organized crime, the cartels, and drug and human trafficking, which have made the region one of the most violent in the world? Are we on the threshold of a change in international relations in which the distribution of areas of influence by major powers will return?

The twenty-first century has been witness to an extraordinary change: the millenarian Middle Kingdom—*Zhongguo*—has entered an unprecedented expansion phase. This new China owes more to great-power nationalism than to Maoist communism. It also owes much to both the strategic shift in U.S. foreign policy toward China that Nixon and Kissinger made in 1972 and the mistakes made by the leadership of the West in regard to Russia, which finally has brought these Eurasian powers closer together in Toynbee's nightmare of a united world-island. Their conflicting strategic interests are being resolved under the aegis of the Shanghai Cooperation Organisation, whose reach extends to our hemisphere.

China, under the leadership of Xi Jinping, not only aims to dominate the heart of Eurasia and beyond with the imposing vision of the new Silk Road but has set its sights on the domain of seas and strategic steps with its "string of pearls" policy.

Both expansions require the support of large diplomatic, technological, military, and intelligence apparatuses. The global impact of this Chinese overflow has led to a challenge to the power of the U.S.-led world order in Latin America and elsewhere.

The Chinese consider that democracy and pluralism are inventions of the imperialist West that are promoted with double standards. The nature of its regime allows China to make decisions about longer-term investment projects and respond to other profitability criteria. Indirect American financing of this Ozymandian Chinese ambition is arguably one of the greatest strategic mistakes of all time. Donald Trump's strangling of the Chinese trade surplus has done much to undo this mistake.

It is not surprising that in Latin America too many governments of weak or constrained states see more rewards than risks in dealing with China. Reluctant democracies have ideological affinities or outright autocratic tempers and consider the Asian giant, along with Russia and Iran, as a strategic ally in their confrontation with the United States. Supposedly neutral countries, members of the "nonaligned" group and G77, illustrate the truth in George W. Bush's aphorism: "You are either with us or against us."

The wish of many in the world, as Parag Khanna explained, is to see a decline of America. Khanna warned that America's fear of the future and the reactions it provokes can lead to its fall. Those people believe that as in many other states in a position of primacy, the process will result from the contradictions generated by what international expert Parag Khanna calls the "militarist expansion and the degradation of the creative minority," which in turn allows the advance of the "barbarians that each empire deserves."

That vision is underpinned by the quasi-religious belief, based on Marxist philosophy, that history has a certain inexorable direction that should be interpreted only for the purposes of placing oneself "on the right side," which is the assumed to be "advanced and progressive."

The United States has proved itself by the polyarchical nature of its institutions and the pluralism of its culture, which has a great capacity to reinvent and relaunch itself, overcoming the deepest and most complex crises. Recently, this was confirmed by the fracking revolution that has been leading to energy independence and by the overcoming of the subprime mortgage crisis of 2008. At this historic crossroads where the greater Caribbean once again has become the theater of global rivalries, the risk of fomenting violent antagonisms in the region is real.

Trump has taken note. It is necessary that all the nations of the continent, beginning with the United States, be aware of the enormous challenge of recomposing inter-American relations on solid foundations, with the aim of creating a shared space of stability and prosperity, of democracy and liberties, of security and peace. The price of not doing this can be very high for everyone. Trump has said that national sovereignty must correspond to and rest fully in a free, democratic, and plural exercise of popular sovereignty. The American continents must be a space of peace and harmony and never become a space of the struggles of the extra-continental powers for world domination.

Trump is seizing the opportunity but has been careful not to overplay his hand. Taking on ascendant Chinese ambition is a start. Changing relations with Cuba was a good, if modest, first step. Backing change in Venezuela is mandatory; ensuring it is the hard part.

Globalism Is the New Tower of Babel

The Tower of Babel—in the Hebrew language לְבָב לַדְגְמ—was real.

Today that tower is the European Union and other globalist organizations. Globalists in the European project have been building their tower for decades. Their punishment of Europe has been biblical in scale.

Babel is part of biblical literature and is recorded in the book of Genesis 11:1-9.

The structure, reaching far into the skies, was built in the land of Shinar in Babylon. It was constructed some years after the deluge, or what is commonly called Noah's flood.

To prevent the wrath of God, Europeans must keep their faith in the system the Lord gave them.

Historically, Babel has been explained as an attempt to comprehend the existence of so many diverse languages, an allegorical myth. In truth, it represents the sinful pride of humankind and an act of ultimate hubris—wanting to reach the heavens, where humans could become gods.

This warning has been ignored by the Eurocrats in Brussels and Strasbourg. They speak of building a European empire with their sons and daughters drafted into the European Army going off to die for Angela Merkel.

In this sense, the tower broke God's covenant and his commandments, unifying people in sin. Similarly, Brussels's Babel is rapidly becoming the gate through which hell itself spills onto the continent.

It was on account of this sin, the same as that in the original Garden of Eden, that God divided humans and made them speak different tongues, as a result of which they could not understand each other.

The law of Europe—whimsical, unenforceable, and ill advised—is no substitute for the Holy Writ.

The Flemish master Pieter Brueghel's influential portrayal of that scene is based on the Colosseum in Rome, whereas later conical depictions of the tower (such as Gustave Doré's illustration) resemble much later Muslim towers observed by nineteenth-century explorers, notably the minaret of Samarra.

Towering over the nations of Europe, Brussels does not promote a culture. Instead, it favours a universalist anticulture, a sinful attempt to standardize every nation.

The composer Anton Rubinstein wrote a powerful opera based on the same story, *Der Turm zu Babel*.

The conservative political philosopher Michael Oakeshott surveyed at great length historic variations of the Tower of Babel story in different cultures and produced a modern retelling of his own in his important 1983 book *On History*. In his retelling, Oakeshott expressed disdain for human willingness to sacrifice individuality, culture, and quality of life for what he called "grand collective projects." He attributed this behavior to fascination with novelty, persistent dissatisfaction, greed, and lack of self-reflection and/or self-governance. Oakeshott was of course right, and his critique on this, as on so much else, was prescient.

Today the new Tower of Babel is the European Union and globalism. This is the prevailing ideology of the global elites and the institutions and machinery they deploy to make themselves gods.

Setting aside all tradition, all past custom, often rewriting history, and most notably eradicating the nation-state, these globalists and the crony capitalists and socialists who fund them and all their doings seek one thing: the power to control.

Zbigniew Brezinski, former national security adviser to President Carter, put it this way in his book *Between Two Ages: America's Role in the Technetronic Era*: "The technetronic era involves the gradual appearance of a more controlled society. Such a society would be dominated by an elite, unrestrained by traditional values. Soon it will be possible to assert almost continuous surveillance over every citizen and maintain up-to-date complete files containing even the most personal information about the citizen." Reread that and you have the doctrine of globalism in a few short sentences.

In the words of globalist in chief Jean-Claude Juncker, president of the European Union, "In these [May 2019] elections, those who promote foolish nationalism will pay the price for it."

Hating the common man and woman while elevating their own self-righteousness and power, the global elite at places from Davos to Bilderberg and from the United Nations to the European Union and especially in the mainstream media and the deep state want to end life as we know it—in the "little platoons," as Edmund Burke called them.

As was explained above, they abhor freedom, family, and especially faith. They want one huge psychobabble and one-world government controlled by them.

The conservative worldview is founded in the dignity of persons and their flourishing in freedom; in contrast, globalism is a worldview of domination. This new order would be neither democratic nor representative; it would be what Oakeshott termed an "enterprise" association: a unitary Leviathan.

It bears mentioning that Leviathan, a mythical sea monster whose defeat precedes civilization, is syncretic with Ouroboros, the snake that ate its own tail. This description fits the Eurocrats perfectly.

Like the Tower of Babel, today's acts of global arrogance run contrary to the very nature of humankind. Defeating it will allow the flourishing of a new Europe of sovereign nations. It sounds lofty, perhaps even idealistic, to bring people together and facilitate some far-reaching new do-good international order. It always does. But it is just the same sin over and over.

Nimrod's tower fell, as did Alexander's, Cyrus's, Attila's, Napoleon's, Hitler's, Stalin's, and Mao's. They all fall, and the European Union is next.

Why? Because such global geopolitical projects, even when buttressed with so-called noble reasons, are utter vanities. They are not noble at all. So too globalism itself must and will fall.

Once nationalists overrun Brussels, we can begin freeing the rest of the world. The recent European elections are the next place to watch for the death of globalism.

Europa, Eurabia, and the Last Man

Europe is full of "Last Men" (and perhaps women, we are now forced to say, given the incessant demand for political correctness). Why is this so, and who will come to dwell in these territories we have hitherto called our ancestral homes?

We are not talking about some imagined community. The point of contention is a real place with real peoples and real nations that have existed for centuries on end, perhaps thousands of years; it is called Europa.

Trends in immigration suggest what can only be termed a self-imposed European death wish. Look at any demographic map, preferably an interactive color one. Among the 7.5 billion people currently on this earth, the vast majority, mostly in the southern hemisphere, of a generally destitute status, are trying to get to the northern hemisphere, where there are greater opportunities. In recent polls seven of ten people from those lands said that given the chance, they would flee their plight.

The last decade has seen more refugees, migrants, and economic immigrants than at any point in human history: The UN High Commissioner for Refugees (UNHCR), charged with keeping up with such things, puts their number at 60 million or so. They are dying in transit, drowning in the Mediterranean Sea, and dying in the back of trucks, as was the case in Texas recently. Human trafficking is big business. The International Organization for Migration estimates that more than 1 million migrants arrived in Europe by sea in each of the last three years, along with tens if not hundreds of thousands more by land. The numbers are astounding and are only increasing. Some 5,000 new migrants arrive on the shores of Italy alone every day.

The United States estimates that it is now populated by millions of illegal and undocumented immigrants. In fact, about one-fourth of the 42.4 million foreign-born people living in the United States today are illegal immigrants. This amounts to roughly 10.5 million, according to an objective study by the Center for Immigration Studies. Other estimates cite much higher numbers. Geostrategists cannot comprehend billions (yes, potentially *billions*) of people moving from south to north. They can't comprehend the risk or the total effects of this world without borders.

Yet it is something that globalist political leaders and flat worlders actually seek and actively endorse.

Europe will change. This will happen and indeed is happening now, with globalist elites endorsing it as benign or even praiseworthy. The "Anywhere" crowd with no attachment to place, custom, or religion favors such open borders. The "Somewhere" folks who still have some degree of loyalty to national identity, tradition, and religion do not share that attitude.

As the global elites get their way, we are witnessing the end of Europe and the emergence of the Last Man. And who is this Last Man?

The Last Man (in German, *der letzte Mensch*) is a description used by the philosopher Friedrich Nietzsche in *Thus Spoke Zarathustra* to describe men tired of life who take no risks and seek only comfort and idle security. They exist without purpose or direction. Their lives are pacifist and comfortable. There is no longer any distinction between strength and weakness, excellence and mediocrity. Social conflict and challenges are defined out of existence. Everyone lives equally and in a superficial harmony of no consequence. There is no originality or flourishing social trends or ideas, merely fashions. There is no innovation or creativity. Individuality and thinking are suppressed.

Ironically, migrants are much more Somewheres than Anywheres—and are not Last Men either. Anywheres share a universal culture born of Western civilization, which they take with them wherever they go. Somewheres, in contrast, value their roots and take their distinctive specialness with them even when they are halfway around the world. Look at any of the *banlieues* of Paris, Brussels, and London and the replication of their cultures of origin is evident. Migrants bring over their wives and children, contrasting with the childless European Last Man and Woman, who may very well be literally the last of their lines.

According to Nietzsche, the Last Man is the goal that modern society and western European civilization have set for themselves. Nietzsche warned that the society of the Last Man could be too barren and decadent to support the growth of healthy human life or great individuals. The Last Man is made possible only by humankind having bred apathetic persons who are unable to dream, who are unwilling to take risks, who simply earn their meager living and try to keep warm. Even having children or concern for future generations is too much of a challenge and an inconvenience. Leadership is nothing more than a greater amount of things and creature comfort. They are willing to make any temporary compromise to maintain their ease.

The Last Man, Nietzsche predicted, would be our response to the problem of nihilism: Death is coming for you anyway, so enjoy the ride.

Is Europe today getting closer to what Nietzsche described? Has European decadence and anomie, adrift from its original moorings and spirituality and more and more awash in a sea of unassimilated and perhaps unassimilable immigrants, with yet more on the way, brought us to this state?

Others have described the onslaught of Islamist immigrants who come to the West to exploit its wealth and flee the scourge of poverty and war in the places they have vacated. They bring with them cultures of hate and the practice of terror as they find no way to immanentize their eschaton and instead end up hating the new places they inhabit and the way of life that has sustained it for centuries. Picture the Jungle, the notorious migrant camp outside Calais that typifies this result.

In their stead, they create what Raheem Kassam called separatist "no-go zones" of sharia law, ISIS recruitment, and so-called honor killings. They are discontented, are unattached to the host society, and strike out in terror, rebelling against life itself. Such horrific events, we are told, are now "normal" in places such as Nice, Paris, Munich, Madrid, Cologne, Manchester, and London. Our political elites, the very globalists who have opened the borders, say we should accept this new reality as the way of life, the new normal. It is less disturbing to analogize this problem to the older problem of assimilating "European" immigrants.

This is what the British conservative philosopher Roger Scruton lamented when he said, "Put simply, the citizens of Western states have lost their appetite for foreign wars; they have lost the hope of scoring any but temporary victories; and they have lost confidence in their way of life. Indeed, they are no longer sure what that way of life requires of them."

If present trends continue, and all the evidence—from Merkel to Macron, from Sweden to Canada—suggests that it will (Trump excluded), the tide of migrants will not abate. The incoming team of EU honchos have already made the requisite noises about being more welcoming. The migrants (overwhelmingly male) will continue to come en masse to open and willing arms.

Make no mistake: If the trend continues, Europe will suffer complete transformation into Eurabia, a cultural and political appendage of the Arab and Afro–Muslim world. This Eurabia will be fundamentally anti-Christian, anti-Western, anti-American, and anti-Semitic. The Cross held the line for hundreds of years against the incursions of the Prophet Muhammad and his heirs all the way through the Barbary corsairs and the Ottoman Empire, which was turned back at the gates of Vienna in 1683 and wouldn't crumble for another two centuries or so.

With every passing day we see the further demise of the cradle of the West, the onslaught of Eurabia, and the nihilism of the Last Man.

A Nation at Prayer

In the bleak, bitter cold winter of 1777, at Valley Forge, Pennsylvania, the encamped troops of General George Washington were gloomy, nearly defeated, and forlorn. They were in despair, and things did not look good for the ragtag, newly created nation. The Revolutionary War was decidedly not going their way. Night was closing in.

Contrary to what is taught in our schools today, the Founding Fathers, to a person, were not secular or atheist in the least. George Washington, like the overwhelming majority of the Founders who signed the Declaration of Independence, were Christians in both principle and practice. We need to recall and understand that those leaders, who were responsible for the birth of America, actively practiced the Christian faith. They had a profoundly theological understanding of hope.

In this, our hour of need, we too should abide in the steadfastness of their faith. The battle rages on, and victory remains elusive.

The most inspiring and iconic portrayal of American history and patriotism is that of George Washington on his knees in the snow at Valley Forge. "The moving image personifies and testifies to our Founder's dependence upon Divine Providence during the darkest hours of our Revolutionary struggle," said President Ronald Reagan.

The following passage was taken from Nathaniel Randolph Snowden's (1770–1851) *Diary and Remembrances*. Snowden was with the Quaker Isaac Potts when he recounted how he found General George Washington praying alone in the woods at Valley Forge:

> In that woods, pointing to a close in view, I heard a plaintive sound as of a man at prayer. I tied my horse to a sapling & went quietly into the woods & to my astonishment, I saw the great George Washington on his knees alone, with his sword on one side and his cocked hat on the other. He was at Prayer to the God of the Armies, beseeching to interpose with his Divine aid, as it was ye Crisis, & the cause of the country, of humanity & of the world. Such a prayer I never heard from the lips of man. I left him alone praying.

America and the West are in a similar place today: in the middle of a war, with renewal of its spirit and the revitalization of its great historic mission the sign of victory.

The promise of defeat is a turning away into an abyss of godless socialism and radical secularism clothed in leftist hatred of everything George Washington stood for, of everything Reagan reflected, of everything God breathed into our very founding.

Pray with all the saints in heaven that His justice will rain down and that His people—We the American people, as proclaimed in the preamble to our Constitution—achieve the victory and keep our republic.

We cannot turn our backs and deny our maker and His will for our exceptional country, this unique city on a hill, a beacon to all peoples regardless of color, gender, ethnicity, or creed. Lincoln called America "mankind's last best hope on earth." As the Constitution puts it:

> We the People of the United States, in Order to form a more perfect Union, establish Justice, ensure domestic Tranquility, provide for the common defence, promote the general Welfare, and secure the Blessings of Liberty to ourselves and our Posterity.

That is why we fight even as our allies fail us and our friends think treasonous thoughts. Trump puts himself squarely in this American tradition.

Losing Faith

Does America depend on its religious faith for its greatness? This is a legitimate question, and Trump has a definite answer.

Polls from the Pew Research Center suggest that the Christian share of the American population is declining and that the number of U.S. adults who do not identify with an organized religion is growing. Surveys show that these changes are taking place across the religious landscape, affecting all regions of the country and many different demographic groups.

The drop in Christian affiliation is particularly pronounced among young adults, but it is occurring among Americans of all ages. The same trends are seen among whites, blacks, and Latinos; among college graduates and adults with only a high school education; and among women as well as men.

Are we living on the fumes of our past, on the spiritual legacy that was the bedrock of our civilization and of American democracy? *The Economist* recently said, "If you want to avoid an argument over religion at your next dinner party, you might suppose it safe to invite an economist or two. They of all people could be expected to stick to Mammon." Well, maybe not.

We are living through that proverbial next dinner party, and we need to stir up some controversy and explore the influence of religious belief and observance on economic growth, nation building, democratic norms, and social life.

Without a spiritual foundation we do not have a country, a civilization, or a soul.

Well, then, what is spiritual capital? It is an emerging concept that builds on recent research on social capital that shows that spirituality is a major factor in the formation of social networks and an impetus for economic and social progress.

There is growing recognition that religion is not epiphenomenal. It is not fading from public significance around the world. Indeed, it is a critical factor in understanding every facet of life from the radius of trust to behavioral norms, all of which have vast economic, political, and social consequences.

The so-called positivistic desire for a "waning of religion" was wrong—dead wrong.

Scholars such as Gary Becker and Robert Fogel, both Noble laureates, have used the term "spiritual capital" to refer to the aspect of capital that is linked with religion and/or spirituality.

Robert Putnam's influential work on social capital found that religion is by far the largest generator of social capital, contributing more than half of all the social capital that can be accounted for. Clearly, spiritual capital is a major subset and thus an area worthy of attention on its own.

This is not the first time economists have held forth on this subject. A century ago, Max Weber, a founder of sociology, observed that the Protestant work ethic was what made northern Europe and America rich. More recently, Niall Ferguson, a British historian, argued that the current economic stagnation in Germany and elsewhere in Europe owes much to the decline of religious belief and church attendance during the last four decades.

Is that work ethic really dead? We need to look at the effects of spiritual and religious practices, beliefs, networks, and institutions that have a measurable impact on individuals, communities, and societies in America.

Here are four questions (you can add more) to address this critical issue concerning spiritual capital:

1. To what extent is or should religion be considered in various experiences of nation building in America and elsewhere?
2. Can one measure the state of national spirituality and do comparisons over time and across countries?
3. How do society, public policy, and the mediating structures actively generate more spiritual capital?
4. How are economic growth, democracy, and social development linked to spiritual capital founded in faith?

Trump knows that unless we address these questions and truly rediscover our spiritual legacy while practicing freedom of religion, we are, well, doomed.

Trump is tuned in to America's spirit and its religious heritage. He taps into it and depends on his base of followers to project his message to both the nation and the larger world.

Trump as Tragic Hero

Think *Dirty Harry*: "Make my day." Yes, Clint Eastwood. An even better example is his character Walt Kowalski in the movie *Gran Torino*. Trump is all of them and more.

Like the famous gunslinger in the classic Westerns who rides into town, shoots up the place, kills the bad guys, and rides off into the sunset. Trump is a real action hero. *Rawhide* and *Unforgiven* come to mind unless you are a fan of the John Ford classics in this genre.

Trump is a tragic hero precisely because he embodies the tragic reality created by decades of progressivism and statism and its internationalist dimension: globalism. He has seen those evils face to face and to each of them he shouts emphatically, "No."

He is a self-styled disrupter who knows that the thanks for his deeds will come in the afterlife. He seeks no reward or monetary prize. His palace on earth has already been built; now he builds his mansion in heaven.

Sophocles, born 496 BC in Colonus, near Athens, wrote the foremost dramas in golden-age Greece. He was, with Euripides, one of the greatest two playwrights of the ancient world. His works include *Oedipus* and *Antigone*, both tragic heroic epics.

In his *Poetics*, Aristotle writes that the purpose of tragedy is to arouse pity and fear in the audience and so create a *catharsis*—a cleansing of emotions—that will enlighten people about life and fate. Each of the plays of the Oedipus trilogy achieves this catharsis that Aristotle defined as the hallmark of all tragedies.

Think of Trump in this vein. Trump is a modern Oedipus, destined to slay the rigged system that produced the backdrop for his victory just as Oedipus slew his own father to get the crown. Parricide was among the highest crimes of ancient Greece, just as is defeating the Democrats today: The cops will come after you with a crusading zeal whether you colluded or not.

The ancient world was full of such tragic heroes. Another one was Ajax, son of Telamon, grandson of Zeus, and king of the island of Salamis. As described in Homer's *Iliad*, an ancient poem about the Trojan War, Ajax was large, strong, and fearless—just like Donald Trump. After Achilles's death he fought Odysseus over who should wear the mighty suit of armor Achilles had left behind. Ajax, the military hero, tragically committed suicide by falling on his sword.

In an important apologia, *The Case for Trump*, noted historian Victor Davis Hanson of the Hoover Institution at Stanford University provides a robust argument for Trump and his policies. He too sees Trump as a tragic figure come to fix the broken nation. Hanson explains how a celebrity businessman with no political or military experience triumphed over sixteen well-qualified Republican rivals, a Democrat with a quarter-billion-dollar war chest, and a hostile media and Washington establishment to become president of the United States—an extremely successful president. A heroic feat, to be sure.

We see Trump in the grand theater of politics, both domestic and international, almost daily. The world, not just America, is digesting Trump and Trumponomics.

He is an earthly demigod, a Geo Deus, to coin a term. He has raised the profile of the presidency to an unheard-of level. He uses Twitter and the media to prevail on every subject 24/7. The entire news cycle, not occasionally but all the time, responds to him and his every partial sentence or proclamation.

Already in his historic inauguration address, breaking with all tradition, Trump used words such as "carnage" and "crippled" and said that the real problem was the entrenched establishment of both political parties sitting directly behind him on the dais at the Capitol. America is under threat, and only a hero like Trump can save it.

The true promise and the solution stood in front of him: the American people. Our own tragic hero loved his country so much that he would sacrifice his wealth, lifestyle, and fame to make America great again.

Now he wants to keep America great.

The Christian Idea of the State

In May 2019 President Trump welcomed Viktor Orban, the prime minister of Hungary, to the White House. Orban is the present leader of the Hungarian national conservative Fidesz Party. That word means *civitas* or "civic alliance" in Hungarian and signals what Orban and his ilk stand for.

Handshakes apart, it was a particularly warm meeting of minds and souls. Orban is "probably like me," Trump announced in a joint appearance at the Oval Office with the visiting dignitary. "A little bit controversial, but that's okay. . . . You've done a good job, and you've kept your country safe," Trump sighed while suggesting that Orban, a controversial leader, "has done a tremendous job" and is "respected all over Europe."

In fact, they are remarkably alike. The two leaders not only share strong conservative and nationalist patriotic zeal, they express a similar fondness for what could be called the Christian idea of the state.

What is that political philosophy? Biblically, the state is an institution ordained by God, embracing both government and citizens, organized for the administration of justice and based on a monopoly of coercive power over a particular territory. The structure of the state is obtained by understanding the normative, political way the state functions in the basic ontological aspects of reality.

This "principled realism" has its foundation in the Old Testament and the moral foundation for legitimate government, the ten precepts, or commandments, given at Sinai.

According to the Christian worldview, human government was instituted by God to protect our unalienable rights from our own selfish tendencies (Genesis 9:6; Romans 13:1-7).

Human nature is of course capable of both vice and virtue. We recognize our tendency to infringe on our neighbor's rights to improve our own lives. Therefore, we know that government and political systems must exist to protect freedom and keep evil tendencies at bay. The right of self-determination and the governance of nation-states allow for a more civilized society.

In this definition in the New Testament and for the long centuries called Christendom, the ruler served as protector of his population. But rulers were not above the law. This definition also secured the biblical vision of independent nations we have come to know.

Since the Westphalian peace in Europe (1648) this vision has witnessed a variety of regimes, but the notion of limited government and separation of powers guides all those which endure.

Threats have come from those with imperial designs, whether ancient kingdoms, the Third Reich, or communist revolutions.

The Christian centuries were marked by religion taking a prominent place in public life and a thorough and open debate about just policies.

In this post-Christian era of globalism and totalitarianism—from the left and the right—the basis and facts of both of these principles have been more or less eradicated.

There is less and less freedom, and the state increasingly has imposed a monolithic and bureaucratic stranglehold on both persons and families and on the other mediating structures so critical to a Christian definition of life. This includes the church itself.

Trump and Orban start from a totally different and nonliberal place. They are conservatives and nation builders, not leftist socialists who decry all countries and want none. Their very definitions are radically diametrical to the prevailing globalist elite's cosmopolitan ideology of no borders, no nations, and no limits to governmental control.

The Trump view of the world would alter all this and return us to the sound and just sovereignty of nations. The world is taking notice of this and the worldview it represents.

5

Trump's Policies

I was elected to represent the citizens of Pittsburgh, not Paris.
—PRESIDENT DONALD TRUMP

The Unsurprising Rise of the Foreign Policy Voter

There is a truism about foreign policy within the larger politi-cal community: Nobody cares about foreign policy. This is an assumption that bears examining.

Donald Trump inaugurated his campaign in June 2015 with a speech that covered a lot of ground. The media focused on one statement: "Mexico isn't sending their best."

Immigration was the linchpin of those first couple of weeks of the campaign to be the Republican nominee. Fortunes (political and economic) were made and lost on either side of the argu-ment. Back when Donald Trump was a humble front-runner in the Republican primaries of 2016 (he was never lower than first place), he had put that issue on the agenda.

Can one truly call immigration a matter of domestic policy? It is, after all, an international affair by definition. One struggles to justify the notion that nobody cared. Both the left and the right of the spectrum (even the anti-Trump right) have a lot to say about the matter. The debate has evolved into questions of foreign aid (a matter strictly of foreign policy) and the eligibility of Mexico as a safe third country—the sort of definition quibbled about in meeting rooms at the United Nations in Geneva. It focused on building a wall on the border of two countries.

Once candidate Trump became the Republican nominee, he was faced with Hillary Clinton, the embodiment of the "Blob," as President Obama had denominated America's foreign policy establishment. She was a former secretary of state, senator, and first lady, and Trump never hammered her on Hillarycare, the 1993 version of the Democratic Party's plan to reform American health care. Why focus on such historical footnotes in the face of her failed intervention in Libya ("We came, we saw, he died," she quipped about Colonel Gaddafi), the orgy of corruption in Haiti's earthquake relief effort, and the retraction of her support of the questionable Trans-Pacific Partnership (TPP) trade deal with Pacific nations?

Imagine the laughs you would have gotten ten years ago if you told them that people would care about trade agreements!

The Democrats may quibble about Trump's tax plan, his attempt to undo Obamacare, or any other number of domestic matters, but the fact remains that foreign policy is at the center of this administration's record.

This trend is evident elsewhere. Is Brexit not essentially a foreign policy matter? When a Frenchman and an Italian vote for Eurosceptic parties, are they not taking a strong stance on a major issue of international relations?

Pulling out of the Iran deal, standing up to China, any number of trade issues, North Korea, ISIS, Israel—Trump's record of putting

America first is clearly a matter of international relations. The first Trump term has been dominated by a debate about American relations with Moscow, hardly a kitchen table issue in the heartland.

When an American votes for Donald Trump, it is chiefly a vote against the Blob. Whatever they think America's role in the world is, it is distinct from the massive money sink that the departments of defense and state have pushed us into in Iraq and Afghanistan. Whether it is the fat, contented Europeans living off of American largesse in their generous welfare states or the unrelenting demands of Middle Eastern kingdoms fighting proxy wars, there is no end to the demands the world continually makes on America, with the all-too-willing participation of the DC lobbyist set and unenforced Foreign Agents Registration Act regulations.

Is it prejudiced to think that taking away government money from foreign adventures—the never-ending pageant of monsters to destroy—should come before the draining of government aid to the American poor? The answer is moot. American voters spoke in 2016 against the sellout trade deals that hollowed out the American economy and swelled the numbers of people on Medicaid, the poor person's health-care plan.

Why indeed should America subsidize the rich European welfare states to the detriment of its own citizens? What exactly was the benefit of Obama's Syrian, Yemeni, and Libyan wars to the average citizen in the heartland? The Blob has no good answer to these questions.

Through the lens of foreign policy, a political discipline that considers itself above political considerations, President Obama had one thing right: America's strategic interests in this century lie mainly in the Asian and Oceanic areas. The fight for the Eurasian world island is the locus of the twenty-first-century struggle for primacy in world affairs.

Joe Biden, President Obama's veep, along with another two dozen Democratic presidential candidates in 2020, consider President Trump's record to be deplorable. Nancy Pelosi, the unofficial head of the Democrats since 2016, managed to flip the House of Representatives by focusing on health care.

Winning in 2020 means bucking yet another major piece of received wisdom. America's voters do care about foreign policy; they just think the Blob's contempt for their anti-interventionism and antiglobalism is as deplorable as the Blob thinks they are.

TR and Trump on Immigration

Almost all Americans agree that Theodore Roosevelt was a great president. That's why his face is carved into the side of Mount Rushmore. Read the biographical trilogy by Edmund Morris if you want to learn more about the man, his life, and his many accomplishments.

More than any previous president, TR grappled with the issue of immigration, an issue of government policy that is both foreign and domestic.

As with President Trump today, in many ways it came to define his presidency.

"We should insist," the ex-president said in a statement read at a meeting of the American Defense Society on January 5, 1919, the day before he died, "that if the immigrant who comes here in good faith becomes an American and assimilates himself to us, he shall be treated on an exact equality with everyone else. For it is an outrage to discriminate against any such man because of creed, or birthplace, or origin. But this is predicated upon the person's becoming in every facet an American, and nothing but an American. . . . There can be no divided allegiance here. Any man who says he is an American, but something else also, isn't an American at all. We have room for but one flag, the American flag. . . . We have room for but one language here, and that is the English language . . . and we have room for but one sole loyalty and that is a loyalty to the American people."

This statement encompasses a view of the government's role in managing population flows. Rather than negligently allowing foreign states to determine (or fail to determine) how many of their people meander toward the lower forty-eight, TR advocated a more selective approach.

When you examine the facts, you will find that Trump agrees with Teddy.

TR advocated, as he put it, for "a Scandinavian, a German, or an Irishman who has really become an American." Before the woke reach for their phones, it bears repeating that none of those three ethnic groups mentioned had a very nice time in America when it arrived: Germans were routinely the subjects of suspicions of double loyalties (to the Kaiser/Führer), as were the Irish (supposedly loyal to the pope). The "whiteness" of certain groups was put into question by groups such as the KKK, and Catholics (like one of the authors of this book) were decidedly not part of the in-group.

Trump has repeatedly made the same point and is certainly not opposed in the least to people of any and all creeds, colors, and backgrounds coming to America legally to help make it great. Remember, TR also said emphatically that there is no such thing as a hyphenated American. For him it was all about allegiance.

Think about that. Now think about the various caravans of migrants that have swarmed the southern border waving the flags of various Central American republics, to say nothing of our southern neighbor.

We need to stop defining ourselves in identity political terms and return to this core belief in citizenship. By doing so, we can revive the important Latin notion expressed on the back of the dollar bill. It has been on our coinage since 1796: *E Pluribus Unum*.

It translates as "out of many one." It is in fact the motto of the United States of America. Men and women of many nations coming together to form a new one. This respects our diverse origins but suggests a higher calling: our Americanism.

Tons of immigrants flowed into the United States from Eastern Europe, Western Europe, Southern Europe, and elsewhere at the turn of the twentieth century. Jews flocked into America at the same time. All came legally and helped make America greater after spending forty days of quarantine on Ellis Island, hardly a low bar to clear in many cases.

America would not be what it is without all of them! But they were all screened and came legally, and assimilation was the key.

TR put it plainly. "Laws," Roosevelt said, "should be enacted to keep out all immigrants who do not show that they have the right stuff in them to enter into our life in terms of decent equality with our own citizens."

The Immigration Act of 1907 was the first federal statute to restrain immigration on the grounds of health, moral character, and criminality. It led to the establishment of the Dillingham Commission, which recommended literacy tests and quotas for all immigrants. Not just anyone could come. The legislation was bipartisan. Roosevelt and Woodrow Wilson both backed it. Republicans and Democrats supported it.

TR sought to combat xenophobic criterion or any form of racism as a basis for immigration. He was also decidedly opposed to anti-Semitism. He wanted all new Americans to be accepted and welcomed for their potential for assimilation and their economic benefit to the rapidly industrializing country. That was his definition of American nationalism. It is not unlike what some, including President Trump, are advocating today: a merit-based system for immigration.

Should we return to the TR notions of legal immigration rooted in citizenship? The answer from this president and his party is yes.

Trump's Clever Use of Economic Warfare

Economic warfare has been defined in textbooks as the use of, or the threat to use, economic means against a country in order to weaken its economy and thereby reduce its political and military power.

Such nonmilitary yet essentially warlike activity includes the use of economic means to compel an adversary to alter its policies or behavior or to undermine its ability to conduct normal relations with other countries.

These economic means stop short of outright and overt physical engagement or battle, but they seek a remedy and have real, measurable consequences. Some of those measures today take an electronic or digital form in the case of cryptowar.

The most common means of such economic warfare are trade embargoes, boycotts, sanctions, tariff discrimination, the freezing of capital assets, the suspension of aid, the prohibition of investment and other capital flows, and expropriation.

Trump has deployed all of them and done so more often than past U.S. presidents. They have come to define both his image and his foreign strategy.

Of course, countries engaging in economic warfare want to weaken an adversary's economy by denying that adversary access to necessary physical, financial, and technological resources or by otherwise harming its ability to benefit from trade, financial, and technological exchanges with other countries.

The United States is no different, and Trump and his team have become wizards at these kinds of actions. Trump has utilized all these measures to bring about shifts in policy and to get a country, a party, or a person to the negotiating table or impose a degree of harm short of military engagement to protect or defend our national interests.

Economic warfare is now more or less synonymous with Trump's foreign policy as a tool, a stick as it were and a carrot to induce desired behaviors. How is it working?

According to *Foreign Policy*, "a year into his presidency, President Donald Trump has become an aggressive practitioner of economic sanctions. So far, the Treasury Department has added over 700 people, companies, and government agencies to sanctions lists." They claim this is unsustainable for that list.

The *Financial Times* goes further and castigates Trump for using too many sanctions too loosely, thereby hurting world trade. The left-wing *Guardian* goes further yet, saying, "Since taking office last year, he has repeatedly resorted to draconian economic sanctions and trade tariffs, launching them like missiles at countries and people he does not approve of. Trump did not invent the practice, but it has become his foreign policy weapon of choice."

However, according to the brilliant international legal expert Professor Ingrid Frankopan in her opus *The Law of War*, "the reaction of international society to a breach of international law is often that of imposing sanctions on an offending State."

She goes on to say that "one of the most common forms of sanctions during conflict has been a declaration on trade or, more prominently, on the purchase of weapons."

In other words, embargoes are an important and forceful type of economic sanctions. So are tariffs, sanctions, and prohibitions.

Trump is proving that they can work, yet many mainstream economists oppose economic sanctions or related measures, saying they don't work or they violate the system of free trade.

They are wrong. Economic sanctions are a most attractive political tool for the U.S. government to use to express dissatisfaction even if they don't always totally achieve the change envisaged.

They are greatly preferred to military intervention. Generals and admirals don't always understand or comprehend economic warfare because they know little about the economy or business and therefore too often decry or downplay those options.

Economic warfare does not always prevent armed conflict. It can escalate if not used appropriately and effectively. It could be said that the higher the level of ambition, the harder it is to achieve the impact when it comes to economic warfare.

Here are a few general rules on economic warfare that Trump seems to be learning:

1. Use them on a short-term basis, not as a long-term solution.
2. Take full measures that bite seriously, not halfhearted ones. Maximize pressure.
3. Get as much international and diplomatic support as possible.
4. Realize that practice differs radically from theory.
5. Because of increased international interdependence and global supply chains, know that some means are less likely to work or more difficult to implement.
6. Because of the variety of sourcing and mobility of capital, any sanctions need to be tight and duly enforced.
7. It all comes down to the teeth. Monitor and enforce.

Trump knows that economic measures as a form of warfare are powerful foreign policy instruments. They are not merely economic tools. They also have a domestic political aspect that should not be discounted. Trump uses them in a fashion that supports his political base. He doesn't want to shoot America or Americans in the foot, but as he has shown in Syria, Iran, Venezuela, North Korea, Cuba, China, Russia, and the European Union, he means business.

Trump is in effect becoming the master of economic warfare.

The Saudi Sword Dance

When President Trump and his large entourage of cabinet executives, family members, and advisers went to the desert kingdom of Saudi Arabia for its first venture abroad in early 2017, the media and foreign affairs pundits were puzzled. Why would he go there first? What was up? He was breaking with tradition. He was disrupting norms. Mecca, Rome, and Jerusalem, the trinity of Abrahamic holy cities, was the first order of business for Geo Deus.

Swaying from side to side, brandishing swords with the Saudi king, Trump appeared at ease and was enjoying himself in a reenergizing of the relationship with a longtime and traditional ally, a major oil supplier. The supposed Islamophobia that liberal journalists insist they can see in POTUS's heart was nowhere to be seen.

The larger Riyadh diplomatic conference that ensued not only included billions upon billions in valuable new business agreements and defense spending but also involved a first-ever collection of Sunni leaders from all over the Middle East. This signaled a new day in U.S.–Arab relations after a tense period under President Obama, who they feared would abandon traditional allies for a rapprochement with Tehran.

The Sunni divide with their Muslim minority counterpart Shias was at the heart of this new U.S. alliance. POTUS put in place a larger policy revolving around Iran and renouncing the Joint Comprehensive Plan of Action (JCPOA), the centerpiece of Obama's Middle East strategy. It also set new hopes for potential peace accords with Israel, an ally of both America and many of the Sunni countries represented, loath as they may be to admit it in public.

This was a high-stakes game, and it was significant in at least two regards: what it portended in terms of future relations and who will be part of that movement. If Trump and his team were able to pull it all off in its many pieces and parts, the Middle East would indeed become a different place: a rich, peaceful oasis of markets full of wealthy consumers and investors.

With the wind-down of U.S. activity in Syria and the later end to the much-dreaded Iranian deal, Trump is extricating the United States and its armed forces from the region while pushing the Sunni-Israeli bond to seize the day. Offloading security commitments by increasing the weight carried by our allies is the watchword.

The 2018 campaign slogan was "Promises made, promises kept." Pulling out of commitments in the Middle East while balancing regional powers to keep the peace was a centerpiece of the 2016 platform. As Trump takes troops out of the theater, which he promised to do, every priority and ambition to put foreign interests in front of America's cries out for attention.

After the debacle of the Khashoggi murder at the hands of identified Saudi parties probably tied to Prince Mohammad bin Salman (MbS), the king's son and recognized heir, putting America first has become more difficult under close media scrutiny and international pressure.

The arms sales and business relations remain paramount for Trump, and he is unwilling to give them up. His son-in-law Jared Kushner has been tasked with forging a better and more complete plan for peace involving Israel and the Palestinian Authority, a plan that will need buy-in from Israel's neighbors. With Saudi help that plan could have teeth, but its details have been slow in coming forward.

The Saudis have been noticeably helpful on oil production and in dealing with the countries in the region that follow Riyadh's lead. They want a quid pro quo for this behavior, and some of that involves their internecine battles with both Qatar and the Houthi rebels in Yemen. Along with his hard-line national security adviser, John Bolton, Trump is adamantly punching back on Iran.

However, this White House is not at all unique in protecting the American alliance with Saudi Arabia.

At the close of World War II, Ibn Saud, the founder of modern-day Saudi Arabia, met Franklin Delano Roosevelt on the USS *Quincy* to forge that alliance. The relationship was, is, and will be about fairly narrow interests. The steady flow of oil and the recycling of petrodollars makes up one side, and Saudi Arabia's survival makes up the other.

Trump has doubled down and cemented good relations with the view of befriending the Saudis to get more business and therefore jobs in America and a permanent settlement to the Israel problem, which has gone on for decades. This is political and economic realism and remains unchanged even if it has a Trump twist. Trump will see to it that this general policy remains stable.

The sword dance was a visual metaphor for that fact and opened a personal chit with the wider Sunni leadership. Trump will not pander to the Saudis but use them in his larger vision for America first. That doesn't mean just selling more weapons ($110 billion in sales was announced in May 2017); it means a deeper form of cooperation that is centered on counterterrorism and the moderation of the extremist strain of Islam, which is controlled by certain elements of the Saudi royal family.

This deepened Faustian bargain involves both parties and has been stress tested, particularly with the human rights concerns surrounding MbS. They are being weathered, but the benefits are still in many ways to be fully realized, though the steep political cost of supporting an ally who murdered a *Washington Post* journalist in cold blood has been paid up front and in full.

The Saudi government's drive to diversify its economy, converting the public investment fund into a $2 trillion sovereign wealth fund, is the centerpiece of this strategy. By selling state assets and divesting a stake in the state-owned Aramco oil company, MbS is offering America a share of the pie. It is the art of the deal.

Iran Regime: The Persian Problem

President Trump has a number of advisers who seemingly have very different strategies for dealing with the long-standing radical fundamentalist nemesis Iran.

Trump has shown insight and deliberation on Iran as he has attempted to renegotiate what was a horribly bad deal made by the Obama team and his secretary of state, John Kerry. It was a sellout that did not achieve what it sought, failed in many areas, and sent money—in cash—to a terrorist state without getting sufficient benefits in return. It was, in other words, what Trump has termed "a very bad deal."

Let's face it: Iran has been a thorn in the side to America and the West since it overthrew the Shah in 1979 and went down a path of radical political Islam of the Shia sect. It has put into place what is unquestionably a terrorist state and exports that terrorism everywhere in the region and around the world. The facts are well documented, and any deal needs to fix this.

Iran's people have repeatedly chanted "Death to America" since they first stormed the U.S. embassy in Tehran and seized American hostages. Things never got better, and through the years Iran has become synonymous with the very word "terrorism." It spews hate at Israel and all who refuse to accept its evil regime. Lebanon, one of the few relatively progressive, developed, and democratic Arab states, has been ruined by the radicalization and militarization of the Shia population by Hezbollah, an armed militia that doesn't even bother to keep its political wing separate as the Irish Republican Army and Basque nationalists (both terrorist groups to be sure) have done.

Not only has Iran terrorized its own citizens, it has become the prime exporter of terror against its neighbors and in the rest of the Middle East. It has funded and extolled the Hamas radicals in the Palestinian territory, the Houthis against Yemen, and the Hezbollah armies in Lebanon, Syria, Afghanistan, and elsewhere. It literally has funded as much terror as possible.

The Quds Force is a unit in Iran's Islamic Revolutionary Guard Corps (IRGC) that is directed to carry out unconventional warfare and intelligence activities and is responsible for extraterritorial operations.

It is commanded by Major General Qasem Soleimani. They have prominent private sector fronts all over the world and operate both a clandestine intelligence force and a standing army semiseparated from the Iranian military. The Quds Force supports nonstate actors in many foreign countries, including the Lebanese Hezbollah, Hamas and Palestinian Islamic Jihad in the Gaza Strip and the West Bank, Yemeni Houthis, and Shia militias in Iraq, Syria, and Afghanistan. The United States has designated the Quds Force a supporter of terrorism since 2007. This was reaffirmed by the United States when the IRGC as a whole was designated as a terrorist group in April 2019. Analysts do not know the Quds Force's exact size but estimate it at about 20,000 members. It reports directly to the supreme leader of Iran, Ayatollah Khamenei.

One approach to Iran of U.S. hawks is military engagement and a counterstrike policy that could escalate and embroil the region and America in a long, costly, and devastating war, as was the case in Iraq.

John Bolton, Trump's former national security adviser, allegedly "never met a war he did not like." He seems ready to bomb or even use troops to bring about regime change. His hands were all over the Iraq strategy.

However, people such as the dovish Republican senator Rand Paul, a libertarian who opposes the use of American force and its military-industrial complex, also have Trump's ear. They don't want America engaged in Iran or elsewhere and don't see any cost-benefit analysis that suggests that there are sufficient upsides to risking war. Tucker Carlson, the Fox News host, is a recent addition to this list of peacemongers.

In the middle, Secretary of State Mike Pompeo has straddled the options and suggested a halfway approach that lists twelve conditions Iran must meet to be welcomed back into the community of nations and uses maximum economic sanctions to bring Iran to the negotiating table. That these conditions are unacceptable to Tehran is beside the point: The status quo is unacceptable to Washington. Pompeo sees a proportional use of strength and has argued for more sanctions as well as crypto-actions against the radical Iranian regime, its armed forces, and its economy.

After an incident involving the use of sea mines or torpedoes against two foreign tankers and the downing of an American unmanned drone, Trump decided to take the Pompeo route and stopped short of retaliatory measures involving the loss of many lives, instead opting for more thorough and damaging sanctions. This wise and measured response has been well received by the international community but roundly criticized by the neocons and some Democrats as showing a lack of American resolve and decisiveness.

What Trump is doing on Iran is trying to fix decades of bad policy and to deflect that nation's atrocious behavior in the region as the world's foremost state sponsor of terrorism. The mullahs are reluctant to change their evil ways even if there are variations in their political views.

The pressure Trump has applied and the persistence to stay the course are increasingly likely to achieve a positive outcome. The Iranian economy suffers and suffers and then suffers some more. Inflation is out of control; the currency has fallen precipitously, goods are hard to find and expensive, oil revenues have plummeted, and GNP continues to decline. All this in time could cause implosion or regime collapse.

If Trump keeps his nerve and implements measures that cut off Iran's last foreign economic lifelines, that nation's prospects will be grim. Iran's population is already suffering under the incompetent rule of an oppressive theocracy. That explains its silly brinkmanship, but the country's leaders also know that blowing up the nuclear accord, as they continually threaten to do, will only push the Europeans reluctantly into Trump's arms and further worsen Iran's economic plight.

A patient course gives Iran no option but to play Trump's game at no cost or bloodshed for America. This is another potentially winning strategy. Trump is good at tough talk and bold diplomacy, but he does not seek war. The mullahs would be wise to bring their reasonable faculties to bear.

The End of ISIS

When Donald Trump assumed the U.S. presidency in January 2017, ISIS controlled a large swath of Iraq and Syria that accounted for approximately a third of those two countries, hijacking the peace in Iraq and the rebellion against President Assad.

The self-declared Caliphate was strong and vibrant and commanded vast territory, resources, and armed forces. ISIS enforced strict sharia law on local populations, took their wealth, and even ran land registries and tax administrations: a serious challenge to the states it usurped.

The Obama administration had been thwarted in its efforts to eliminate ISIS, and it seemed to accept the facts on the ground. Although America and the militias under its influence wanted to curtail ISIS and take back land, not much was happening. By any honest assessment, ISIS was stronger than ever.

With frustration running high amid a confused state of policy, Trump and his generals stepped into the void and sought just one thing: the total and complete end of ISIS. They put together a battle plan to annihilate the enemy and take back all of the ground, if not destroy the extremist ideology itself.

Kurdish fighters and the U.S. Air Force were able to virtually annihilate ISIS in roughly eighteen months. Week by week we took back large portions of territory. This literally changed the contours of the map. The last battle, in March 2019, after the fall of Raqqa, ISIS's spiritual and military headquarters, was in Baghouz, an enclave in the Euphrates valley on the border between the two countries.

ISIS, of course, is registered as a terrorist organization by the United Nations and is known for its beheadings and brutal executions of soldiers and civilians, including journalists. It is also responsible not only for gross human rights violations but for war crimes. It committed ethnic cleansing and genocide in the northern parts of Iraq.

ISIS was the outcome of the disastrous Iraq War, which was a roll of the dice. It was not a war Trump sought or thought necessary. He called it Bush's neocon exercise. It was a bad theory with very high costs, and it had an atrocious outcome.

The U.S. surge in Iraq in 2007–2009 put a damper on the enemy, which was then named al-Qaeda, the precursor to ISIS. But once it was reconstituted, ISIS ran wild. Barack Obama referred to it as the "junior varsity," but it was a JV squad he couldn't beat. Al-Qaeda never tried to administer territory, but the ideology was mostly the same: Islamic chauvinism with revanchist claims stretching from Kazakhstan to Mali.

Daesh, as it is known in Arabic, or IS (Islamic State), was a nonstate actor that adhered to fundamentalist Salafist doctrines. The organization gained prominence in early 2014 when it drove Iraqi government forces out of key places in western Iraq and captured the significant city of Mosul.

As a caliphate, ISIS claimed authority over all Muslims world-wide on religious, legal, and political matters. Operating in eigh-teen countries, including Afghanistan and Pakistan, it had an estimated budget that exceeded a $1 billion, mainly from selling stolen antiques and slave trading. With a fighting army of over 30,000 battle-hardened combatants, ISIS was a foe to contend with. The long-term goal of ISIS was stated clearly: to conquer the world. Headed by Abu Bakr al-Baghdadi, the self-styled caliph, ISIS was a potent enemy and excelled at extremist propaganda.

In the last months of the war against ISIS, the United States had around 2,000 troops in Syria mainly to support the Syrian defense forces in fighting the Islamic State. That number is slated to go down to about 400 now that the mission has been com-pleted as Trump disentangles the United States from the region.

Trump said: "You kept hearing it was 90 percent, 92 percent, the Caliphate in Syria. Now it's 100 percent gone. We did that in a much shorter period of time than it was supposed to be."

Trump, using American might, bombing, and some boots on the ground, did what no other president had been able to do. How did he do it? He took the fight to them and gave his generals and com-manders in the field the prerogative to exercise control—to win.

For Trump, winning is everything. Simple but effective.

Our Israeli Brethren

President Trump's victory in 2016 was excellent news for Israel. America has always been on the side of its staunchest and only democratic ally in the Middle East, but during the Obama administration that relationship was cast into doubt. The United States became anti-Israel, as the Democrats have been since Hillary's defeat.

The Obama foreign policy was a rebuke to Israel, nowhere more than in the dying days of President Obama's second term. He abandoned Israel in the UN Security Council, letting that body pass a resolution that can provide the legal basis for international prosecution of our allies. Ths was a far cry from the days when Taiwan wielded China's veto on behalf of Tel Aviv.

The Iran deal—extremely disliked by Tel Aviv—was the very centerpiece of the Obama administration and especially of Secretary of State John Kerry. Obama traded our pro-Israel stance for a flimsy nuclear pact with a terrorist regime that sided with our enemies and was out to destroy Israel one way or another.

Faced with this set of policies, when Trump became president, he immediately did an about-face, changing the policy 100 percent. Not only did he sink the doomed Iran deal, he went to Israel and made the deepest of commitments.

Unlike so many U.S. presidents before him, Trump actually delivered on his promises. He kept his word. That became evident when, against State Department thinking and lobbying, he moved the U.S. embassy from Tel Aviv to Jerusalem, shocking the Palestinians and the whole world. No one believed he would actually do it, but he did. The Israelis were elated and most grateful.

He delivered on all the commitments to defend Israel and to sell them the top caliber of U.S. defense systems and aircraft. Trump then went one better and recognized the Golan Heights—land taken during the Six-Day War decades ago—as sovereign Israeli territory. What was once Syrian territory used by Hezbollah to fire on Israel from on high probably will be part of a wider negotiation of the Syrian peace and set the precedent for land changing hands in the Middle East.

Unlike Obama, who sent campaign advisers to the Israeli opposition, Trump solidified a long-standing commitment to Benjamin Netanyahu, a leader who loves America almost as much as Trump does (he was born in Philadelphia).

Trump, along with his Orthodox Jewish son-in-law Jared Kushner, has examined the contours of a peace plan that would bring something that has been missing for many decades: a durable peace and settlement of the Palestinian issue.

It would be difficult to imagine a more pro-Israel administration than the Trump team. It has cast its lot with Israel and brought the friendship to new heights. It has challenged old assumptions and delivered in powerful and unexpected ways.

The land for peace formula never worked, and so it has been discarded. Trump's historic policies instead make peace itself the reward for peace. Meanwhile, the increasingly more leftist Democratic Party has abandoned support for Israel and become blatantly anti-Jewish.

Secretary of State Pompeo, a true Trumpian, said it is possible that "God raised up Trump to protect Israel from Iranian aggression."

The Antidote to Globalism: A Better, More Localized Economy

Many people, particularly on the North American side of the Atlantic, have never heard of Wilhelm Röpke. That is a shame: He was one of the most important economists of the twentieth century, a true Renaissance man, a polymath, and a father of the "economic miracle" after World War II. His thinking is particularly valuable today as we move away from globalism and corporatism and return to more local supply chains, give greater significance to small and medium-sized businesses, and move toward a humane economy.

Röpke displayed unique moral courage. He was often politically incorrect and was perhaps the sharpest critic of the failure of Keynesianism ever.

Ludwig Erhard claimed that he "illegally obtained Röpke's books . . . which I absorbed as the desert drinks life-giving water." (His classic, *The Humane Economy*, was translated into English in 1952.)

Röpke, a full professor at the early age of twenty-four, was also the first German professor to lose his job in 1933 when the Nazis came to power. They despised him, as did the communists. As an exile who would not cave in to Hitler and the SS, he never returned to his native land, living instead in the cantons of Switzerland that practiced what he preached.

He is less well known to the English-speaking world than Friedrich Hayek, Ludwig von Mises, or Milton Friedman, and there have been few book-length treatments of his contributions, although numerous biographies exist.

As the intellectual author of Europe's post–World War II economic resurrection, Röpke is an underappreciated thinker who informed policy making. We could use his thinking today!

He could rightly be called a Smithian (Adam Smith, that is), as he was adamantly against the unlimited power of the state, but he was much more. Röpke was an economic humanist of the first order. He historically showed how the Great Depression came to limit economics as a science and how collectivism is incompatible with authentic human freedom. This is unquestioningly an exercise in historical recovery that is also much needed today.

Four subjects concerned Röpke until his early death in 1966: the challenge of business cycles, the unending growth of the welfare state, full employment and inflation, and international economic relations.

Röpke's political economy was attuned to "interdependence," in which empirical analysis is not separated from normative judgment. With a profound focus on "human flourishing," Röpke was enlightened beyond today's narrowly trained economists and econometricians because of his scope and vast intellectual and multidisciplinary horizons.

By returning modern economics to the Aristotelian realm of ethics from which it originally emerged, Röpke achieved a new synthesis. For him the market economy allowed people to exercise their "natural liberty," which was rooted in the Christian realism of Saint Augustine.

As part of the promarket Austrian school, as opposed to the historical school, Röpke can best be placed in the context of major modern economic thinkers such as Walter Eucken, Alexander Rustow, Franz Böhm, and Alfred Müller-Armack. Breaking with the dirigiste past together, they sought to articulate an economy rightly framed on order. For them economics was a normative social science as Marx wished it to be. They discerned values beyond utility.

This is a style of political economy that needs to find a revival as it is sorely lacking in today's boring mathematized treatments and small-gauge discussions about trends in data.

It is something we need if we are to overcome the economism of the present and reengage with true human flourishing.

For Röpke, economics unfortunately often had a "restricted vision." This view parallels the better-known thoughts of Hayek, who also warned about the scientism of economics and was an equally harsh critic of Lord Keynes and his overly ardent followers who favored constant government intervention. Both witnessed what they called the failure of intellectuals and their nearly total surrender to the evils of socialism portrayed as a road to serfdom inhabited if not dictated by arrogant government bureaucrats.

With liberty constantly under attack, Röpke's "Christian humanism" is a perfect antidote or remedy to the crisis that surrounds us on every front in both Europe and America. It appears even more urgent in light of our most recent economic collapse and massive government interventions cum bailouts.

Röpke would appreciate the unleashing of deregulation and the economic growth rooted in freedom we are seeing in the United States today, but he would go much further.

Many of our politicians, especially the Marxist Democrats, still seem plagued with an incessant belief in what Röpke termed "the folly of human perfectibility." Our newly anointed leftist political saviors have an unflinching belief in the ability of the state to solve all our problems and cure all our ills. If only they knew. If only they had read and been taught by Röpke.

There are clear connections to the Scottish Enlightenment thinking in Röpke's opus. Röpke sought to avert welfare statism but held a conservative attachment to tradition, especially to the all-important mediating structures of civilized life. They included for him the family, the school, civic associations, churches and temples, and the local community.

Röpke realized that the space between the individual and the all-powerful state is where life is actually lived. This variety of what is called ordoliberalism owes a great debt to the Scottish Enlightenment. Indeed, this tension between social conservatism on one side and economic liberalism, even in Republican politics, on the other continues into the present era. Until it is resolved, perhaps by reemploying the likes of Röpke and his seminal ideas, we will be one-handed and fail to see the full dimensions of ordered liberty.

Such division also undercuts potential conservative political power, unnecessarily dividing it into warring camps of social versus economic conservatism.

A cohesive model of the market economy and its social dimensions offers a useful and viable alternative. Trump seems to be going down this path.

We seriously need to bring back interest in both Röpke and his humane economy. We would all be the beneficiaries, especially those critical of the left and the Keynesian models that have led to damaging globalism and the elitism of the party of Davos.

Trump, No Chump on Trade

Recently, President Trump tweeted: "The U.S. is doing very well with China, and talking."

The press has hammered him mercilessly for being tough on trade. Guess what? It is working.

Trump's trade policy is focused on these key elements as it succeeds at the overarching theme of his presidency: making America great again. His attention is fully on putting America first.

Trump is a free trader by instinct, and as he has stated, he has no plans to return to the failed Smoot-Hawley plan of the 1930s. The economic reality is that tariffs usually don't work. Countries retaliate, and all parties lose in a trade war.

Of course, in the past, the United States has always backed down and caved in. Not Trump! We are negotiating this time to get real results, not just more promises and blather.

There are supposedly 142 items on our list of demands to China.

What realistically can be done by Trump on trade vis-à-vis China and other predatory mercantilist nations?

On the supply side, surely the United States must get more competitive. This includes more research and development, constant innovation, advanced technological manufacturing, improved access to capital, renewed skills training, and bench-marking. Upping wages, which can never happen in the presence of competition from slave-wage sweatshop workers in places like China, is one of the best and most reliable sources of innovation.

A progrowth agenda and a deregulated environment are being sought earnestly by Trump and will lead to prosperity and rising standards of living and increased wages for all Americans.

On the demand side, Trump has already cooled off on all the Obama globalist trade deals. Now he has put them on ice permanently. They are history. The Trans-Pacific Partnership (TPP) with eleven Asian countries was a bad deal. Trump killed it.

The one with the European Union is no better. It is dead in the water. Its socialist bonanza with MERCOSUR, a leftist trade bloc set up by Brazilian President Lula (in jail for buying off fellow socialists all over Latin America), is not the right model to install permanently in the international system.

Next, continue to confront China on its currency manipulation. This is rarely discussed but is at the heart of our trade imbalance.

The Treasury Department's biannual report to Congress on the exchange rate practices of our trading partners confirms Trump's analysis that foreign countries are eating our lunch and that the U.S. government is doing little or nothing about it. Under current procedures, by the time we finish pleading with them to halt their unfair practices, there will be little or no industrial economy left in this country.

Under enhanced reporting criteria set forth by Congress in the Trade Enhancement and Trade Facilitation Act of 2015, the U.S. Treasury names five countries—China, Japan, Korea, Taiwan, and Germany—whose trade policies pose a threat to the U.S. and global economies. This is nothing more than a "name and shame" document since each of these countries meets only two of the three criteria necessary for (ineffective) action.

Thus, all Treasury does is put the countries on a new monitoring list. Big deal! That means that we watch them while they continue to steal factories and jobs from the United States and its workers. Even if these countries did meet all three criteria, the potential penalties are toothless and can be reversed by the president basically at will.

We need a concrete plan that fixes this situation with immediate action.

Currency misdealing can no longer be tolerated. If need be, we can play the same game.

Make no mistake, China and other countries also routinely break the rules by dumping their products (not just steel) below cost in the U.S. market. Some also specialize in making counterfeit products, costing the companies that make the authentic products over $20 billion a year.

We were told that Larry Kudlow and the Trump team were negotiating on this and that further tariffs were postponed for 90 days, and then the talks broke down and new tariffs were instigated on larger sums.

This is not a sound idea. China reacts only to real threats and real tariffs, and so we have to keep up the pressure, not relax it.

If we fail to do so, they will game us again just as they have for the last three decades.

Trump needs to tell China and anyone else doing this that we will add up the bill and assess the tariffs accordingly.

They also need to police their producers on their end. That goes especially for illicit goods, including fentanyl, which is killing thousands of Americans.

The same countries also use illegal transshipping by changing documentation to avoid duties. The penalties on such behavior should be raised a thousandfold. A few shamed examples that are severely penalized would work to end the practice.

It is true that Trump will need congressional approval for the imposition of any lasting and sizable tariffs on imports. This he can get with a Republican-controlled Senate. He does not need approval for short-term sectoral retaliatory tariffs or negotiations. This he can do himself and indeed has.

Trump also can block U.S. companies from shifting production overseas by taxing them identically at home and abroad; abolishing the foreign tax credit, which allows companies to avoid double taxation; and jawboning them, as he has already done with Carrier Corporation, which planned on moving 1,500 jobs from Indiana to Mexico. These actions should set a precedent.

It will be imperative for Trump to work with Congress, which has jurisdiction over many trade matters.

Honestly, our elites on both sides of the political spectrum have been lying about the exaggerated benefits of globalization for decades. It, like free trade, is in reality a mixed bag.

As in any equation, there are inevitably winners and losers. The losers have unfortunately been Americans, particularly the middle class who work in manufacturing and reside in the Rust Belt.

Free trade, you see, as nice as it appears in theory and in economics textbooks, does not benefit everyone. The United States has lost one-third of its jobs over the last fifteen years—over 6 million real workers gone.

In 2018 the United States ran a $365 billion merchandise trade deficit with China alone, which translates to 2.4 million jobs lost to Chinese imports over the longer period.

Trump's tariffs should be used as what they are: a threat. They are a stick, and they can be removed when the culprits change their behavior.

The point is that we want reciprocity. Play by the rules that were set up by the World Trade Organization or we will react. Those rules also must be bent in our favor, as they are uneven at present.

This will keep more jobs at home. Open up or we will close down. That means that Japanese and European car markets, Chinese financial services, and access to every other market must change or we will reciprocate and impose on them exactly what they impose on us.

Isn't that fair?

We have been stupid for far too long, so now, under Trump, we are starting to get smart. After all, global trade is not a zero-sum game.

Trump is putting together a comprehensive plan to uphold his promise to the American voters. This will involve tough negotiations by professionals who know what they are doing and coordination between the United States Trade Representative and Commerce, Defense, Energy, and Treasury as well as all other government agencies.

Trump has named a trade czar, the brilliant Ambassador Robert Lighthizer, who will work for him alone—not for any special interests—and who is producing immediate and measurable results. He won't fall for China's empty promises.

A new index on MAGA called the Trump Prosperity Index should capture how we are doing, measuring all new jobs created, all jobs returned, economic expansion, the employment participation rate, and all trade balances moving in our direction. This single combined number will prove Trump's economic benefits in a telling way.

He has started, and now he must finish the job. Trump is producing results and moving the needle in the direction it needs to go. The entire country is counting on it. The result will be a more inclusive capitalism, higher economic growth, and improved employment numbers for every worker.

A New United States–Mexico–Canada Trade Deal

Trump ran against the NAFTA trade agreement—"the worst deal ever"—and sees it as the embodiment of everything that is wrong about the direction of America, its trade patterns, and its negotiation skills.

From the day he went down the escalator in Trump Tower, announcing he was running to become U.S. president, Trump has decried and lambasted the NAFTA agreement. It has crippled America, he has said.

Never a fan of the multilateral pact that seemed to trade America's jobs for cheap goods made south of the border while giving Canada access to our markets without much reciprocity, Trump has demanded either a change in or the end of NAFTA.

Recall that the United States entered into a bilateral trade negotiation with Canada more than thirty years ago, resulting in the United States–Canada Free Trade Agreement, which came into force in 1989. In 1991, bilateral talks began with Mexico, which Canada then joined. NAFTA followed—the North American

Free Trade Agreement—which came into force in 1994. Tariffs were eliminated progressively, and all duties and quantitative restrictions, with the exception of those on a small number of agricultural products and goods traded with Canada, were eliminated by 2008.

NAFTA also included chapters covering rules of origin, customs procedures, agriculture and sanitary and phytosanitary measures, government procurement, investment, trade in services, protection of intellectual property rights, and dispute settlement procedures. It was a fairly comprehensive treaty.

However, its effects were not as promised. The rules and flow favored Mexico and Canada more than the United States. Mexico especially had benefited from its exports to the large and affluent U.S. market. The "giant sucking sound" that Ross Perot was ridiculed for naming turned out to be prophetic.

So much was this the case that underdeveloped Mexico had a $63.6 billion trade surplus with the United States in 2017. Canada likewise saw a swing in its favor because of oil imports by the United States.

Trump saw this relationship as problematic and harmful to the United States, particularly to its manufacturing base, the very people who had swept him into office. He said that NAFTA was "the worst trade deal the U.S. has ever signed" and that it "has and continues to kill American jobs."

Trump decided that one option was just to pull out of NAFTA, to drop it in one fell swoop. He threatened to do just that, to pull the plug. Another option was to renegotiate a new, improved, and better (for the United States) agreement with a new name and rules.

When he put hawkish U.S. Trade Representative Robert Lighthizer on the case, a complete overhaul was envisioned. A new United States–Mexico–Canada Trade Agreement (USMCA) was hammered out and signed in November 2018 at the G20 meeting in Argentina.

Trump wanted the new agreement to replace "the catastrophe known as NAFTA" and "deliver for American workers like they have not been delivered to for a long time."

Awaiting congressional approval, what has been called NAFTA 2.0 has had a few new tweaks and appears to help America more than its predecessor did. Notably, it changes rules of origin, especially benefiting U.S. automakers by requiring that 75 percent of components be made in the treaty countries to qualify for zero tariffs. By 2023, 45 percent of automobile parts will have to be made by workers who earn at least $16 an hour.

Mexico has also agreed to pass laws giving workers the right to union representation, extending labor protections to migrant workers, and protecting women from discrimination. Importantly, U.S. farmers will get greater access to the Canadian dairy market. This was a big issue for Trump and his rural supporters.

The new deal extends the life of intellectual property to seventy years and protects pharmaceutical drugs from generic competition, a major win for American companies. There are many new provisions to deal with the digital economy. However, there are no Section 232 protections in the new bill. Trump insisted that the agreement contain a sixteen-year "sunset" clause. The deal is subject to a review every six years, at which point the United States, Mexico, and Canada can decide to extend the USMCA.

Trump negotiated hard, particularly with Canadian Prime Minister Trudeau. In the end, President Trump tweeted about the pact, calling it "one of the most important, and largest, trade deals in U.S. and world history." And now we have the new USMCA deal, thanks to Trump.

Geo Deus—the world of God—is a world where America comes first and delivers to its people the bounty of their efforts.

MERCOSUR, the European Union, and "Free Trade"

After twenty years of negotiations, Paraguay, Uruguay, Argentina, and Brazil signed an agreement with Brussels for the elimination of tariffs on a number of exports in either direction. Pedro Sánchez, the failing socialist prime minister of Spain, is leading the charge for this free trade agreement between the European Union and MERCOSUR.

Who cares?

The domestication of Jair Bolsonaro is a Brazilian problem. That he would sign a document committing him to break multiple campaign promises is a betrayal of Brazilian democracy but is sadly par for the course. Uruguay has been a leftist stalwart since the election in 2010 of José "Pepe" Mujica, an old lefty with a decent record. Argentina's President Macri, on the centrist end of the right-wing spectrum, is trying to have his rightist cake and eat it too, mainly to win elections. Paraguay hasn't had its own agency since Brazil and Argentina devoured its richest provinces in the nineteenth century.

Is it safe to ignore the leftist machinations behind this?

The treaty is meant to lift tariffs on US$4.5 billion worth of goods, a rounding error in American eyes. The ratification of the treaty remains up for grabs: As with the EU's free trade agreement with Canada, the agricultural and environmentalist lobbies are playing the bootlegger and the Baptist. South American agriculture is too dirty and disrespectful to its workers to compete in the European paradise.

Indeed, it remains to be seen if the treaty can make it through the over two dozen national legislatures (and subnational legislatures), to say nothing of the European Parliament, where the agricultural lobby remains the longest-established force and the Greens are a new power to contend with.

MERCOSUR was established under center-right governments in 1991, another project of the globalist Washington Consensus. It started out with good intentions—nobody really opposes free trade on its own merits—though important details remain unresolved.

The rise of the "pink tide" in the early 2000s, with leftist governments sweeping to power all over Latin America, did what leftists always do: take over the creations of others and repurpose them for their own ends.

With the accession of Chávez's Venezuela, it became an important forum for the internationalist efforts of the Latin American left. A number of other countries joined as observers, the first step toward membership. Bolivia, another leftist stalwart during the pink tide era, remains a candidate country.

Venezuela's membership has been suspended for offenses against democracy. Caracas surely will come back to haunt this and the other regional integration mechanisms Chávez established during his long rule (CELAC, Petrocaribe) if Caracas is allowed back into the international system without repenting.

If the MERCOSUR-EU FTA is ratified, the only thing standing between Nicolás Maduro and access to the European markets will be a formality in the MERCOSUR assembly and his own ratification of the final agreement. Not quite what he deserves for forcing over 15 percent of his population to flee the country as refugees.

This is an unacceptable state of affairs. Rewarding *Chavismo* with the pocketbooks of Western civilization would make a mockery of what remains of the international system. That Pedro Sánchez would expose Europe to this possibility speaks volumes about his intentions.

MERCOSUR is the last gasp of the pink tide that bought off governments all over the continent (fourteen and counting), swung decisions in the Organization of American States (OAS) with corrupting oil money, and wrecked the notion of a peaceful hemisphere that America has worked so long to build.

It is not irrelevant to mention that another force behind this effort is Josep Borrell, an unreconstructed 1970s hard-core socialist who is President Sánchez's minister of foreign affairs. He is now running the EU's entire foreign policy apparatus. His links to *Chavismo* are aboveboard and one of the reasons previous socialist governments shelved him. That he would try to preserve the achievements of international socialism in Latin America is hardly a surprise.

Why anyone should let him do so remains an open question. This is why Trump is and needs to be more suspicious of both the European Union and Latin American governments and their blatant anti-Americanism.

A Defense Buildup

During the 2016 campaign, Donald Trump decried the poor state of America's readiness and military prowess. In fact, it had been run down and depleted over the course of the previous eight years. His budgets did away with the failed sequester—which only succeeded in starving active-duty soldiers of vital supplies—increasing the Navy to 305 ships and replacing Air Force planes that had been flying since World War II.

Obama famously despised generals and admirals and cared only about "don't ask, don't tell," transgender rights, and other such social policies of political correctness. That our troops needed new armaments, increased troop levels, or grand strategies was of lesser importance than the social agenda. Obama's animus against the military was a hallmark of his administration and took a toll on the military's capabilities and readiness, as was made clear in the fight against ISIS and the never-ending lawn mowing in Afghanistan.

The Army was weaker, the Navy had far fewer ships, and the Air Force was stealing parts from older planes to keep newer ones in the air. Obama had presided over what could be called a defense "builddown" or, more precisely, the opposite of what America needed and what Trump was elected to do.

After years of devastating cuts, we're now rebuilding our military "like we never have before," Trump said without apology. "We are a country that's respected again," he declared. "There's a big, beautiful difference."

Trump boasted that we would see a military "like we never had before." The massive $717 billion defense spending bill is truly without precedent.

President Trump has also brought a budding new doctrine to bear: space dominance. With the establishment of the sixth branch of the U.S. military, the Space Force will bring America's dominance in the use of force to the final frontier.

No other limb of the federal government is as qualified and ready to take on the challenge of dominating space. The military already has the advanced rocketry capabilities needed for intercontinental ballistic missiles that would launch a payload into space before the reentry vehicles descended back onto the planet, devastating enemy targets.

Republicans on the Hill, like Trump, are hawks. They argued that we needed to have steep and steady funding to meet growing worldwide threats and foes. This position is not incorrect. Specifically, the results are demonstrable. The ranks of active-duty military will grow by over 15,000, and the Navy will procure thirteen new warships, more than it requested. Troop pay will rise by 2.6 percent.

But this raises the question of what capabilities America is buying with this money. Our Navy is the unparalleled heavyweight of the world. America's Air Force could literally win a matchup against the entire rest of the world, including privately owned fighters. Our enemies usually frag only American infantry, Marines, and tanks with sneak attacks with improvised explosive devices. Nobody wants to fight America fair and square. New investment should be directed toward space, where all the new challenges will come from and America's dominance is comparatively unimpressive.

The defense cuts are over. This is Trump's fighting force now. His original secretary of defense, Jim Mattis, sought to preserve readiness as the highest priority, modernize, and enhance the force structure. Mattis wasn't sold on the Space Force, however.

Trump agreed with everything the general and the Joint Chiefs of Staff wanted. The United States was going to be stronger—far stronger—on his watch. Nevertheless, they attempted to slow-roll the inauguration of the Space Force and have folded it into the Air Force, that guardian of all aeronautical kinetics. This battle seems to have a few more seesaws back and forth to go before it is won by either side.

President Trump has bolstered the military by reassessing foreign alliances too. "We are getting other nations to pay their fair share," he said, referring to the budgets of NATO allies. South Korea, Australia, and Japan have also seen major gains in force readiness and numbers.

The National Defense Strategy that the Department of Defense published was very forward-leaning, calling for "a Joint Force that possesses decisive advantages for any likely conflict, while remaining proficient across the entire spectrum of conflict." Needless to say, the major gap in "spectrum" remains space to this day. Issued in January 2018, the document bluntly depicts a U.S. military that is losing its edge over potential competitors and urges "increased and sustained investment" for "long-term strategic competition with China and Russia." Space remains the unfair advantage that only America can exploit better than the land-based Eurasian powers that America will have to face down in the future.

Until the invention of the airplane, land powers such as Russia and sea powers such as the British Empire competed asymmetrically in their domains. Establishing air superiority—taking out enemy planes and antiaircraft capabilities—is the first step in any serious American strategy anywhere in the world. America became the one and only air power the world has ever seen, dominating the skies with that uniquely American invention, flight.

It is time to bring this edge to the twenty-first century. Bringing a workhorse to the space battlefield—what the biplane was to the World War I strategic picture—will represent a major advance in humanity's war-making capacity, completely monopolized by one power: the United States.

Geospatial capabilities based on satellites are advanced enough to marry space-based targeting with land-, sea-, and air-fired ordinance. All the near-peer adversaries America potentially faces—China, India, Russia—have satellite-killing missiles that could easily blind some of our smartest bombs and highest-tech weapons. Capabilities to defend our satellites and offensive possibilities against enemy spacecraft would change this dynamic to America's advantage.

Securing these kinds of advantages while moving forward with developing and fielding further capabilities in the space arena will perpetuate America's edge in war fighting for another generation.

This is Trump's might in the world and proves we are back and leading once again. America will be more secure with Trump as commander in chief, and so will the world.

Trump Pounds the United Nations Again

As this book went to press, President Trump joined other world leaders in New York for the opening of the UN General Assembly session. He was also to chair a Security Council meeting on Iran, as the United States is president of the council this year.

Everyone expects another round of confrontation. Trump will make his views on Iran, trade, North Korea, and America first policies the thrust of his remarks.

Other world leaders generally stand in awe but detest him and the United States, with few exceptions. Does it matter?

In his book *Tower of Babble*, former UN ambassador Dore Gold accused the United Nations of fueling global chaos because of its moral relativism. Well, how bad is the United Nations?

Donald Trump has said he will send a message to the organization and it is not going to be one it want to hear or will swallow well. He said in a campaign speech, "The United Nations is not a friend of democracy. It's not a friend to freedom."

Only 75 of the 193 members are real democracies, according to Freedom House, which ranks such things. They are in for a shock because President Trump wants to cut our payments (25 percent of the whole budget) and drop out of much of what parades as internationalism but is truly a movement toward one-world government.

He has already removed the United States from UNESCO, reinstituted the Mexico City doctrine on not funding abortions or population control, and cut the U.S. contribution to the UN Relief and Works Agency (UNRWA), which is responsible for the Palestinian refugee debacle.

Make no mistake, the ideology of the United Nations is globalism, and it has not worked. With seventeen specialized agencies, fourteen funds, a secretariat with eighteen departments, over 40,000 overpaid employees, a budget of $5.4 billion a year, peacekeeping missions costing $9 billion a year, and another $28 billion a year for disaster and development, the United Nations is by any measure an utter and complete catastrophe.

Most of us have heard about the UN Population Fund that pays for forced abortions and sterilization, but few know of the UN's far-reaching tentacles, let alone its Human Rights Commission that is against human rights. The members on that commission include wonderful and open states such as Algeria, Bolivia, Congo, Cuba, Maldives, Qatar, Russia, Venezuela, and Vietnam.

I know this up close and personal because during part of the Reagan administration I had the top UN job in Europe.

The fish stinks. Believe me, the United Nations is a vast and highly politicized bureaucracy with a nondemocratic character that is the most ineffective of all international organizations.

In all honesty, it has had very few real successes since the days of U Thant. The United Nations has missed just about every opportunity given to it and especially the more recent ones aimed at reforming it. It can't stop ethnic cleansing or genocide and certainly has had zero effect on Islamic jihadism. It can't glue together failed states such as Syria or stop bloody wars in places from Rwanda to Sri Lanka.

All attempts to restructure its leadership, finances, infrastructure, and the system itself have had little to no effect. However, it has done everything in its power, flying in our face, to establish a Palestinian state despite the well-founded allegations of anti-Semitism. Resolution 3379 is a case in point, equating Zionism with racism.

When it comes to scandals, the United Nations tops the all-time worst list. It's oil for food fiasco (watch the movie *Backstabbing for Beginners*), many peacekeeping atrocities, and child sexual abuse scandals, to name but a few, have led to a nearly total lack of accountability.

When I was in the United Nations, nearly everyone was on the take, and Mr. Ten Percent in the form of kickbacks was all over the institution.

One fact is certain: Corruption abounds. So, more than 70 years on and about half a trillion dollars later, Trump is right to ask: For what?

The United Nations is bloated, undemocratic, expensive, and fragmented and produces few tangible results beyond platitudes and unattainable left-wing goals. It is a sinecure for aging diplomats and a dumping ground for cronies. Its permanent employees after five years get grandiose tax-free salaries, free education, and duty-free alcohol, cigarettes, housing, and petrol. You'd love such a gig, right?

All the audits of the organization turn up the same evidence, but nothing comes of them. Dag Hammarskjold, the second UN secretary general, once remarked about the United Nations that it was created not to lead humankind to heaven but to save humanity from hell.

Trump needs to ask if this is actually true or if instead the United Nations is a kind of hell on earth. Is it a drag on world peace, and does it resist all suggestions of reform because of its entrenched elites and do-nothing high-minded globalist civil servants?

One establishment school of thought keeps saying that if you didn't have the United Nations, you'd have to invent it. Trump should take up the offer and pronounce the 1945 folly dead on his arrival in New York. Read it its last rites and build a new, vibrant Council of Democracies that is more suited to the twenty-first century.

This bipartisan idea, which was backed by the late Senator McCain, among others, suggesting a league of only democratic member states that met certain requirements, has its philosophical basis in Kant's notion of "perpetual peace." Autocracies would be excluded, and the new body could provide a very modest multilateral vehicle and end the nonsensical Security Council veto in instances as far-ranging as Sudan's Darfur, North Korea, and Burma.

Controversial former U.S. ambassador John Bolton, now Trump's national security adviser, was absolutely right when he said, "Quasi-religious faith in 'engagement' and the UN has run into empirical reality." We should "become more cognizant of that organization's moral and political limitations."

Trump should listen to Bolton, not to his unfaithful Never Trumper former ambassador Nikki Haley, who liked her expensive curtains and title too much.

In truth, Bolton, not known for his diplomatic demeanor, was being too polite. Trump should sever the cord and stop paying for an anti-American institution that does not fulfill its original mission. That tower on East 42 Street in New York City should be put out of business and could be turned into a new Trump edifice with a good water view.

Climate Change or Not

In June 2017, President Trump went to the Rose Garden at the White House with the then-director of the Environmental Protection Agency by his side and announced that the United

States was withdrawing from the Paris Agreement on climate change. His stated reason was that it was "an agreement that disadvantages the United States to the exclusive benefit of other countries." China in particular is still classified as a "developing" country with very few obligations despite being the world's biggest source of CO_2.

"As of today, the U.S. will cease all implementation of the non-binding Paris accord and the draconian financial and economic burdens the agreement imposes on our country," Trump said. In a much-quoted line, he said, "I was elected to represent the citizens of Pittsburgh, not Paris." He went on to say, leaving the door open just a crack, "We will see if we can make a deal that's fair, and if we can, that's great." But, he concluded, "If we can't, that's fine."

America cannot unilaterally withdraw until the end of the notification period—conveniently, just after the 2020 election—but the groundwork has been laid.

On the campaign trail candidate Trump had already denounced the Paris Agreement as both wrongheaded and contrary to American interests. Another treaty whose rules only America follows while the rest of the world cheats is another treaty America doesn't need.

He sees it as a way for some countries, namely, China and India, to game the system and hamstring our economy. It probably isn't a Chinese conspiracy, but it may as well be. The "science" is not nearly as settled as claimed. How much carbon exactly will warm how many degrees? The range is vast and full of horrors. Meanwhile, America and American jobs are hurting.

Coal miners in particular were named by Trump as a group that the global elite and the Hillary campaign explicitly wanted to put out of business. He did not.

The Republican Party's 2016 platform opposed the idea of climate change and cast doubt on its urgency. It was viewed as an outright attack on America's oil and gas industry, a strategic asset that is among the best performing exports since America first came back.

The entire Paris apparatus and the funders behind it, both NGOs and largely European countries, realized that the agreement is based on a voluntary approach.

Recall that President Obama took the United States into the Paris Agreement along with 195 other countries and considered it the apex of his environmental policy, calling it "a turning point for our planet."

What is the Paris Agreement? In its own words: "At COP 21 in Paris, on 12 December 2015, Parties to the UNFCCC reached a landmark agreement to combat climate change and to accelerate and intensify the actions and investments needed for a sustainable low carbon future. The Paris Agreement builds upon the Convention and—for the first time—brings all nations into a common cause to undertake ambitious efforts to combat climate change and adapt to its effects, with enhanced support to assist developing countries to do so. As such, it charts a new course in the global climate effort."

The Paris Agreement's central aim is to strengthen the global response to the threat of climate change by keeping the global temperature rise this century well below 2 degrees Celsius above preindustrial levels and to pursue efforts to limit the temperature increase even further to 1.5 degrees Celsius. Except that Trump said, "No thanks."

The Paris Accord relies on the fear of being "named and shamed," but Trump doesn't care. Shame is precisely the wrong incentive for the Trumpian worldview; dollars and cents are the only relevant matters here.

Environmentalist NGOs are never going to like Trump or any decision he makes. The hard-core environmental lobby is on the left of the political spectrum, and many groups advocate outright GDP reduction. It is overtly anti-industry, is against economic growth, and does not correspond with Trump's political base. No pressure group is more antithetical to Trump's values.

He frankly doesn't care if they call him out. It probably helps his political status to be on the receiving end of their ire, and they feed off his indifference for their own benefit.

Truthfully, even the most solid adherents to the Paris accord say that the approach is unlikely to be very effective. Witness Germany's flip-flop on its commitments to the agreement.

Clamoring to get off fossil fuels and adopting a Green New Deal are things Trump will never buy. The cost of ending air travel and rebuilding every single skyscraper in New York City is not reasonable ($93 trillion).

Climate misinformation is something Trump and his cabinet are trying to combat. Scare tactics won't work, and the divide between Republicans and the far-left Democrats on this set of issues gives Trump plenty of cover. Between the jobs Democrats want to get rid of and the businesses these policies will hurt, environmentalists might as well be campaigning for Trump!

Trump's moves amount to a reassertion of American sovereignty. As such, they are a hallmark of his overall America first plan.

Transatlantic Affairs in the Era of Trump

Since the election of President Trump, a worrying trend has manifested and grown among some of our European allies. Worries have been voiced over our commitment to the postwar international order built by the United States after the capitulation of the Third Reich and the Japanese Empire.

In trips to Munich and Brussels, Vice President Pence has recalled the sacrifices of our soldiers, who paid the ultimate price to guarantee the freedom of our European allies. Starting with the blood of those American soldiers, the United States has long devoted itself to ensuring a peaceful Europe.

It is important to remember what those brave young men died for.

Democracy is messy and sometimes disappoints. As Sir Winston Churchill once said, it is the worst system except for the alternatives. Churchill himself was on the wrong end of electoral surprises, not least when he lost at the ballot box months after defeating the fascist menace. Tellingly, he is a figure claimed by Eurosceptics and hailed as a "founding father of the EU" by Europhiles. We will never know all his private opinions but cannot imagine him ignoring resounding public mandates.

The Brexit vote that took place on June 23, 2016, represented such a mandate.

Once again, recalling our darkest moments serves a didactic purpose: France once abandoned NATO and did not reestablish full participation in the allied forces until 2009 under then president Nicolas Sarkozy. Despite this, the organization has survived and thrived and remains the cornerstone of the American-led world order even as we push to update it and get others to pay their fair share of the burden.

EU President Juncker's office published a vision of the five ways the European Union can move forward. Recognizing the right of sovereign member states to decide which direction they will pursue, it remains to be acknowledged as a more effective representation of President Juncker's constituents.

It is not for the United States to say how Europeans should vote in any election, but I for one congratulate President Juncker for this rare act of humility and hope he will continue to recognize diversity of opinion among Europeans.

Very few apparently desire his and President Macron's United States of Europe that would place sovereignty in the European Union itself and not in its member nations.

America remains committed to the exercise of democratic prerogatives by the citizens of the European Union. Their votes should count. However, it behooves us to address the alarmism to which some European figures are resorting.

Comparisons to dark historical figures are far too common. The time has come for all parties to accept the results of the elections of May 2019, preparing for an improved future of U.S.–EU relations.

Scoring cheap political points by insulting the president of the United States or his representatives is no way to show commitment to a "Europe whole and free." It was, after all, an American president who coined the phrase, and it was American military power that enabled Europe to emerge whole and free from the Cold War. We are and remain Europe's best friend and staunchest ally.

One of Secretary Clinton's greatest mistakes was comparing President Putin's actions in Ukraine with those of Hitler in the Sudetenland. It behooves us to remember that the Soviets lost nearly 30 million of their citizens in their war with the Third Reich. Only 11 million of them were soldiers; the rest were civilians. Refraining from those comparisons is a taboo worth keeping. Any Russian alive today will have lost family to the Wehrmacht.

European nations large and small suffered at the hands of fascists, from the victims of Guernica, through the horrors of the Holocaust, to the Balkan successor states of our modern time. Cheapening their memory is a calumny.

As an American who is a strong friend of Europe and a strong believer in the liberal democratic ideals that unify the West, I find it baffling that we should now be considered an enemy. Those who spent the years after the fall of the Berlin wall spreading democratic values across the former Soviet Union can always count on our admiration and respect.

I was one such party.

We clearly have more in common than the Europeans like to admit. It would be wise to focus on what brings us together, but it must be said that the Trump administration has its own political priorities: the American people.

President Reagan—another Republican accused of insufficient commitment to Europeans—famously won the Cold War by outspending the Soviets in the arms race.

Little remembered was the commitment he extended to NATO: 2 percent of the GDP of every alliance member should be dedicated to defense. This commitment went unheeded over the course of every presidency since that time.

My fellow Republicans heavily criticized President Obama when he called some of our allies "free riders," but as Vice President Pence said last year in Munich, "the patience of the American people is finite."

We welcome recent commitments by our European allies to increase NATO spending, but America must insist on results, not mere blandishments. Europe, a rich continent, should shoulder its fair share of the burden for its own defense.

Almost thirty years has passed since President Reagan's exhortation; we are entering the sixth presidency since the 2 percent commitment was made. Yet still Europeans say "later." Even the nice Canadians fail to pay their share.

The extenuating circumstances are always convincing. German reunification was miraculous. Having defeated communism, the allies wondered what NATO was for until the Bosnian wars provided an answer.

The post-9/11 world led to controversial out-of-area operations. Then the bugbear of modern Europe—financial crisis—carried them to the present day. Yet in 2018, Germany posted a €6 billion budget surplus.

It is difficult to see that figure and accept the gradualism with which NATO's 2 percent target is being achieved. During the financial crisis, the European Union used its powers to decide on spending priorities. I'm sure the great minds of the European institutions will find creative ways to direct those powers toward our common objectives. If they won't, there should be consequences.

It remains to be said that some notions need updating. The burden sharing evidenced during the Libyan intervention was disastrous. President Obama set out to "lead from behind" and ended up supplying the bulk of the hardware as well as the vital logistical functions: in-air refueling, submarine-launched missiles, and other mighty pieces of American muscle.

Without American political commitment to the mission, it was a failure. Malta and Italy bore the brunt of the costs for that failure, but the European Union paid in political legitimacy during the ensuing bickering over refugees. Syria offered a redux: Again European failure to address issues that primarily affect Europe fostered infighting among member states while millions of refugees streamed into neighboring countries, not the least into Europe itself. This was a problem tailor-made for Europe to step up and solve.

President Trump won on a platform of noninterventionism.

The Founding Fathers of the American Revolution did not believe in foreign entanglements. Indeed, every successful revolution tempers its resolve to enlighten the globe. As George Washington said, "Let us raise a standard to which the wise and honest can repair. The rest is in the hands of God."

President Washington did not believe in spreading the revolution he led to other countries.

The European Union has expanded very quickly but hasn't been raising a standard toward which its own citizens can look with admiration. Now they want a new EU army on the cheap, and some call America the enemy.

We say this as friends who wish to see a successful and free Europe. In a different context, President George W. Bush once spoke of the "soft bigotry of low expectations." By expressing high expectations for European leadership in Europe's backyard, President Trump shows himself to be a true friend.

When the Soviets became tired of Leninist vanguards and permanent revolution, they invented the concept of "socialism in one country." President Trump will raise the standard to which the wise and honest can look. His platform is "Freedom in one country." That country is the United States first but not alone.

We are committed to defend democracy where it exists, especially in Europe, but have renounced the liberal interventionist, neoconservative notion of spreading democracy throughout the world.

Make no mistake: America under Trump is Europe's best friend, security shield, and trading partner. But no longer are we silent participants, a cash machine, or a quiet do-nothing idle partner.

America has a new mission: greatness. This mission need not clash with Europe. Indeed, it should revolve around a continued alliance and common Western values that have served Europe and the United States well.

In August 2019, when President Trump tweeted about buying the autonomous territory of Greenland and later jokingly promised not to build a gold Trump Tower there, many pundits called it "absurd" or "crazy." Trump called off a long-planned visit the next month to Denmark after the prime minister of that country, Mette Frederiksen, called his idea of the United States buying Greenland, an autonomous Danish territory, "absurd" and dismissed it completely.

But is it absurd? Greenland, the world's largest island, is a territory that is not physically connected to Denmark (population 5.7 million) and has been for a millennium.

It has a population of just 57,000—89 percent of whom are Inuit (Eskimos). Socialist Denmark does next to nothing for them, and the rates of unemployment, alcoholism, and suicide are exceptionally high. Geographically the island is considered part of North America, not Europe. It is and has been an important part of the Arctic, an area of significant interest to both Russia and China.

With considerable mineral wealth, gold, and potential oil and gas reserves, Greenland is not something to sneeze at. It is absolutely strategic.

The United States already has valuable bases there, including the vitally important Thule Air Base, which is critical in the forward positioning of nuclear bombers and surveillance radar systems. More crucially, Greenland has known and current production of rare-earth minerals that are critically important to the high-tech manufacturing of everything from computers, to iPhones, to sensors and batteries.

China is the dominant player in this market and has threatened to cut the United States off from its supply. The West badly needs alternatives. In 2018, the People's Republic of China offered to fund three airports in Greenland to develop minerals. It wants to control this strategic output and bring Greenland into its fold, perhaps extending its mercantilist Belt and Road Initiative there.

President Trump is no fool and has had a long career as a real estate wheeler-dealer. This would be the legacy deal of a lifetime. Is obtaining Greenland really such a "crazy" and "absurd" idea?

Remember, the United States bought the U.S. Virgin Islands from the same Kingdom of Denmark in 1917, and Greenland also was on the table. U.S. history is replete with important land deals. "Seward's Folly"—the purchase of Alaska from Russia in 1867— turned out to be one of the best purchases of all time. The 1803 purchase by President Thomas Jefferson of the Louisiana Territory from France greatly expanded the size and wealth of the United States and defined its westward expansion.

Leftist critics have denounced everything Trump and see this as a colonialist enterprise or a mockery of native rights. Well, Denmark is in fact the colonizer and pays over $700 million a year to carry the island of Greenland, something its own citizens loudly complain about. This is Denmark, which is a nearly non-paying member of NATO that has never met its 2 percent obligations and allows the United States to pick up the tab for defending it (and Greenland). Why not put a plebiscite to the actual native peoples of Greenland since they are not an independent country and are not integrated into Denmark proper?

Here is the question: Would you like to become citizens of the richest country on earth and develop while receiving a direct nontaxable payment from the U.S. Treasury for your island, paid as a sovereign fund allotting you a significant stipend every year for perpetuity, or do you want to remain a colony of oppressive Denmark and receive nothing? I think I can guess the answer.

Matteo Salvini on the Shores of Tripoli

The slow escalation of Franco-Italian tensions has so far been relatively amicable. Demands for paintings and sculptures looted during the Napoleonic wars can be dismissed as brotherly banter and resolvable. A proxy war in Libya, in contrast, is something quite different.

Khalifa Haftar, the French-backed head of the Libyan National Army (LNA), decided to engage in hostilities and start shelling Tripoli, the capital of the rival Government of National Accord (GNA). They were supposed to sit down with the United Nations to negotiate a peace accord, but Haftar chose the path of war. Salvini has accused the rebels of carrying out a military coup.

Italy's interest—as well as that of its hard-line interior minister, who is in charge of border security—is clear. Destabilizing Libya for the third time in ten years will lead to yet another influx of migrants fleeing from the unnecessary conflict. Salvini has declared his certainty that terrorists would abuse the relief corridor to infiltrate Europe.

An EU statement condemning Haftar was blocked by Paris for advocating a UN-mediated solution to the conflict. EU policy on Libya has failed to stop the flow of migrants. Bucking the multilateral approach, Salvini tried to negotiate a bilateral deal with Tripoli.

Safeguarding the widespread Italian-owned gas infrastructure is another. Haftar, an old Gaddafi hand, is trying to replicate Colonel Muammar's old racket—the bizarre hostage situation: Pay me or you get a boatload of hostages. All in all, Haftar's greatest mistake may have been failure to win quickly.

Matteo Salvini's statement that the "blitz has failed" left a little twinge of regret for what could have been. The Tripoli government relies on thick networks of organized crime to keep the peace.

France's efforts to impose Haftar aside, there is one more bit of historical backdrop to consider: President Sarkozy's initiative to unseat Muammar Gaddafi in 2011, which was opposed by Silvio Berlusconi.

Fate has inverted those positions. France now wants to let Haftar off the hook, and Italy wants to intervene in defense of Tripoli. There are ways this could escalate. Italy has the planes to impose a no-fly zone, which would decimate Haftar's air superiority. The Tripoli-based GNA has no planes. If Salvini could even that score or even provide air support for a GNA counterassault, the narrative would be very different.

United Nations support and recognition of the Tripoli-led GNA is another factor to consider. An Italian incursion into this conflict would have the blessing of the international community, to say nothing of the Italian gas giant Eni, whose Libyan operations are extensive. Ensuring that one of Europe's main supplies of oil and gas stays stable is certainly in America's and the EU's self-interest.

Macron, already isolated in EU diplomatic circles on issues such as climate change and trade with the United States, would become even less of a consensus leader for the bloc. The story of Salvini's ascendancy in Europe would include defeating Macron in a proxy war in Europe's neighborhood and stopping more migrants, perhaps the first of many victories to come.

A Roman triumph could be organized to celebrate his victory: Salvini Africanus Invictus.

Little Rocket Man and the Prince of Peace

North Korea has for decades been a thorn in people's side, not only in the United States but also in South Korea and the entire Asian neighborhood. Its involvement in nuclear proliferation, terrorist financing, and the international drug trade makes it a foe of everything American policy stands for.

The formal end of the Korean War never came even though there was a cessation of hostilities and a division of the country on the 38th parallel after World War II.

The so-called Hermit Kingdom, while propped up by the Red Chinese, was a place no one went, with which no one traded, and where the ugliest form of familial totalitarian autocracy reigned: the ancient Asiatic dictator. Leadership was passed down in primitive monarchical fashion, and any opponents of the regime met instant doom. The communist country to this date runs an extensive gulag of prisonlike camps and has been known to execute its adversaries on flimsy grounds. There are no human rights and no economic development except to keep the ruling class in power.

The last four American administrations had to deal with the growing threat of the Democratic People's Republic of Korea's nuclear proliferation, and they were all found badly wanting.

The devious DPRK regime was intent on just two things: its own survival and the buildup of a nuclear threat to ensure the former. According to the CIA's World Fact Book, "Kim Jong-il was the second leader of North Korea. He ruled from the death of his father Kim Il-sung, the first leader of North Korea, in 1994 until his own death in 2011. He was an unelected dictator and was often accused of human rights violations."

The Bushes, Clinton, and Obama all failed in their delicate and deliberate diplomacy, thwarted by the masterful evil empire that repeatedly lied, cheated, and promised things but never delivered. Money didn't work, UN sanctions didn't work, military exercises didn't work, assistance didn't work, and kindness didn't work. Nothing worked.

With North Korea, Trump inherited a dangerous and escalating disaster in the making. Obama told him it would be his biggest challenge. The risks were high, and the prospects bleak.

North Korea over the last decade not only had built up fissionable materials and delivery vehicles but was testing intercontinental rockets to send miniaturized nuclear weapons of some sophistication into trajectories that could strike South Korea, Japan, Guam, Hawaii, and even the mainland United States.

Trump took a radically different approach. It started with calling the North Korean leader out. In a vehement UN speech Trump said, "Little Rocket Man is on a suicide mission for himself and his regime."

The president warned that the United States was prepared to "totally destroy North Korea." The military card—indeed, a first strike—was on the table. The toughest international sanctions ever were then deployed with agreement in the Security Council that involved both Russia and China, which in the past had been reluctant to challenge their ally.

When the effect sank in and North Korea was crippled even worse than before, they blinked and said they were open to negotiation and, most important, to denuclearization. With good cop–bad cop diplomacy involving South Korean President Moon Jae-in, Trump, and his forceful secretary of state Mike Pompeo, it looked like a whole new ball game.

Without the bellicose rhetoric of fire and fury (but not the lifting of sanctions), the new approach trumpeted diplomatic efforts to resolve the looming nuclear crisis. There was realism but a degree of optimism surrounding the planned summit between Trump and Kim that took place in Singapore. A process was started and a gate was opened to a potentially defused situation that could lead to the final and ultimate goal: denuclearization.

After a colorful love-in between the two parties and a number of letters between them, it was Pompeo who did the shuttle diplomacy to try to move concrete proposals forward in good faith. It was the most progress U.S. policy on North Korea had made in decades!

The second summit in Vietnam was arranged in order to sign a more formal agreement, a deal that would begin the road to an agreement. The branding and communications led the world to believe that the decades-old war footing would change. The parties would sign a formal end to the Korean War, denuclearize the peninsula completely and verifiably, and start a longer-term policy of lifting the sanctions regime piece by piece and helping North Korea become a more open economy even if the communist madman stayed in power. After all, for over a year there had been no testing of nuclear devices or ballistic missiles by the DPRK. They had stood down.

The reduced tensions in the region were very well received. In fact, the prime minister of Japan, Shinzo Abe, even drafted a letter recommending President Trump for a Nobel Peace Prize, which would be richly deserved should he turn such a foe into a friend.

Then, at the last minute, on the final day of the second summit, Trump walked away. He said the North Koreans had failed to move sufficiently and had asked for a total relaxation of global sanctions. It was not a deal to be done. He wasn't going to cave.

This disappointed some parties and the media, which had expected something more fantastical. But as a principled realist, the president and commander and chief of the United States was unwilling to do a bad deal, notably one in which we got hoodwinked. Peace was the goal, but not at any price.

This means denuclearization is still on the table; the next steps and concrete details and time line are still to be determined. South Korea maintains a Ministry of Unification, and its powerful chaebols are ready for the day when cheap North Korean labor is dumped on its heavily educated, capital-intensive economy. It'll be a payday to remember.

The Korean saga, which is still unfolding, shows Trump at his best. He was willing to risk meeting a notorious and brutal leader, change course, and befriend an enemy, but only if there was a real deal in America's favor. He has become the first American president to enter North Korean territory, a fantastic achievement with echoes of Nixon and Kissinger's trip to Beijing in the 1970s.

This is America first foreign policy. It is in line with the decades-old nonproliferation commitment that America has upheld along with its allies, applied to the hardest case of all—a rogue state with nuclear weapons.

The ball is now in North Korea's court. They want the benefits, so the remaining question is: Are they willing to pay the costs? Will they ever reunite with Seoul as they both claim to want?

With Trump at the helm, you have to pay up.

O Canada!

Sleepy Canada is up to its snowdrift in scandal.

Arrogant, hypocritical Prime Minister Justin Trudeau, a hyperliberal archglobalist and Trump nemesis, is facing repeated demands that he resign. If he won't, his liberal government may fall or be defeated.

What's up in the frozen north? Maybe it is time to call in Sergeant Preston of the Yukon and the Mounties of television fame.

Trudeau now regrets what he calls "the erosion of trust." He caused it himself. He has put at risk the entire liberal establishment, his government, and his very office.

What happened? It is spelled *corruption*.

It appears that the former minister of justice and attorney general was pressured to help a crooked Quebec construction company settle a criminal case and avoid prosecution over allegations that it bribed officials in Libya to obtain large government contracts.

How much? you ask. Lots. Fifty million dollars.

The AG (Jody Wilson-Raybould) faced veiled threats and pressure from Trudeau to fix the deal. That would mean doing injustice—not exactly her job title.

Trudeau denied the allegations, but it has all backfired and come tumbling down on him. It has caused a national outrage from St. John's, Newfoundland, straight across the country all the way to British Columbia. The AG has resigned from the cabinet, and so have others.

The fresh-faced baby Trudeau (his father, Pierre, was PM in 1968–1978 and 1980–1984) is now scorned by the people. His troubled image plasters all the news outlets 24/7. It is not going well.

He can't find any sympathy. Remember, his trip to India a year ago was widely mocked and his negotiation with Trump over trade was an embarrassment and a failure.

His government is in disgrace, and his political life is probably over.

Can you hear the Canadian national anthem? Somebody better be "standing on guard for thee." With Trump in the Big House, Canada is getting a new treatment.

When Amazon Rules the Whole Wide World

Do we need to defang the FAANGs (Facebook, Amazon, Apple, Netflix, and Google) before it is too late?

The stock valuation of those companies exceeds $4 trillion. They dwarf the real U.S. economy and that of almost every country on earth. Their power is growing exponentially with cloud computing, e-commerce, artificial intelligence, blockchain, machine learning, robotization, and now space travel.

They believe that they own and will dictate our future. They have a normative belief in their own goodness. Do they require antitrust action? What about their unruly collusion? Their alarming labor practices? Or the fact that they avoid paying taxes?

These are perhaps the most rapacious enterprises ever. Yes, they rape the public; that is the very meaning of the word.

Look at how intertwined Amazon is. It is imperial. And its leader is cultlike, a cyberoligarch of the largest pretensions.

This is a serious political, cultural, deeply societal question. We pose it in all seriousness. Don't censure it or shy away from asking it yourself.

President Trump's endgame seems to be to get a real-world free and fair trade agreement going on all sides even as he bashes a few players along the way. That may work to America's benefit as long as it maintains a technological advantage over the emerging Asian powers.

It is abundantly clear that the Chinese in particular have ambitions not just to take over but to run the world by 2030, including its technology, its military, and its political and trading systems. They have said so. Some day we will all awake to the danger of all this, one hopes not before it is too late to do something about it.

Trump gets it, and that is why he refuses to kowtow to China and its not so covert project that literally translates as "global domination."

We should, however, be equally if not more concerned about another rising tide that seems to be gathering greater power with every passing day. It is FAANG power.

You use a mobile phone and a laptop, go on social media, conduct searches, and view the Web to buy stuff and entertain yourself, right? Think about who controls every link in that chain.

Jeff Bezos better than anyone represents FAANG power. He is the poster boy of tech monopoly. Recently, he was worth only $66 billion. Today, that number tops $150 billion. If you add up all the wealth of the mightiest in the world today, it might eclipse most government coffers. We are sure Bezos believes in low taxes (at least for himself and for Amazon, which pays almost none) and free trade too, as do most of the other techno-entrepreneurs now classified as the world's wealthiest people.

But his intentions are very sinister. Bezos wants to dominate our lives every bit as much as the Chinese do. He is a real monopolist, and that is threatening. He is already getting there, from his websites, to his services, to his media outlets, to even what you eat and how you medicate. Make no mistake: Bezos's strategy is to own you and control you and do so vertically. That is his strategy: vertical integration of our entire supply chains and our life cycles.

When confronted at the BENS (Business Executives for National Security) annual meeting, where he was given a prize for his contributions to America, Bezos stated his ambitions boldly. Asked what he was going to do with his many, many billions, he replied that he wanted to take humankind to the outer planets. He wants to own space, too.

At some time in the near future, there will be a tipping point after which these new multinational corporations (the FAANGs plus their Asian equivalents), but particularly Amazon, which realize they control the financial world and can influence the political and governmental worlds, will come to full power.

Watch for the takeover. It is coming sooner than you think. There are signs. Having spent years working within the G7 leadership community, we realize more than most political observers that the elected leaders of governments have been losing influence on affairs. They can barely run their own offices and get reelected most of the time.

Cabals of civil servants and lobbyists (a deep state) now control every step in the process from writing speeches, to creating policies, to passing laws and enforcing them. From the most powerful governments down to the majority of puny little states, these leaders have become pawns of the other, more powerful bureaucrats in regional bureaus and corporate research labs.

Unelected so-called experts working on behalf of and dictated to by the FAANGs will in time decide everything: what you buy, where you buy it, who you vote for, and what you read and see. It is absolutely Orwellian and portends nothing less than the end of freedom.

Trump alone is ripping up this matrix and delivering his own speeches and executive orders, which are understood and accepted by a populace heretofore left out of the political process. He is succeeding but against all the odds and in the face of massive opposition and racial and political hatred, most of it fueled by the mainstream very liberal media and the tech giants (in Amazon's case they are one and the same).

The question is: Can he sustain this barrage long enough to continue these efforts? Can he possibly win? Or will they destroy him?

This is the new geopolitical battleground. Global (called transnational because they owe no allegiance to any country or nation) corporations are moving in their sole-sourced directions (Jeff Bezos, Mark Zuckerberg, Tim Cook, and hundreds of others worldwide). Central banks and governments are pushing in another direction.

The fault lines are cracking around these forces.

Trump stands in the middle, but alone he may not have the power to influence the change he so dearly wants and shares with the majority of ordinary voters, ordinary citizens—the masses.

Many remain unaware of the dangers, willing to follow their leaders over a cliff. Too often the technology and influence of FAANGs grow beyond anything we have previously experienced. Their biased algorithms control what we do, buy, and view. Their gadgets and platforms shape elections, markets, and ideologies.

Who polices them? Who has oversight over them? Nobody.

This extraordinary shift in power away from governments and into the hands of a few corporate markets and their highly paid lobbyists, along with the weakened powers of the governed, makes for a battle zone bigger than that of any past world war. Even the press has become a subsidiary of this model, just one more "content creator" for the universal platforms.

When we see the wimps who make up most of the governments around the world and realize that they are mere puppets in the hands of their handlers, we fear that Trump will fall into the same trap. Even he can't control the vast government he presides over—more than the military-industrial complex that Eisenhower warned us about some sixty years ago and that President Lyndon Johnson manifestly crash-landed into Vietnam. Trump's own justice department and FBI colluded to take him down and impeach him.

The media, the bureaucrats, and all who oppose him do not see that he is the one true altruist trying to turn this tide.

Can he alone do it? The angry haters who oppose him grow in strength. Their shrill voices of resistance fill the airwaves and the streets. Silicon Valley and the Bezos crowd want him to vanish. They even tried a clandestine coup to overthrow him.

Those who continually and vociferously oppose him, such as the almighty Bezos, buy an organ such as the *Washington Post* to critique and defame him day in and day out. It is hard to compete with such power and wealth. They censor their opponents and deprive them of their voice.

It is a war of words for now, but governments will soon bow to the forces of manipulated markets, which can overpower them. Europe is just the most recent example.

Amazon could rule not just the United States but also the whole wide world by 2030. Teddy Roosevelt avoided this fate the first time it reared its head by breaking up the railroads.

Rue the day when Amazon and a clique of all-powerful tech giants run the world. It will make the Matrix look like child's play.

We will all be mere serfs in their techno-grip.

NATO Dogfight

President Trump came, he punched, and he drove his point home. NATO will never be the same after Trump challenged the organization to its core and read it the riot act by delivering an ultimatum.

Following his America first philosophy to make decisions on the basis of U.S. and no other interests or multilateral concerns, Trump went to Brussels with both fists swinging.

At a breakfast meeting with NATO Secretary General Jens Stoltenberg, who was previously prime minister of Norway, Trump laid down the law and reinforced his main point: Pay up or shut up.

Only five of the twenty-nine NATO allies are meeting their pledges to spend 2 percent of GDP on defense. Germany is the worst culprit and is in effect "taking the American taxpayer for a ride," as Trump said. Trump went one step farther, saying that Germany was a "captive" of Russia's oil and gas pipeline and was spending billions on an unreliable source, the very adversary NATO exists to deter: Russia. In a single exchange Trump won the war. He caught them off guard and hit them right between the eyes. It was a knockout punch.

All the mainstream media said Trump got it wrong, his figures were inflated, or NATO gives the United States other benefits, but they missed the point. Trump sucker punched the German juggernaut and its chancellor, Mrs. Merkel, and showed Germany's hypocrisy in one fell swoop.

The formal NATO meetings were no less contentious. Trump had a series of bilateral meetings and changed the whole agenda to return on the final day to his major topic: burden sharing. His efforts seemed to work. He strong-armed the entire cabal to admit that they needed to do more and do it immediately. Trump said in his news conference that they should be paying 4 percent of their GDP if they want a real defense.

Trump in effect single-handedly told our allies that if they want defense, they have to pay for it. We are not their piggy bank. The United States has your back but needs to see a serious commitment or else. No other president since Harry S. Truman started NATO in 1947 has stood up and made the American case so forcefully.

Trump did not capitulate. As a result, NATO will be more focused, more deliberate, and better funded and America and Americans can be proud. The hell with diplomacy, said Trump. It hasn't worked for decades, and so it's time to try something new. America is leading the world again after a long hiatus and an apology tour during the previous eight years. Leadership means having the courage to lead. Trump gave a two-day seminar on leading to the NATO heads of state. Some didn't like it. Tough love is what they got, and he is watching defense budgets for 2019. The result will be noted, and already the cash registers are ringing. Those who don't meet the pledge will be cut out.

When Donald Met Vlad

Just after high noon on July 16, 2018, in historic Helsinki, Finland, a meeting (not a summit) between the presidents of the United States and Russia took place to repair what some have called the worst relations between the two countries ever. (Putin was an hour late; this is the diplomatic equivalent to icing the kicker in football!)

President Trump blamed the "foolishness" of past U.S. administrations, particularly Obama's, for the deplorable and dangerous state of affairs with Russia. Downplaying expectations in advance, Trump said he had "low expectations" for the meeting while the mainstream media castigated him for even holding such a session, condemning him for his supposed collusion and failure to be "tougher" on Russia. Damned if you do, damned if you don't. Trump strode confidently into the Finnish palace.

The results of the leaders' time revolved around five items that truthfully deserve more time and attention to detail and an ongoing structured working dialogue. They include the extension of the Strategic Arms Reduction Treaty on nuclear weapons, the end of the Syrian civil war, the annexation of Crimea, the hot violence in eastern Ukraine, and the "meddling" in U.S. and other elections. All these issues were discussed, and Trump added one more: China and by implication North Korean denuclearization.

Through it all Trump made it abundantly clear that two realities color U.S. thinking about Russia.

First, Russia is weak. The United States is a superpower, alone in the world. Russia, by contrast, is a middle power aspiring to be greater. Militarily the United States is far stronger than Russia, has bases around the world, and is far superior technologically. It also has a robust alliance of allies, which Russia lacks. Legally, institutionally, and freedom-wise, the United States is in a league far beyond Russia. The United States is a vibrant democracy; Russia is not. Economically, the United States is fifteen times larger than Russia and Russia has been declining. The United States ranks far above Russia in education, technology, and intellectual capital and is and remains unsurpassed as the leader of the free world.

Second, Russia has a complex. After its loss in the Cold War, under Putin Russia has two related goals. The first is to be respected as a proud nation with a long history as an important European power and a superpower. The country still has significant military might with nuclear weapons, a thriving navy, and many troops.

With 1 million active military and 2 million reserves, Russia is a formidable fighting force. The commander in chief is the Russian president. Their navy consists of four fleets and a standing flotilla that includes nuclear submarines. Some 1,765 deployed nuclear strategic warheads and another 2,700 nondeployed strategic warheads are ready for fire. Another 2,510 warheads are available but under dismantlement. Many of them are stationed in Kaliningrad, a Russian enclave sandwiched between Germany, Poland, and the Baltic states. Russia spends some $70 billion a year on its military budget, a twentyfold increase in the last decade.

The second goal is at times obscured and at other times "weaponized" in an information war and not so secret diplomatic and counteractive measures. That goal is simply the demise of the West. Moscow wants a reversal of the historical process that began in 1989 when Eastern and Central Europe peacefully reclaimed freedom and eventually brought down the Soviet empire.

As James Kirchick put it, "Shorn of Marxism-Leninism, the Kremlin today is driven by an ideologically versatile illiberalism willing to work with any political faction amenable to its revisionist aims."

Russia wants to reset the Transatlantic Alliance by using destabilizing efforts. Exploiting every crisis, Russia exacerbates nearly every situation by its malign intentions. Its motives revolve around predatory strategies to divide and conquer.

Using aggression and subversion, Russia no longer has to depend on the deployment of the Red Army on its western flank. The Communist ideology equally has no sway and is out of fashion. This means Russia meddles constantly to incite confusion and the demise of Western governments and societies. The plan to supplant the West and achieve a restoration of Russian power and influence arose from Russia's deep-seated inferiority complex.

The meeting in Helsinki was not a huge breakthrough or the disaster that many of Trump's opponents had declared in advance. It was instead a pragmatic entrepreneurial dose of realism about the need for serious relations with Russia where it is and who it is. It offered constructive dialogue as a way forward.

Trump, as always, put his own spin on the situation and upset the global elite with his America first approach to foreign relations. He called the meetings frank and fruitful and very future oriented. Putin himself said that the Cold War is over. They both seemed desirous to jointly rebuild the bilateral relationship around mutual interests.

Trump in a prepared opening statement said that "diplomacy is preferable" and that new pathways to improve stability were on the table.

The questions from reporters from both sides yielded interesting replies on matters ranging from oil and gas markets and supply to Russian accountability and collusion. Putin said Russia would allow Robert Mueller's team to come and interview the intelligence agents it has indicted, using an existing treaty to do so. The leaders shed light on Syria and said they want to help Israel and aid humanitarian efforts.

In a football handoff, Putin gave Trump a soccer ball from the World Cup and said that the ball was now in his court.

The most amazing part of the summitry, however, was the completely biased, vengeful CNN coverage. They called it in conclusion "the most disgraceful performance by an American president ever."

Jim Acosta, David Gergen, Anderson Cooper, Chris Cuomo, and Christiane Amanpour literally mugged the president for lacking so-called Western values and exhibited unprecedented anti-Trumpism. They complained repeatedly about the survival of the present order: the globalism that Trump was eroding right in front of their eyes.

Google Makes Merkel Its Leader of the Free World

Google, the world's leading search engine, has pushed a false fact—that Angela Merkel, the chancellor of Germany, is now the "leader of the free world," a position or title typically accorded to the U.S. president, at least since the end of World War II.

Is she?

Merkel, the longest-serving leader in Europe, and her CDU/CSU party were narrowly reelected in a turgid campaign with only 33 percent of the vote and 218 seats to an unprecedented fourth term. But the election was really a setback for her party, which needed the socialists to create another grand coalition to form a weak government.

Her growing opposition, given her self-created immigration debacle, is an ascendant populist Alternative for Democracy (AfD), which won 13 percent of the vote (eighty-seven seats) and came in third. This is hardly the stability of the past, let alone the leader of all of Germany, let alone the world.

Indeed, there is sufficient reason to believe that Merkel's overly dominant Germany is the real reason for the demise of the critical and long-lasting transatlantic alliance and the fallout over Brexit. This is not leadership but sabotage.

German culture is an odd combination of pride and penance. Germans cannot resolve their deep inner conflict, which is submerged and crosses generational lines even if they do not or cannot mention *Mein Kampf* or Hitler's name.

Germany may appear uncomfortable in its own skin, as well it should. Their tormented minds—adrift between *Schmerz* and *Angst*—exhibit a high degree of what psychoanalysts used to refer to as repression, except that it is not all that repressed any longer.

Today Merkel's strident Germany is the decidedly dominant reunited bullying European power in every sense of the term. It can't help itself. But a world leader it is not.

The Iron Chancellor (who is referred to as *Mutti*, or "Mom," in German) is trying to push all of Europe around. You see, Germany is no longer a defeated, reluctant, insignificant power.

Ironically, Germany is also the biggest NATO laggard at 1.2 percent of GDP even though it has the most robust economy on the Continent and a current account surplus of over $285 billion, the largest in the world. In effect, American taxpayers, by paying so much (70 percent of the current NATO budget), are subsidizing European and particularly German welfare states. Such free riding can't continue, and we need to read the Germans the riot act, as the president repeatedly has, and not just about cheating on Volkswagen emissions.

It is noteworthy how stubbornly Mrs. Merkel adroitly played her anti-American card throughout her tedious campaign. She said: "Europe must stay united because it cannot fully count on the United States." Her socialist former minister of foreign affairs, Sigmar Gabriel (a Putin crony), said in no uncertain terms that Trump is "a threat to peace and prosperity."

Germany is on a collision course with Trump's United States politically, socially, and economically even if it is a weakling militarily. It is also clear that it is totally dependent on Russian energy. In fact, Germany's former social democratic chancellor, Gerhard Schröder, is the chairman of Russia's Gazprom. Trump exposed this risky business at a NATO meeting, but even opposition from other EU members hasn't been enough to force Germany's hand.

While notable German magazines (*Der Spiegel* and *Stern*) despicably portrayed a severed Trump head on their covers, Germany was marching to its own dangerous drumbeat, trying to drag the entire European Union along. Merkel calls the shots and has said she wants an integrated, unified, and federal European Union with Germany at the helm and always benefiting from the euro currency play. In all honesty, that's what the euro is: a German ploy for its own export-led growth. Trump exposed that as well.

Did you know that Merkel was born Angela Kazmierczak and is part Polish? Her grandfather was a Ludwig Kazmierczak, born 1896 in Poznan, which was then part of the German Reich. The family was proud of its Polish roots. After World War II, however, they changed their name and moved. She ended up residing in the DDR—the Soviet part of Germany (East Germany)—where she was raised speaking Russian as a pacifist Lutheran pastor's daughter.

Merkel's values are therefore very divided, as was Germany itself. She embodies in ways the dark soul of Germany's anguished history. But underneath the boring demeanor is a will to power, a German ambition to reign over Europe.

Maybe Google should have listed her for what she truly is: a European tyrant.

Gone are the common Atlantic values of the past. Peace, security, and economic growth are sacrificed for raw German ambition camouflaged in European clothing.

Germany is in effect becoming a de facto bully. What it could not win militarily in the last war, it is achieving in a not so secret attempt to take over Europe and all its institutions, money, and culture, using the façade of the European Union as its Trojan horse.

Decades ago, a cabinet minister to Margaret Thatcher named Nicholas Ridley was forced to resign after he said that the European Union was "a German racket designed to take over the whole of Europe." He went on to say that giving up sovereignty to that body was as bad as giving it up to Hitler. Back then such language caused shock; today it is as obvious as Wiener schnitzel and apple strudel.

Merkel is now the leader of the world? Really? Which world? She can barely run Germany. Before it is too late, the United States and the United Kingdom, and Europe too, have to step up and call Germany what it is. Merkel is a threat to freedom, not its leader.

The transatlantic alliance in this century demands honesty and burden sharing as well as common principles and purpose. If Germany is not on board, it can go it alone, realizing that the United States no longer will pay for it, defend it, protect it, or watch idly as it transforms the continent into a German panzer-like machine and puppet state to which it dictates orders.

European nations should come to their own conclusions, but America cannot appease or deny reality any longer. We have a leader, and he has taken on the challenge even if the likes of the techno-giant leftist Google deny it. Google needs to fix its algorithms lest we all see what they are: just another form of anti-Trumpism.

There is only one leader of the free world, and his name is Donald Trump.

How Do You Say Uncle in Chinese?

When you have your opponent in an unbeatable hold and literally wrestle him to the ground, you release him only when he cries out "uncle."

Donald Trump now has China in such a position. Chinese communist leader Xi Jinping will cry out *shushu* ("uncle" in Mandarin) any time now.

Why? According to Secretary of Commerce Wilbur Ross, China is "out of bullets." It can't retaliate because its exports to the United States are four times larger than U.S. exports to China.

Do the math. Trump and his able-bodied trade representative, Robert Lighthizer, have.

Peter Navarro, one of the president's top trade advisers, said that China is in a zero-sum game with the rest of the world when it comes to trade. "We have to defend ourselves," Navarro said, citing alleged Chinese theft of U.S. intellectual property involving technology. "They're attacking our crown jewels. They make no bones about it."

Trump has made it abundantly clear that as China plays this game of chicken against U.S. farmers and industries, we will move to phase 3, which is tariffs on approximately $267 billion of additional Chinese imports. This means that *all* Chinese imports will be affected, the whole damn lot.

The United States imported $505 billion worth of goods from China in 2018.

China is already suffering. Its economy is contracting. Its export order index is falling steeply. Its currency is weaker. Its stock market has dropped by 20 percent. Its nonperforming loans are skyrocketing. Its growth rate is way off its normal numbers.

More tariffs will bite even harder. Do you hear *shushu* yet?

Friends, it is time to tell the truth about Red China, a communist country with a pretend form of crony capitalism that is the foremost adversary of the free market, bar none.

The expansion of China's international trade has been the most noteworthy aspect of that nation's rising prominence in the world. China's exports have grown at an average rate of 15 percent a year since 1979.

China is a predatory nation. That has greatly benefited China and hurt places such as the Midwest and Europe.

Trade reforms and the general opening of China's economy that have led to a surge in foreign direct investment and increased integration with the global trading system, especially since China joined the World Trade Organization in 2001, have facilitated this process. Globalists promoted this, and we have paid a high price.

In light of China's very large population and still substantial development potential, as reflected by its current per capita income, China could have a bigger impact on the global economy than all the other Asian economies combined. But will it, or will the bubble burst? Is China imploding?

Face the facts. China dumps its products, subsidizes its production, is rampant with corruption, and steals an estimated $600 billion a year in intellectual property from anyone who does business with it. And it employs slave labor.

The Chinese should be called out for what they are: cheats.

For decades after the 1949 revolution, Red China followed a policy of socialist economic development that was based primarily on the centrally directed allocation of resources through administrative means. By the late 1970s, that approach was increasingly recognized as being untenable and unsustainable, and an overhaul of the economic system was initiated.

But China's approach to economic reform has been gradual and incremental, without any detailed liberalized blueprint guiding the process. This incremental approach is best depicted in a metaphor attributed to Deng Xiaoping: "crossing the river by feeling the stones under the feet." It is still applicable to many of the slow-walked reforms being carried out by China today.

There is no freedom. China is not a democracy. There is no religious freedom, and the national ideology remains Marxist-Leninist-Maoist. China continues to be a communist dictatorship playing with marketization. The two things are incompatible. Eventually they will break apart.

Trump has called their bluff.

A great deal of recent debate has focused attention on China's exchange rate regime. China maintains a de facto fixed exchange rate, with the renminbi linked to the U.S. dollar within a narrow trading band. China's strong export growth, expanding market shares in major trading partner countries, and rapid accumulation of reserves have raised questions about whether the renminbi's link to the U.S. dollar may have resulted in an undervaluation of the currency.

Clearly, China does manipulate its currency to benefit its export-led regime. Even Mitt Romney—no Trump lover—hammered this point home in 2012.

The Chinese government faces a number of possible obligations associated with potential losses in the state-dominated banking system, the future funding requirements of the pension system, and rising expenditure pressures, especially for education, health, and other social programs. Resolving the substantial quasi-fiscal liabilities poses more than a significant challenge. China could go bust, especially if it can't export.

This challenge increases substantially as macroeconomic conditions, especially growth, become less favorable or when structural reforms are not forceful enough to prevent the accumulation of new contingent liabilities. This highlights the urgency of undertaking real reforms since many of those liabilities could pose an even greater burden in the future. But domestic politics in China won't let this happen.

China never does real reform or liberalization. It pretends to so that it can placate Westerners. The Communist Party and its leader for life dominate China. It has militarized the South China Sea, imperiling trading routes, and exerts its force anywhere it can to America's detriment and future demise. To date we have looked the other way.

China's stock market is relatively thin, and there is a small corporate bond market. Banks have a crucial role in intermediating the substantial amount of private saving, which is estimated to be around one-third of total household income.

Bank lending has supported the high level of investment growth, which has made an important contribution to China's growth performance in recent years. Stability of the banking system is therefore crucial for promoting sustained growth. Financial sector reforms undertaken recently highlight the challenges. The urgency of those reforms has increased as domestic banks are facing intense competition under WTO accession commitments; the financial sector opened up to foreign banks in 2006. Chinese banks appear to be increasingly insolvent and teetering on bankruptcy.

Many of the inefficiencies in the Chinese economy are ultimately manifested in labor market outcomes. Unemployment and
underemployment of a significant proportion of the rural population remain pressing concerns as the economy adjusts to the
effects of reform of state-owned enterprises and WTO accession.
Even with strong output growth, the unemployment problem has
worsened. The divide between rich and poor is as extreme as anywhere in the world.

Watch what happens next as China collapses. Yes, China boasts
one of the longest single unified civilizations in the world. All of us
should have enormous respect for China's rich 5,000-year history,
which has long been characterized by dramatic shifts in power
between rival factions, periods of peace and prosperity when
foreign ideas were assimilated and absorbed, the disintegration
of empire through corruption and political subterfuge, and the
cyclical rise of ambitious leaders to found each new empire.

For the last 300 years China has seemingly more or less been
asleep except that the horrible mistake of Mao's disaster are all
too evident today. (I offered to help find funding for a Museum of
Mao's Killings, but China refused the offer.)

Wake up! Trump has. China is still red and is our preeminent
enemy. We need to adjust our strategies in trade and in defense
accordingly.

It appears the sleeping dragon empire has indeed reemerged in
a new dynasty. They think this is "their century." They are on the
rise, and we are in decline.

Until they call out "uncle," we cannot let them escape Trump's
hold. The dragon has met its match in the American eagle: Donald
Trump.

How to Lose Friends and Influence:
United States–Turkey Relations

Over a generation ago the acclaimed motivational speaker Dale
Carnegie penned a best seller titled *How to Win Friends and*

Influence People. It was chock full of good advice that any leader could readily use: Do not be overly critical. Give honest, sincere appreciation. Get the other person's point of view. Show genuine interest. Smile. Be a good listener. Make the other party feel wanted and important.

This isn't rocket science, just good policy and plain common sense. It is something sorely needed today in U.S.–Turkish relations.

It is worth stepping back from the current downward spiral and reinvesting in a long-term, rock-solid good relationship with Turkey before it is too late. That is the way it was for decades and the way it should be for decades to come. The consequences of deterioration in the relationship are just too great for either side. Yet the United States appears to be doing precisely the opposite of what Carnegie suggested and is losing Turkey as a good friend and ally.

For a while, President Trump and President Erdogan seemed to be forging a strong personal relationship. The national interests of the two strong NATO allies, which have long cooperated and held each other in esteem, appeared to be, even with a few bumps and irritants, headed in the right direction. "I think right now we are as close as we've ever been. And a lot of that has to do with the personal relationship," said Trump on the sidelines of the UN General Assembly. "He's getting high marks," he said of Erdogan.

Turkey was a friend, a trading partner, and a close military and intelligence partner, and the bilateral relations between the two world leaders had been going relatively well. After all, the two countries truly need each other.

This is in spite of the fact that the United States has failed to meet a reasonable demand of Turkey, its dear friend and ally. What demand is that? The return and extradition of Fethullah Gülen, a known terrorist operator who it has been established played a leading role in an attempted coup of President Erdogan's government in July 2016 that killed 250 people.

Even when presented with reams of information and dossiers of evidence, the U.S. State Department and Justice Department have been reluctant to act. If the shoe were on the other foot, would it be so? Of course not.

Turkey has a treaty with the United States and has extradited numerous assailants to the United States over the years. If Turkey harbored a terrorist who tried to overthrow the legitimately elected government of the United States, would we demand his head? You betcha!

What's at work here, then?

The problem appears to be the deep state and long-standing political IOUs.

Former U.S. ambassador to Turkey John Bass, a career foreign service officer and Obama loyalist with no ties to Trump or his policies, overplayed his cards and did unthinkable damage to United States–Turkey relations.

He appeared to want to destroy what took seventy-odd years to build. His outright disdain for Erdogan and his AKP (Justice and Development) Party are most newsworthy, and we are witnessing the horrible fallout.

It includes the suspension of visas between the two friendly countries; putting Turkey in the ranks of Syria, Yemen, and other terrorist states; harm done to trade, investment, and tourism is potentially irreparable; a loss of Turkey in the fight against ISIS, our common foe; the possible removal of U.S. troops and nuclear weapons from the strategic Incirlik Air Base in Turkey; the denial of papers to Turkish VIP invitees to the Trump inauguration; and the brouhaha around the arrest of a Turkish citizen who is accused of espionage who worked in the U.S. embassy.

Certainly, it is not Trump's policy to chase Turkey into the willing and open arms of Russia and its Iranian partners. But is it the policy of the deep state and its agents, such as Bass, who work to thwart everything Trump is doing in foreign policy?

The IOU is the dirty money Gülen and his FETO network have paid for years to obtain support and cover in the United States. That so-called spiritual network, which is a known terrorist Islamic threat, has funded lots of congressional campaigns and donated millions to the Clinton Foundation. Such political favors have bought influence and safety in the conclave of Pennsylvania's Poconos, where Gülen maintains his nerve center, undisturbed. Exposing the history of such doings and payments would further implicate the deep state.

Therefore, President Trump needs to get involved to resolve this situation. His state department is not doing it. He should call President Erdogan urgently and revert to the late Dale Carnegie's well-advised policy.

He should personally offer to work to extradite Gülen soon, close down his terror network, and expose its doings and even its connections to Democratic Party politicians. The visa window should be reopened immediately, and a special hotline should be installed to keep Turkey on our side as a loyal friend and willing ally ally—including buying our missiles and not Russia's. He should offer to replace Russian S-400 missiles with our preferred systems.

We do not want a diplomatic war or worse with Turkey, and the president can avoid one if he steps up to the plate (big league) now. If the Turks don't listen, he can sanction them and ditch them as fair-weather friends.

Breaking the Cordon Sanitaire: A Long Telegram for Our Time

The French prime minister a century ago, Georges Clemenceau, used medical terminology to argue for a quarantine against the Bolshevik tide spreading from Moscow. As revolutionary communism began to spread into newly independent states that had been parts of the Russian Empire, Clemenceau's cordon sanitaire policy—a precursor to the Truman–Kennan "containment" doctrine—remained relevant to understanding European politics.

Today, the ideological threat perceived by Western European states lies within them. National parliaments across the Continent struggle to fend off rebellions from upstart political parties that have upset the established order. Incumbent and opposition parties have resorted to the tactic that Clemenceau named: excluding "extremist" parties from the legislative process and coalition governments. The threat to the centrist mainstream comes from both right and left. Many far-left outfits have broken past their own containment zone and are currently in power both as part of coalitions as in Sweden or on the throne as was the case of Greece. Italy arguably could be included in this category, as the Five Star Movement isn't particularly right wing and is technically the senior coalition partner.

The cordon sanitaire and its role in the European elections that saw Eurosceptic victories all over the Continent are no less relevant today for the United States' relationship with Europe.

Europe's friend across the pond vacillates between calling the current European order a "foe" of America and insisting that nothing has changed in the relationship. The only thing everyone agrees on is that the transatlantic relationship is at a crossroads. What's wrong? President Trump abandoned the controversial rhetoric surrounding NATO well before Election Day in 2016. The national security strategy and national defense strategy both contain every commitment expected of America. After applauding President Obama's strategic pivot to Asia and ridiculing Senator Romney's warnings about Russia in 2012, Senate Democrats now insist that countering Putin's active measures should be the focus of transatlantic affairs; this has become a bipartisan consensus. Think tanks speak of a "fringe insurgency" of ethnonationalists coordinating internationally to affect one another's elections, but the establishment is unmoved.

These takes ignore a crucially significant factor: the Europeans themselves. It is in small states that are themselves fiercely divided politically that the direction of the Euro-American alliance will be decided. It is unfair to treat those states as passive, lacking agency, only acted upon by outsiders, be it Russia or any other influence. The decisions of their plebiscites should always be respected as examples of free peoples exercising self-determination.

What would it look like if the cordon sanitaire failed to contain surging populist movements? Consider the recent history of the other legislative body in Brussels: Belgium's federal legislature. The Flemish separatist party won the largest share of seats in the 2010 election for the Belgian Federal Parliament but fell well short of a majority. Having come out in first place, the New Flemish Alliance (N-VA) had the right to form a government, but with the establishment holding fast to the cordon sanitaire, coalition negotiations repeatedly failed to result in a deal, setting an ignominious record for Belgium, which went 541 days without a government.

The emergence of the centrist ruling coalition proved to be a pyrrhic victory. Having wasted half the term bickering, the N-VA was in a position to gain seats in the election of 2014. Seeing the writing on the wall, three center-right parties came into power with N-VA by elevating the leader of a junior partner to the premiership, breaking the Belgian cordon sanitaire. And so Belgium, with its government of mostly Dutch-speaking parties headed by a Francophone prime minister, demonstrated just how an antiestablishment party can go from outsider to kingmaker in one election. Past a certain threshold, the political imperative of getting into office and governing outweighs establishment parties' desire to maintain the cordon sanitaire.

The European Parliament, whose 751 members were elected by their domestic constituencies, also chooses the president of the EU executive branch, the European Commission. In 2014, members of the European Parliament (MEPs) voted in Jean-Claude Juncker on the strength of a "grand coalition" of the two largest political groups. Juncker's center-right European People's Party (EPP) and the progressive Socialists and Democrats (S&D) were especially strange bedfellows since European Parliament political groups are already big-tent alliances of national-level parties in member states. Since they lost over 100 seats, there is little reason to argue that they can stem this hemorrhage.

Indeed, the 2019 elections returned an even worse result for the center. The mainstream parties now need at least one more party to come up with a majority for installing Germany's Ursula von der Leyen as Juncker's successor—a closer-run thing than even these numbers predicted—and also to pass legislation.

In March 2017, mere months after President Trump's disposal of America's cordon sanitaire, a rattled European Union struggling to get a grip on a rapidly changing political landscape made its first move toward finding its feet in the Trump world order. The office of European Commission President Jean-Claude Juncker set out a white paper on the future of the European Union. Five scenarios were outlined, two of which we can discard out of hand for their inherent reduction of power concentration in Brussels (very unlikely under EPP leadership). One was fantastical in its advocacy of quick, deep federal integration, and the remainder were essentially status quo proposals. As far as adaptation went, it was consistent with the ethos once famously expressed (in protest) by Daniel Hannan, a Eurosceptic British MEP: Whatever the question, the answer is always more Europe.

French President Emmanuel Macron, widely seen to have claimed the mantle of European leadership from German Chancellor Angela Merkel, appears to have decided which of Juncker's five scenarios he envisions for the Continental bloc: a "multispeed Europe" in which groups of countries form a vanguard in taking measures to begin the deeper integration process and then pull the rest of the member states toward their position over time. Astute observers pointed out that the status quo is largely reflected in this position: Some countries use the euro; others don't but have committed to adopting it eventually, to point out only one example.

There is no shortage of proposals: President Macron's personal list was surprisingly mainstream for a new party. Critics would say that this is to be expected from a former finance minister in the government of France's Parti Socialiste (which Macron unseated). Speaking at the Sorbonne University in Paris, Macron outlined his vision of a reformed Europe. A significant component is attitudinal change; Macron denounced the technocratic modus operandi that Brussels currently employs, calling for true participation from the European citizenry. Citing the slew of terrorist attacks, Macron emphasized the need for Europe to provide its own security: an EU intelligence agency, a European Defence Fund (EDF), and a European version of DARPA. Exceptionally, he invited military service members and officers from other EU countries into the ranks of the French military, a step toward integration into one big EU army. Without exception, parties beyond the cordon sanitaire object to at least some of this package, though agreement with Macron does exist elsewhere.

A few months after his inauguration, President Trump visited Warsaw to celebrate the twenty-fifth anniversary of President George H. W. Bush's visit. The symbolism was powerful: President Bush came to Warsaw shortly after Poland's emancipation from Soviet domination. During President Trump's visit, Poland brought all its friends to the party. Twelve EU member states were present at the Three Seas Initiative, a forum encompassing the three Baltic states (representing the Baltic Sea), Romania and Bulgaria (representing the Black Sea), and Croatia and Slovenia (representing the Adriatic Sea), along with Austria, Czechia, Slovakia, and Hungary (the "Intermarium" between the three seas).

Although the Three Seas conference was ostensibly an energy and infrastructure cooperation group—and they certainly went through the motions of soliciting American investment in rail and energy projects across the Three Seas—the subtext was clear: Poland sought the imprimatur of nationalist, antiglobalist legitimacy that only President Trump could bestow. Their Visegrad (V-4) group represents the most ardent opposition to Brussels's federalist agenda, and the battle lines on this side have been clear for some time.

Unlike the postwar Germanies, where the denazification process purged the Nazi Party's political influence, there was very little decommunization after 1991 in Poland (the ruling Law and Justice Party [PiS] is trying to change this). Attempts at "lustration" (de-Nazification for communists) were frustrated until the parliament passed controversial judicial reforms, ending the domination of the Polish judiciary by ex-Communist Party apparatchiks. Close observers of this issue will point out that Poland's new system borrows heavily from America's federal bench appointment system, but this is hardly an offense against the rule of law, as Brussels alleges.

Since Poland has been a "double victim"—oppressed by Nazism and then by communism—the suspicion of big, powerful, centralized government runs deep in that country. They see no reason to feel guilt for colonialism or slavery, which they had no part in and derived no benefit from. In their last election, none of the country's left-of-center or leftist parties got any seats in the parliament. The most left-wing party with a seat (PSL) calls itself a Christian Democrat (center-right) party, and they have only a paltry 16 seats (out of 460). Needless to say, the current government has continued the commitment to spending 2 percent of GDP on defense, one of the few European countries that take this responsibility seriously enough to comply.

Other countries in this group are much less ideological in their opposition to Brussels. Romania, governed by a socialist party, has balked at the prospect of having to integrate Middle Eastern and African refugees into a society that already has a large itinerant underclass of Roma who live outside mainstream society. The Czech Republic's recent electoral result expelled some surprisingly Eurosceptic socialists from government in favor of populists, speaking to the general direction of this region and its future relationship with European federalism. With the exception of Austria, which recently installed a right-wing coalition and banned the burqa before that, every member of the Three Seas Initiative was dominated by communism and is keen to retain its independence as a sovereign state. Romania, Bulgaria, Greece, and Hungary (which has militarized its southern border), at the forefront of the migration crisis, bear no illusions about what it means to cede control to Brussels. If Brussels can decide who you have to let into the country, what can't it decide?

Indeed, the status quo in which these countries reject Brussels's diktats amounts to a "soft exit" from certain "mandatory" EU integration mechanisms. The rigidity with which the European Union opposes these developments reveals an impolitic inflexibility that serves neither side well. Adding to this will be the sharp reduction in EU funds as the east develops and Britain's substantial contribution to the common budget disappears. Where Brussels's funds once greased the wheels of cooperation with European federalist policies, many Intermarium countries will now be expected to foot the bill for policies they fundamentally disagree with.

Rounding up a trend in the Three Seas Initiative (TSI), it bears pointing out that both Croatia and Slovenia are former communist Yugoslav states that also suffered under Italian fascism. They owe a historical debt of gratitude to the European Union for recognizing them quickly and to the United States for its defense guarantee against revanchist Serbia in the 1990s. Croatia, the more right wing of the two, is also setting up liquefied natural gas (LNG) terminals on its coastline, aiming to distribute American shale gas farther into the European Union. Despite their having relatively little to complain about (and arguably the most upside from joining the European Union), their presence in the TSI speaks volumes; if the federalists can't hold on to their allegiance, federalism really is in trouble. Swing states like these are where the cordon sanitaire could break for good.

Recently coalesced under the leadership of Wopke Hoekstra, the Dutch finance minister, is a group of eight rich Northern European member states (the Hoekstra 8, or H-8). Claiming to act in concert against future financial consolidation of the European Union by the Franco-German motor, they opened a new front on the battlefield against European federalism. The group includes two countries outside the eurozone: Sweden, which committed to adopting the euro in the future, and Denmark, which secured an opt-out at the same time the United Kingdom did. These eight countries maintain healthy public finances and shoulder a large portion of EU spending, which may limit how deep any potential cooperation with spendthrift rebels might be.

The Netherlands, which leads this group, has traditionally been a hotbed of Euroscepticism. Though Geert Wilders of the Dutch Party for Freedom (PVV) was widely seen to have "lost" the March 2017 election, the parliamentary math doesn't fully reflect the political swing. The supposed winners, the People's Party for Freedom and Democracy (VVD), lost more seats than Wilders picked up and came out of a "grand" (centrist) coalition with the Dutch Labour Party (PvdA) to run on a platform that borrowed heavily from Wilders's PVV. Wilders has pulled the Overton window rightward, forcing mainstream parties to form a fragile four-party coalition with a one-seat majority: classic cordon sanitaire. Unlike his counterparts in Austria (or neighboring Belgium, for that matter), Wilders didn't manage to break through the cordon sanitaire. The election was marked by mass protests by the significant Turkish minority (with embassy involvement), though he singularly failed to deliver during the European elections of 2019. The socialists, who placed a surprise first, were helped by the star power of Frans Timmermans, the Dutchman who led the S&D campaign as its presidential candidate, or *spitzenkandidat*. It remains to be seen which way the wind will blow in The Hague, but Mark Rutte, the prime minister reelected by the narrowest possible margin in 2017, is playing second fiddle to Macron as part of the liberal alliance, which is neither socialist nor Christian Democratic; Renew Europe is what they're calling themselves. Expect fireworks when Macron realizes that his spendthrift plans for a big, bloated Brussels meet opposition from his own troops.

Denmark also has been a traditional member of the home-grown resistance to the European core. It refused to join the euro after the Maastricht treaty, backing the British in their bid for exemptions and securing an exemption for itself in the process. This most right wing of the Nordic countries has been a stalwart NATO ally and was until recently ruled by a sort of broad right-wing coalition, bringing into government the populist right, serving as a model for safely breaking the cordon sanitaire. Former PM and former leader of NATO Anders Fogh Rasmussen pioneered the tactic of counting on this "populist right" as a reliable foil to European federalist plans that he wanted to oppose anyway. Although the Danes are unlikely to back a broad-based rebellion against the Franco-German motor, they will be natural allies to the resistance on many questions, including further fiscal integration, NATO supremacy over common EU defense, and opposition to mass movements of population into the Schengen area.

The Baltic states present interesting cases. Estonia is a model for twenty-first-century governance, pioneering fully electronic public services and competing in the digital economy worldwide. Latvia and Lithuania have both benefited from market-liberal governments, making miraculous recoveries from the 2008 crisis, and all three have elbowed their way into the rich northern European club, going so far as to appropriate the "Nordic" label. Together with Poland, they pioneered the importation of American shale gas as a substitute for Russian pipeline-exported LNG, a major strategic gain for the United States, Europe, and the transatlantic relationship.

All three Baltic states have suffered greatly from a brain drain in which their most talented youth have left their countries and never come back. None is keen to replace its fairly small population with any number of foreigners, European or otherwise; large Russian minorities are enough to handle. All are committed to NATO membership and wary of a Brussels-based European army, fully recognizing the inevitable competition that will arise between a German/French-led international security force focusing on idealistic pursuits and America's more realistic attitude to international relations. Their membership in the H-8 and TSI raises awkward questions: Why did poor but financially well-behaved countries such as the Baltics end up shouldering bailouts for profligate, comparatively rich countries such as Greece? Why should they risk their ironclad relationship with America over Germany's wish to pinch pennies? Sharing a border with Russia historically has been a losing proposition, and the Baltic states have already suffered more than their share.

In the middle of this pack, Finland leans toward the Danish perspective. Although Finland adopted the euro, its contribution to migrant quotas has been much lower than Brussels wants. Finland has been vocal in the more traditional opposition to Brussels over the last ten years that is centered on the fiscal union that transfers wealth from countries such as Finland to the European south. The ruling coalition, which once included the heavily Eurosceptic Finns Party, has managed to tear away from its geopolitical Finlandization in a full embrace of its status as a buffer state between Russia and Europe. The cordon sanitaire was unnecessary. Over the next few years, deteriorating Western relations with Russia will create a window of opportunity to bring Finland into NATO, a position the Trump administration should handle carefully. Finland's election in April 2019 turned out to be a hotbed of Russian cyberoperations; offering a referendum on NATO membership in a formerly neutral state is fighting words. The victory of the socialists guaranteed the status quo.

Sweden, in contrast, has a much more humanitarian bent. Its socialist-green coalition, backstopped by the votes of the former Communist Party, famously prioritizes a feminist foreign policy. The collection of parties in opposition on the (relative) political right would have the seats to govern if they included the Sweden Democrats but is holding fast to the cordon sanitaire doctrine and keeping them out of power at all costs. Ironically, the "populist" and "right-wing" Sweden Democrats would pass for a center-left party anywhere else in Europe and are not particularly Eurosceptical. Sweden is at the forefront of pushing for greater outlays of development aid to migrants' countries of origin as part of its strategy to become a "humanitarian superpower" and is a surprise member of the H-8 despite its longtime status as a net contributor to the EU budget. One beacon of hope, however, is Sweden's uncharacteristic distancing from its traditional geopolitical neutrality; it has recently started making noises about joining NATO in defiance of Russia's bugbear status, providing much political support for the sanctions regime spearheaded by President Obama. On this and other defense matters, they are likely to surprise positively. The Swedes are willing to join only if Finland joins simultaneously, which means it won't happen any time soon. Again, it would benefit NATO to bring in Nordic partners such as Sweden, but too much overt support from the White House is likely to be counterproductive in the current political context.

On the other side of the ledger, Spain and Portugal occupy a special place on the European frontier. Much like the Balkan EU countries, the Iberian Peninsula came to the European Union as a later addition and in a different context: the last gasps of fascism. Portugal occupies the upper end of the small-country sweet spot that allows its higher-ups to aspire to positions of authority from which larger countries shy away: With the backing of the socialist S&D coalition, Portugal produced the most recent president of the commission bar one (José Manuel Barroso) and the new secretary-general of the United Nations, António Guterres (both former socialist Portuguese PMs). There doesn't seem to be much risk of Portugal flipping on Brussels on any major issues. Spain held a bit more promise until the ascension of Pedro Sánchez, who leads the European Socialists.

Spanish and Catalonian left populism is unique. These may well be the only populists in Europe who clamor for more refugees, representing a brand of Euroscepticism comparable only to that of Jeremy Corbyn and Alexis Tsipras in the United Kingdom and Greece, respectively. Podemos, the far-left franchise of GUE/NGL, has taken over city hall in Barcelona and had a good showing in May. Vox, a new outfit that has taken up the right flank, recently accomplished the unthinkable: ousting the ruling socialists from their southern Spanish redoubt, though significantly underperforming in 2019. Spain is a swing state. Both sides of the establishment seem happy to pull votes from outside the cordon sanitaire. Despite this, Madrid and Lisbon remain a reliable part of the federalist core.

No country in the European Union has as much to complain about as Greece. Avoiding "Grexit"—even if it only left the eurozone—had been the main task of the European Union before Ukraine stole the spotlight. Abysmal treatment of Greece at the hands of Brussels gave rise to the first serious Eurosceptic movements in many EU member states, which came to realize that one day it could be them being treated that way. Greece was ground zero for populism and then its reversal by technocratic elites. As Alexis Tsipras—the sort of leftist who opposes the European Union for being too capitalist—won power at the ballot box, won referendums, and won more elections, he still couldn't shake off Brussels's yoke. Having already let the European Central Bank run its monetary policy, as every eurozone member has done, Athens had no choice but to submit.

It is hard to say whether Greece has any fight left in it. Newly installed Prime Minister Mitsotakis seems unlikely to force any confrontations. As one of the few countries that spend 2 percent of their GDP on defense (even after slashing government spending by 25 percent), Greece has received little credit for its contribution to European security as the commission took over its fiscal policy. They fought against federalism for a decade and lost at every turn.

The Greeks have in common with the Italians (and Maltese) the geographic front line of the migration crisis. A strong cross-party majority in Rome sees an idealistic Brussels detached from the reality of having a failed state (Libya) a few miles off the coast. During the height of the migration crisis, Malta and Italy were the loudest opponents of the reigning policy of sending military vessels to rescue migrants. Former prime minister Silvio Berlusconi (now an MEP) famously forced Brussels to relent after threatening to hand out Italian passports to every migrant in full knowledge that they'd all leave for France and Germany the next day. Operation Triton, by which a federal EU maritime border guard patrols the Italian coast, was pried from the promigrant federalist faction only after it became clear that sending out EU-funded rescue missions to save the drowning was only encouraging human traffickers to leave their passengers in the middle of the sea and go back for more.

Rome has since abandoned the Brussels consensus and begun dealing unilaterally with the relevant forces in Libya, wounding regional cooperation, the philosophical cornerstone of the European Union. With youth unemployment at an eye-watering 35 percent, dissatisfaction with Brussels remains high. These were major factors in the Eurosceptic wave that gained in the election in March 2018, which brought populist figures such as Matteo Salvini into the inner sanctum of the EU ministerial council meetings, where he votes Italy's large shares against the federalist agenda. In the places where a Eurosceptic Italian minister might find fast friends, such as the council of defense, finance, or even interior ministers, decision making could be wrested away from the Franco-German motor of federalist integration and taken in completely new directions. No region of the European Union has been hit harder by the downsides of federalism, and no other country apart from Italy can lead the resistance as effectively as Rome. A founding member of every EU institution, Italy has historically punched below its weight but has the scars to prove its legitimacy as a reforming actor. Having busted both sides of the cordon sanitaire, Italy has a historic chance to lead. The former communist countries and other naturally Eurosceptic nations are all too small to lead independently. To achieve anything, they must coalesce under a bloc leadership that only Italy can provide at the moment.

In London, these are the times that try men's souls. Isolated and internally divided, Britain is slowly realizing what it has gotten itself into. David Cameron suffered from a disease that American Republicans will recognize. He campaigned on a platform much more conservative than he was in his heart and ended up surprised by how successful the result was. Having promised his electorate a referendum he doubted he'd have the seats to deliver, Cameron boxed himself into the position of having to fight to remain in the European Union and again was surprised that his electorate delivered a result he wasn't ready for: Brexit. After successfully leading the charge against Brussels's European federalism for so long, Great Britain jumped off the Eurosceptic cliff without waiting to see if its friends were coming. One historical verdict we can already pass: Britain decided to leave too early. The Brexit moment was meant to be the starting gun for a mass exodus from Brussels and was always conceived as such by those "Europhobes" for whom leaving the European Union wasn't enough; nothing short of burning it to the ground would do.

Instead, they got Theresa May. To her credit, she ran on a platform that was a reflection of her true self: a Christian Democratic right-of-center figure. As the old joke goes, a Christian Democrat is just a socialist who goes to Mass. The electorate that gave Westminster a Conservative majority for want of a Brexit referendum (where they then voted to leave) was in no mood for pre-Thatcherite conservatism. Future prime ministers, mulling over a snap election, will be forever haunted by Theresa May's squandered majority. Boris Johnson—finally the Prime Minister— has now made it clear that it is Brexit, "no if, ands, or buts."

The fundamental issue surrounding Brexit is the fiction of equality among nation-states. Brussels is treating London the way it treated Athens during the Greek crisis: Keep them in at all costs or at least make an example of them for their disobedience. The fault in the assumption lies in the UK's elevated status in the international arena as a nuclear weapons state, the emitter of one of the currencies in the IMF's special drawing rights, a permanent member of the UN Security Council, and a member of the G7. With the notable exception of France, every other EU member is thus equal to the United Kingdom only on paper as a diplomatic courtesy.

As it stands, the United Kingdom is currently on the fast lane to a Corbyn government, whose operation declared victory in the 2017 election, celebrating a net gain in seats. The party infrastructure has been infiltrated enough by Corbynistas to ensure a long-term legacy within the Labour Party. Corbyn has been consistent in his opposition to the European Union for entirely left-populist reasons. Starting from his campaigning against the United Kingdom joining the EEC in the 1975 referendum and the more recent Treaty of Lisbon of 2007, he sees EU membership as a straitjacket against the rollback of Thatcherite privatization. In many ways, Corbyn belongs beyond the leftist cordon sanitaire, with GUE/NGL rather than S&D, where the Labour Party currently resides. Rumors of party splits abound, and this fact may well gain salience now that the Corbyn party has sent a delegation of MEPs to Strasbourg—in 2019 and beyond. Corbyn has come out in favor of a second referendum, the only way to keep the party united under him. It is not unimaginable, however, that Corbyn is personally be opposed to his party's policy.

Today's Labour Party is likely to knock out the Scottish Nationalists from their perches up in Scotland; already their bumper 2015 performance of fifty-six seats has been reduced to thirty-five, not quite enough to put Corbyn over the finish line.

The specter hanging over the whole situation is, of course, the Brexit deal. As things stand, it's looking like an ugly shakedown on Brussels's part. London has not fired the heavy artillery yet, but a bungled deal will inevitably result in a Corbyn premiership, with all the anti-NATO, nuclear disarmament, and inevitable slide into socialism and capital controls that entails. The prospect of Britain leveraging its powerful presence in EU bodies such as the European Parliament is without a doubt their best strategy. The EU budget for the next seven years represents an incomparable opportunity to buy votes and goodwill for a better Brexit deal.

One ray of hope lies across the Irish Sea. Ireland, currently run by its establishment center-right party, has the sort of fragile coalition that could crumble at any moment: no majority propped up by an agreement to support bills by a number of independent MPs and another center-right party. No country in the European Union stands to lose more from Brexit than Ireland, a fact Britain has failed to take advantage of. Theresa May's agreement with the Northern Irish Democratic Unionist Party (DUP), the sort of right-wing group that used to have paramilitary squads, was highly controversial. Ireland's lack of membership in NATO puts it in an awkward situation regarding security cooperation with the rest of the European Union. Ireland is not bound by the 2 percent of GDP promise, nor does it have any strategic imperatives surrounding it (like, say, Malta with Libya a few miles away). Ireland is therefore not particularly keen to spend more money on defense or see the EU defense union they might have to pay for with very little benefit to the geographically isolated (and therefore safe) Irish citizenry. Their membership in the H-8 group of fiscally conservative Northern European countries reveals Ireland's willingness to buck mainstream European federalism even under leftist governments.

Brussels maintains a red line in not allowing free movement of goods and people on the Irish border unless London accepts those terms with every other EU country. This raises a potential reimposition of border controls after Brexit, which violates the Good Friday accords. That this inevitably would bring about the return of Irish terrorism to the British Isles illustrates the inflexibility inherent in trying to treat every case equally. Ireland, which already was feeling Brussels's pinch on fiscal and taxation matters, may well find itself joining the barricades on other issues in exchange for support from more habitual rebels against federalism.

The question has been put before: Could core Europe move forward without a core? The "variable geometry" of the past always included France in the center stage, variably pairing up with the United Kingdom on foreign policy aims or with Germany on the internal EU matters such as the euro. Without the United Kingdom, France is left with a functionally isolationist Germany. Even France isn't traditionally on Germany's side on EU fiscal policy; it usually takes the spendthrift southern European stance of pushing for rich northern European countries to pay into public investment projects all over the southern and eastern European Union. Germany's consistent loss of power since 2016 doesn't make anything easier.

Having had their elections within months of each other, the Franco-German engine of core Europe went through tense times after Trump's inauguration. Higher-ups in German politics seemed to take seriously the possibility that Marine Le Pen might pull off an upset of Trumpian proportions as a result of the wave of anti-Brussels sentiment set off by the Paris attacks (which ones? you ask; exactly). Having been abandoned by London and Washington within six months of each other, the only major ally Berlin had left was Paris, which looked to be packing its bags as well. Never again, said some, should Germany ever find itself in a situation in which one election in another country could so fundamentally alter its position in the world.

"Encircled by friends" describes the German position post-1991. No country has benefited so much from the American-led liberal international order, an order it now sees America criticizing. Indeed, Germany has become one of the richest nations on the planet, with a handsome budget and trade surplus, full employment, and the sort of high-value-added manufacturing that once made states like Michigan and Ohio the industrial powerhouses of the world. The recent election result sends this message: Germany wants more of the same—stability.

This is the nub of the current transatlantic disagreement. Germany has optimized its governance model for the pre-Trumpian era, in which America provides security for the Middle East, East Asia, Oceania, Latin America, Afghanistan, parts of Africa that aren't handled by France, and the high seas, as well as Europe. President Trump is right to assert that Europe, especially Germany, is developed enough to provide its own security and powerful enough to justify ambitious roles in upholding the international system from which it benefits so greatly.

The insistence on living in the past is having serious structural consequences within Germany. The 12 percent of Germans who voted for AfD weren't living in a context of underemployment and lack of opportunities like a Rust Belt Trump Democrat. A 2017 AfD voter was a one-issue voter, and that heralded the start of a culture war in Germany.

Merkel's having to form another "grand coalition" and promise not to run again signals weakness. It bears remembering that the Bavarian CSU (nominally the same party as Merkel's CDU) forced Merkel to flip-flop midelection on the migrant issue, taking a "never again" stance on letting so many migrants into Germany; Merkel had acknowledged the existence of "no-go zones" in migrant communities. The Bavarian CSU should be on the list of Eurosceptic parties to poach after the election. They don't belong in the EPP any more than Viktor Orban does.

Another cost of forming Merkel's centrist coalition handed the AfD a major victory: As the largest opposition party, the AfD is guaranteed chairmanships of major parliamentary committees (budget, for example) and other constitutionally mandated roles in scrutinizing the government. This crash course in governance augurs terrible things for the establishment in a couple of years as newly experienced AfD apparatchiks start spreading their Eurosceptic tentacles all over Brussels and Berlin.

It is almost a shame that the tripartite coalition talks failed, as they might have provided cover for much more productive reversals. The recommendations by a group of German foreign policy mandarins come to mind: Getting rid of the Nord Stream 2 pipeline to Russia would ease the tension between Washington and Berlin, solidifying their commitment to the EU's objective of energy independence from Russia, which Merkel's government still ostensibly claims as a priority. Such hypocrisy is inherent in governing for so long, and Merkel's valedictory term will be filled with it as she struggles to shrug off liberal aspirations for her. In pushing for pan-European defense, she will be hobbled by her coalition partner's opposition to the 2 percent of GDP rule.

This leaves core Europe rudderless even with Ursula von der Leyen on the throne.

A weak Germany cements Macron's France as the leader of Europe. In what was already a shaky arrangement, Paris has lost momentum in recent months. Macron's strength—freedom from the old party system—has become a sword of Damocles: He needs the establishment's cooperation with his agenda. President Macron, in the middle of his five-year term, holds a solid majority in the French legislature. Coming out of the French socialist party (which he served in government as finance minister), he has taken to governing as a surprisingly right-wing figure: proposing tough laws on migrants, coming out for universal mandatory military service, and democratizing parts of the European bureaucracy (a popular "populist" position). Insofar as Macron has lost support, it has been mainly for socialist reasons: Tax increases on the middle class sparked the *gilet jaunes*, after all.

Recent developments in the European parliament put pause to this: The unpopular *spitzenkandidat* system to select presidential candidates for the commission was forced through against the will of both Macron and Eurosceptic forces, which then proceeded to ignore the resolution in nominating von der Leyen. If European federalism was ever going to be victorious, it seems inevitable that the Brussels political class would stage this sort of power grab eventually; it might even work next time. In theory, the system cements in place of the current party order, making the European Parliament's cordon sanitaire stronger. In practice, it probably will lead to the fracturing of the seven-party system. Consolidation is logical for many reasons on both left and right, and if having the most seats magically grants the right to the commission presidency, any number of ways to abuse this system will be cooked up.

An uncharacteristically outspoken German (who happens to have been his party's *spitzenkandidat*) leads the ruling parliamentary plurality. Manfred Weber of the EPP lost the internal European federalist fight in a council brawl, but in the meantime, being one of his party members meant having to campaign for him at home, a prospect that added nothing to many candidates and may have cost them votes. President Juncker (also of the EPP) sided with Weber on this issue and muscled his chief of staff, Martin Selmayr, into the powerful top civil servant position in the commission (to loud protests from lesser parties). Merkel and Juncker will live on through Selmayr and von der Leyen.

Macron's stance on the *spitzenkandidat* system saw him on the same side of a major European issue with the Italian, Polish, and Hungarian Eurosceptics for the second time since his inauguration. In his first major foray beyond the cordon sanitaire, Macron teamed up with Italy (unofficially and de facto) to delay drafting the EU budget until after the European elections.

When combined with uncertainty about who the commissioners will be, this all promises to be a wonderful mess, especially if the United Kingdom threatens to withhold £39 billion from the budget. Armed with that much money to spread where it wants while negotiating both appointments and budgets, those appointees will create a delicious plot twist in the Brexit saga; Britain will never have had this much influence on what the European Union does.

Europe has been tried multiple times in the last few years. Most of the time, it has been found wanting in the extreme. From the Arab Spring to the Ukrainian crisis, through Syria's disintegration and Libya's collapse, the European Union has been an incoherent actor in its own security interests. The spectacle of former secretary of state Rex Tillerson standing next to his titular nominal counterpart Federica Mogherini shows the fundamental inequality between them: Tillerson led the state department of a nation-state with plenipotentiary sovereignty; Mogherini responds to over two dozen capitals, most of which possess diplomatic services centuries senior to her operation and none of which take orders from her. It bears remembering what (surprisingly Eurosceptic) Victoria Nuland, President Obama's Assistant Secretary of State for European and Eurasian Affairs, had to say about the European Union while she dealt with the Ukraine crisis in 2014. It need not be repeated, but the sentiment says much about the constructiveness of European participation in transatlantic security initiatives.

Kiev's fundamental question comes down to whether the Ukrainian space is part of the Intermarium or Novorossiya (a term Moscow has since dropped). As Moscow stays intent on keeping Ukraine in Novorossiya by force, the diplomatic effort to sustain sanctions on Russia will stay strong. President Putin's reelection held no surprises. In light of his approval ratings, democratic challenge to his regime doesn't seem to be the way out of the current impasse. One possible exception: Belarussian smuggling of EU and American goods into Russia is a major pressure valve from Western sanctions. Bringing Belarus into the sanctions regime against Moscow would accentuate the pressure from existing sanctions without necessitating new formal sanctions. Only the European Union has the sort of carrots that could bring Minsk to the table: This is one area where greater EU engagement could be useful.

The situation with Turkey has escalated beyond any of America's enemies' wildest dreams. Despite the fact that Turkey is a keystone ally for the American-led liberal international order, both the Europeans and certain sectors in Washington insist on alienating Erdogan's government. Whether FETO is a real terrorist threat to Ankara or not remains to be seen. If nothing else, FETO certainly wouldn't benefit from proving Erdogan right. Kurdish interests have so far received a favorable hearing in Brussels and other European capitals. Abdullah Öcalan's leadership of the PKK, a communist guerilla group from the Cold War days, should not be brushed over, but any revolutionary communist group willing to back democratic socialism and modern leftist concerns such as gender equality should be offered a place at the table until confidence is broken (the Colombian FARC comes to mind). Bringing Ankara and Brussels to Washington's priorities—Assad must go (a policy success for which the White House gets no credit), stability within NATO, and peace in the Middle East—would be furthered greatly by a rapprochement between the AKP and the PKK. Childish episodes such as putting Erdogan on an enemies' list in NATO exercises should be avoided and condemned in the severest terms wherever they occur. Imagine if they had put President Trump there instead.

The most frequently mentioned gripe against Washington in the European Union is President Trump's pulling out of previously agreed initiatives: the Transatlantic Trade and Investment Partnership (TTIP) trade deal, the Paris Agreement, and more recently the Iran nuclear deal (JCPOA). Even the most pro-American part of Brussels, the NATO headquarters, has come out against the White House's hard line on Iran. The prospective coalition of EU rebels could conceivably wrest away Iran policy from Le Berlaymont. Such an alliance at the Council of Foreign Ministers again runs through The Hague, Copenhagen, Rome, the Intermarium, and perhaps some surprise guests such as Madrid. Breaking the cordon sanitaire on foreign policy, major European political figures are coalescing around Washington's position on Iran. Former PM of Spain José María Aznar, a transatlantic stalwart, is leading the charge. President Macron has again bucked the Brussels consensus and slammed Iran's missile program. Iran and to a greater extent North Korea will be issues in which Washington shoulders the burden of leadership alone while it waits for the end of the Juncker administration in November 2019. The political will for a European hard line on the issue could be fertile ground for either side to exploit in coming elections, especially with the special purpose vehicle (SPV) that Mogherini forced through for trade with Iran.

President Trump's intention to move forward on Israel is also clear despite European protests. Though Palestinian sympathies in European capitals have long plagued the transatlantic relationship, they will be resolved in the coming months. A unifying aspect of right-wing parties beyond the cordon sanitaire is their uncompromising support for the Jewish state. There continues to be a European left campaign to impose sanctions on Israel, reflected in many a UN vote by the various European countries (including Germany) that make it their business to oppose Tel Aviv. The mantra of "shared values" is belied by this reality, though it is hardly America's position on Israel that has changed over the years.

On trade and the climate agenda, fundamental differences between President Trump's worldview and the Brussels consensus will remain the Gordian knot. The politically powerful German car industry and its lucrative exports is a weakness even Berlin's influence may not be able to neutralize. Faced with large tariffs on American exports (cars in particular), President Trump has the substance of the matter on his side. Despite the heated rhetoric around the Paris Agreement, America's signature cannot technically be removed for another few years, and the United States is complying with its promised cuts to emissions. Merkel's Germany, which made a political issue of climate during her campaign, is lagging far behind on its promises and dropped its climate campaign promises during the coalition negotiations. Europeans may find it wise to refrain from throwing stones while living in glass houses: The White House wants to renegotiate the Paris Agreement, and it seems only fair to give President Trump a fair shake at a deal that even environmental NGOs were dissatisfied with.

Unifying Europe's militaries will present an awkward situation for the transatlantic relationship. Current plans present a deafening silence on the NATO-EU relationship with the possible exception of the question of where to put a unified military command, which is the wrong question to be asking if the two organizations are to be working together. A headquarters in London might be a good halfway house and represents the sort of ambitious agenda Britain should pursue. Although Permanent Structured Cooperation (PESCO) does seem genuinely aimed at delivering what President Trump has asked of Europe, the 2 percent spending target has received the same nominal bromides and token increases that usually happen when Washington complains. Assuming that the EU army is an inevitability despite what was said during the Brexit campaign, Washington's priority should be to push for an EU-level defense spending floor through mechanisms similar to the public spending caps Brussels imposed during the financial crisis. Managing the migration crisis, which the Trump campaign successfully leveraged to buttress its talking points on ISIS and illegal immigration, will remain at the top of the priorities in Washington, if not necessarily Brussels.

In the "Long Telegram" written at the outset of the Cold War, Ambassador George Kennan underlined the differences between the Soviet and American systems and what the strategy should be to contain and eventually defeat the Soviets.

The European Union is not the Soviet Union; nor is Brussels a new Moscow, offering the world an ideological alternative to liberal free market capitalism and democracy. The Europeans are our friends and will forever remain so.

The source of tension is the halfway house the Europeans currently find themselves in: The European Union is a regional integration mechanism, an intergovernmental organization, and a multilateral political forum with an executive (the council), a legislative (the European Parliament), a judiciary (the European

Court of Justice), a civil service (the European Commission), a diplomatic service (the External Action Service), and a common monetary policy for the eurozone members (but no common fiscal policy).

Unfortunately, the European Union of today is not greater than the sum of its parts. These pillars of the "ever closer union" currently do not add up to a peer for America and will not until and unless the ultimate step is taken.

If the Europeans wish to federalize and unite under one flag, they are free to do so under the democratic rights they retain as free peoples in the international order, and America should neither encourage nor discourage this outcome. However, European federalists are not the only political force in Europe, they do not hold a monopoly on political legitimacy, and the challenge to their primacy will only get stronger as they are forced to accommodate factions beyond the cordon sanitaire that hold opposite views.

Until then, the European Union should be treated as twenty-eight countries with separate nationhoods and sovereignties. To grant implicit recognition of their unity prematurely is to pick a side in a foreign political debate about which America shouldn't have an opinion. This is the side of the argument most at odds with the philosophy of the Trump administration to boot.

President Juncker is not the prime minister of Europe; he heads a regional body that sometimes has legal force and is disobeyed anyway, much like the United Nations. "First Vice President" Mogherini is not the foreign minister of Europe's 500 or so million "EU citizens" (a meaningless category outside Europe), nor are EU missions abroad embassies or the heads of those missions ambassadors. European fantasizing over China's replacement of America as internationalist in chief was swiftly found to be wishful thinking. Similar international organizations (ASEAN, CARICOM, the African Union) would never be treated as equals to the federal government of the United States unless their member states subsumed themselves into a fully federated polity.

The hope of a Europe of nation-states or a revamped European Union with deeper democratic checks on its bureaucratic excesses remains salient. The party line even in the most Eurosceptic political organizations is that Brussels can be reformed. Eurosceptic parties left and right are finding that modern takes on welfare statism coupled with their opposition to globalization can deliver surprisingly high electoral returns. The elements for an antifederalist coalition—breaking the cordon sanitaire—are all in place and lack only the leadership to put the challenge to the current crop of Eurocrats. As Kennan said of America in 1946, winning at home is the key to winning abroad. If Eurosceptics can keep the momentum in their favor, they will triumph. To prove the point, consider three Eurosceptic stories: Salvini, Le Pen, and Farage. Salvini has won at home, ascending into government. Le Pen has won lesser victories, such as making the second round against Macron and getting deputies into the French congress. Farage, unfortunately, is the slacker: He won the referendum but remains the leader of a party with no seats. Farage needs to start winning again, and he may get the chance.

Where differences in political systems do exist, they are mainly the consequence of the Reagan and Thatcher revolutions. Recent political developments seem to be dragging Europe slowly to the right, toward the "bipartisan consensus" of the Democrats and Republicans in Washington, a position not exclusive to President Trump. Dissident federalists and Eurosceptic forces in Europe need someone to lead the caucus of rebels against Junckerian federalism if Europe is to start emphasizing sovereignty, strong defenses, law and order, and strong borders. It remains to be seen what the nonpolitical staff of the European Commission would do when faced with a less than federalist leadership in Le Berlaymont. The battle lines in Europe are drawn, and 2020 will show whether Macron's reformist promises have fallen on deaf ears.

6

The U.S.–UK Special Relationship

The U.S. relationship with the UK is "indispensable."
—PRESIDENT DONALD TRUMP

What Is the Special Relationship?

The "Special Relationship" is a term that has been used to describe the exceptionally close political, diplomatic, cultural, economic, military, and historical ties between the United Kingdom and the United States since its use in a 1946 speech by the British statesman Winston Churchill.

Although both the United Kingdom and the United States have close relationships with many other nations, the level of cooperation between them in economic activity, trade and commerce, military planning, execution of military operations, nuclear weapons technology, and intelligence sharing has been described as unparalleled among major powers. The question AB (after Brexit) is: Will it remain that way? It will if Trump has any say.

Arguably, this relationship has had and could have a bearing on liberty not only in the Anglo-American sphere but also in all the places around the world that are still influenced by civil society.

The United Kingdom and the United States have been close allies in numerous military and political conflicts, including World War I, World War II, the Korean War, the Cold War, the Gulf War, the Iraq War, and the Afghanistan War. A poster from World War I showing Britannia arm in arm with Uncle Sam symbolizes the Anglo-American alliance. It shows a profound Churchillian influence that has undergirded the relationship. But what will it look like in 2030 or 2050?

Although the Special Relationship was most famously emphasized by Prime Minister Winston Churchill, its existence had been recognized since the nineteenth century, not least by rival powers. The two nations' troops had been fighting side by side in skirmishes overseas since 1859, and the two democracies shared a bond of sacrifice in World War I.

Prime Minister Ramsay MacDonald's visit to the United States in 1930 confirmed his belief in the Special Relationship, and for this reason he looked to the Washington Treaty rather than a revival of the Anglo-Japanese alliance as the guarantee of peace in the Far East. However, as the historian David Reynolds observed, 'for most of the period since 1919, Anglo-American relations had been cool and often suspicious.'

America's "betrayal" of the League of Nations was only the first in a series of U.S. actions—over war debts, naval rivalry, the 1931 Manchurian crisis, and the Depression—that convinced British leaders that the United States could not be relied on.

As President Truman's secretary of state, Dean Acheson, recalled: "Of course a unique relation existed between Britain and America—our common language and history ensured that.

But unique did not mean affection. We had fought England as an enemy as often as we had fought by her side as an ally."

Arguably, the fall of France in 1940 was decisive in shaping the pattern of international politics, leading to the Special Relationship displacing the Entente Cordiale as the pivot of the international system. During World War II, as an observer noted, "Great Britain and the United States integrated their military efforts to a degree unprecedented among major allies in the history of warfare." "Each time I must choose between you and Roosevelt," Churchill shouted at General Charles de Gaulle, leader of the Free French, in 1945, "I shall choose Roosevelt."

Churchill's mother was American, and he felt keenly the links between the English-speaking peoples. He first used the term "Special Relationship" in 1945 to describe not the Anglo-American relationship alone but the United Kingdom's relationship with both the United States and Canada. The *New York Herald Tribune* quoted Churchill in November 1945: "We should not abandon our special relationship with the United States and Canada about the atomic bomb and we should aid the United States to guard this weapon as a sacred trust for the maintenance of peace."

Churchill used the phrase again a year later at the onset of the Cold War, this time to note the relationship between the United States on the one hand and the English-speaking nations of the British Commonwealth and Empire under the leadership of the United Kingdom on the other. The occasion was his famous "Sinews of Peace Address" in Fulton, Missouri, on March 5, 1946: "Neither the sure prevention of war, nor the continuous rise of world organisation will be gained without what I have called the fraternal association of the English-speaking peoples. This means a special relationship between the British Commonwealth and Empire and the United States."

The United Kingdom's success in obtaining a U.S. commitment to cooperate in the postwar world was a major triumph in light of the isolation of the interwar period. A senior British diplomat in Moscow, Thomas Brimelow, admitted: "The one quality which most disquiets the Soviet government is the ability which they attribute to us to get others to do our fighting for us . . . they respect not us, but our ability to collect friends." Conversely, "the success or failure of United States foreign economic peace aims depended almost entirely on its ability to win or extract the co-operation of Great Britain."

Reflecting on the symbiosis, a later champion, former prime minister Margaret Thatcher, notably declared: "The Anglo-American relationship has done more for the defence and future of freedom than any other alliance in the world."

The intense level of military cooperation between the United Kingdom and the United States began with the creation of the Combined Chiefs of Staff in December 1941, a military command with authority over all American and British operations. After the end of World War II that command structure was disbanded, but close military cooperation between the nations resumed in the early 1950s with the start of the Cold War.

Since World War II and the subsequent Berlin Blockade, the United States has maintained substantial forces in Great Britain. In July 1948, the first American deployment began with the stationing of B-29 bombers. Currently, an important base is the radar facility, part of the U.S. Ballistic Missile Early Warning System. During the Cold War, critics of the Special Relationship jocularly referred to the United Kingdom as the "biggest aircraft carrier in the world."

After the end of the Cold War, which was the main rationale for their presence, the number of U.S. facilities in the United Kingdom was reduced in line with reductions in the U.S. military presence worldwide. Despite this, those bases were used extensively in support of various peacekeeping and offensive operations in the 1990s and the early twenty-first century.

The two nations also jointly operate on the British military facilities on Diego Garcia in the British Indian Ocean Territory and on Ascension Island, a dependency of Saint Helena in the Atlantic Ocean.

The Quebec Agreement of 1943 paved the way for the two countries to develop atomic weapons side by side, with the United Kingdom handing over vital documents from its Tube Alloys project and sending a delegation to assist in the work of the Manhattan Project. The United States later kept the results of the work to itself under the postwar McMahon Act, but after the United Kingdom developed its own thermonuclear weapons, the United States agreed to supply delivery systems, designs, and nuclear material for British warheads through the 1958 U.S.–UK Mutual Defense Agreement.

The United Kingdom purchased first the Polaris and then the Trident system, which remains in use. The 1958 agreement gave the United Kingdom access to the facilities at the Nevada test site, and from 1963 it conducted underground tests there before the cessation of testing in 1991. The agreement under which this partnership operates was updated in 2004. The United States and the United Kingdom jointly conducted subcritical nuclear experiments in 2002 and 2006 to determine the effectiveness of existing stocks, as permitted under the 1998 Comprehensive Nuclear-Test-Ban Treaty.

The United Kingdom is the only collaborative, or Level One, international partner in the largest U.S. aircraft procurement project in history, the F-35 Lightning II program.

A cornerstone of the Special Relationship is the collecting and sharing of intelligence. This originated during World War I with the "Five Eyes" group and led to the 1943 BRUSA Agreements signed at Bletchley Park. After World War II the common goal of monitoring and countering the threat of communism prompted the UK–U.S. Security Agreement of 1948. This agreement brought together the signals intelligence (SIGINT) organizations of the United States, the United Kingdom, Canada, Australia ,and New Zealand and is still in place. The head of the CIA station in London attends each weekly meeting of the British Joint Intelligence Committee.

A present-day example of such cooperation is the UKUSA Community, which consists of the National Security Agency, the United Kingdom's Government Communications Headquarters, Australia's Defense Signals Directorate, and Canada's Communications Security Establishment collaborating on ECHELON, a global intelligence-gathering system. Under classified bilateral accords, UKUSA members do not spy on one another.

After the discovery of the 2006 transatlantic aircraft plot, the CIA began to assist the Security Service (MI5) by running its own agent networks in the British Pakistani and Asian community. Security sources estimate that 40 percent of CIA activity to prevent a terrorist attack in the United States involves operations inside the United Kingdom. Intelligence officials commented on the threat against the United States from British Islamists: "The fear is that something like this would not just kill people but cause a historic rift between the U.S. and the UK."

The United States is the largest source of foreign direct investment in the United Kingdom; likewise, the United Kingdom is the largest single foreign direct investor in the United States. British trade and capital have been important components of the American economy since its colonial inception. In trade and finance, the Special Relationship has been described as well balanced, with London's "light-touch" regulation in recent years attracting a massive outflow of capital from New York.

The key sectors for British exporters to the United States are aviation, aerospace, commercial property, chemicals, pharmaceuticals, and heavy machinery. British thinkers, classical and modern, have exerted a profound influence on U.S. economic policy, most notably the historian Adam Smith on free trade and the economist John Maynard Keynes on countercyclical spending, and the British government has adopted workfare reforms from the United States.

American and British investors share entrepreneurial attitudes toward the housing market, and the fashion and music industries of each country are major influences on their counterparts. Trade ties have been strengthened by globalization, and both governments agree on the need for currency reform in China and educational reform at home to increase their competitiveness against foreign service industries. In 2007 the U.S. ambassador suggested to British business leaders that the Special Relationship could be used "to promote world trade and limit environmental damage as well as combating terrorism."

Arguably, the Special Relationship is all about personal relationships. It often depends on the personal relations between British prime ministers and U.S. presidents. The first example was the close relationship between Winston Churchill and Franklin Roosevelt, who were in fact distantly related.

Before their collaboration during World War II, Anglo-American relations had been somewhat frosty. President Woodrow Wilson and Prime Minister David Lloyd George had been the only previous leaders to meet face to face but had enjoyed nothing that could be described as a special relationship, although Lloyd George's wartime foreign secretary, Arthur Balfour, got on well with Wilson during his time in the United States and helped persuade the previously skeptical president to enter the war.

Churchill spent much time and effort cultivating the relationship, which paid dividends for the war effort although it cost Britain much of her wealth and ultimately her empire. The architecture of the Special Relationship is practical, revolving around shared goals. It has not always worked well. For instance, Harold Wilson's government would not commit troops to Vietnam, and Wilson and Lyndon Johnson did not get on especially well.

Peaks in the Special Relationship include the bonds between Harold Macmillan (who like Churchill had an American mother) and John F. Kennedy, between Margaret Thatcher and Ronald Reagan, and more recently between Tony Blair and both Bill Clinton and George W. Bush. Nadirs have included Dwight D. Eisenhower's opposition to UK operations in Suez under Anthony Eden and Wilson's refusal to enter the war in Vietnam.

The links that were created during World War II, such as UK military liaison officers being posted to Washington, persist. However, for Britain to gain any benefit from the relationship, it became clear, that a constant policy of personal engagement was required. Britain, starting in 1941 as the somewhat senior partner, found itself the junior. The diplomatic policy was thus two-pronged, encompassing strong personal support and forthright military and political aid.

The two countries have always operated in tandem; that is to say, the best personal relationships between British prime ministers and American presidents have always been based on such an understanding. Most recently these relationships have waned, as could be seen in *The Atlantic*'s account of what Barack Obama really thought of former PM David Cameron. As we have seen, the United Kingdom needs U.S. backing and support and a bilateral trade deal more than ever before.

It is proper to ask: Will this relationship survive the rest of this twenty-first century? What if the world pivots east, the EU achieves supranational status, or the emerging nations finally emerge? Will the United Kingdom have the same significance it once enjoyed? Will the United States be the sole superpower? Does it even need a junior partner?

Trump has said unequivocally that he thinks we do. He has restated that our mutual and abiding interests, common worldview, congruence of sympathy, and undeniably unique heritage of liberty should assure our future together. In my view, a shared Whig history, the King James Bible, the Anglican Church, and a long historical memory make up a valuable Anglo-Atlanticist patrimony. Britain and America belong together, not in Europe.

Taking up the cause of Locke and casting aside the philosophy of the European Rousseau and the practices of Bonapartism, the Brits have with America cemented their place on the side of liberty. The Anglo-Saxon rule of law and democratic spirit has triumphed over statism and the centralization of power even as it faces new challenges.

According to the Trumpists, the future will need such Anglo-American leadership more than ever before. Perhaps herein lie the true sinews of lasting peace.

Contrast the Special Relationship, which is critical to Trump, with the way he views the European Union.

Celebrating the Treaty of Rome at Sixty

Europe and all liberal democracies from America to New Zealand should celebrate the achievements of the Treaty of Rome that was signed some sixty years ago. On a bright spring day of March 25, 1957, at the Palazzo dei Conservatori on the Capitoline Hill in Rome, Belgium, France, Italy, Luxembourg, the Netherlands, and West Germany signed a treaty that established a new institution: a customs union that became known as a common market. Much was achieved in that august effort, and for it the world, and particularly all Europeans and those who love Europe, should give hearty thanks.

Today two different ideas of Europe have come into conflict. One idea aligns to that original Treaty of Rome, and the other to the federalist superstate.

When the Treaty of Rome was written, it developed a confederal basis in the formation of a treaty between nation-states that maintained their sovereignty. The nations transferred upward only the things that were necessary to create the European Economic Community. These were measured, deliberate, and slight additions to national entities.

Because of this and not pour cause, the political reasoning that inspired the treaty combined two equal principles: the principle of sovereignty and the principle of subsidiarity. Both were seen as equally important. Nations were to retain their sovereign status, and only those things which could not be done on a national basis were to be cast in confederal terms.

When America was in a similar situation, building a single polity from a collection of small states, the states agreed to come together under the Articles of Confederation and eventually the Constitution. Key to the political compromise was the Tenth Amendment, which reads: "The powers not delegated to the United States by the Constitution, nor prohibited to it by the States, are reserved to the States respectively, or to the people." In other words, the federal government doesn't have permission to do anything other than what the Constitution explicitly spells out as its functions. To rephrase an adage: If you have to ask, you can't do it.

The European Common Market at the upper level was seen as a mechanism for only that which was considered necessary and sufficient for its establishment. Brussels was conceived as a minimal force for coordination, not as an end state of supranational sovereignty. It was never to become the capital of a new, let alone enlarged Europe.

The political details of the Treaty of Rome had a defined and limited architecture that was based on the twin pillars of peace and prosperity. Considering the recent history of war in Europe, those pillars were well intended and necessary.

This spirit was the essential ingredient underlying the treaty. It brought together the European elites and their idea of a community in the defined region with nation-states with their own democratic governments and varied institutions. The treaty was not an elitist mandate from on high.

In this sense, the Treaty of Rome should be seen for what it was: a confederal design to move Europe in a direction that encouraged peaceful development and economic market-based solutions to everyday problems, particularly in trade.

The second idea of Europe that has emerged is federal. This idea and its attendant consequences, step by step, little by little, over the 1980s and 1990s and into the present, have reversed the basic and sound architecture of the Treaty of Rome. It was not a democratic process when it was tested, but it continued unabated.

In 2016, European regulation measured a total of 151 linear kilometers, equal to more than 30,000 pages. Little has been left untouched by the power of Brussels. Brussels did not do what it should have done under its own Treaty of Rome, instead becoming the managerial center of globalism.

Over the last twenty years, Europe has been buffeted by four political and economic phenomena it has been unable either to understand or to manage. An entirely economic corpus increasingly became a political corpus.

Europe was found unprepared, too busy wrangling various types of economies into its one-size-fits-all paradigm. A series of crises occurred that were not foreseen by any of the European treaties: first a financial crisis, then an economic crisis, and finally a political crisis. Each crisis has shown an inability of states to throw off the shackles of "pooled sovereignty" and act in their own interest. This all takes place within an asymmetrical dialectic in which anxiety grows in the face of external new forms. From migration and Ukraine to the unprecedented pace of change and digitization, there have been winners but also many losers.

This has led to nostalgia and a memory of the romanticism of the early nineteenth century that is based on archaic reserves of memory. Today's politics can perhaps be best understood as a reinsertion into the political circuit of a longing for past order and a restoration of lost symbolic value as society disintegrates and the civic, religious, and family bonds that have held peoples together become unglued. We witness a radical atomistic individualism on the one hand and a Brussels-centric statism on the other. In the process, all the intermediary institutions in which people actually live their lives—in which they flourished in the past—have been disregarded, if not thrown on the proverbial ash heap of history.

Immigration has overtaken us in a global and borderless world of nearly constant mobility and easy transport. It is just in the last few years that immigration has been considered a bonum per se and, accordingly, without any limits. This is transforming nations and most certainly the very definition of European identity.

One thing is abundantly clear for all to see. The existing model of the European Union is in a deep crisis. The Treaty of Rome set a milestone, but it was disregarded, and instead Europe finds itself at a crossroads.

The hypothesis of returning to individual European nation-states isolated from all the others is archaic and fraught with implicit dangers. It is unrealistic in this twenty-first century because states are no longer isolated and are vulnerable to global financial powers that are by definition transnational.

There is, however, a viable alternative to any exit ramps from Europe. It is a known route, tested and historical. Europe could return to the Treaty of Rome, roll back Lisbon and Maastricht, and return to the model of confederation that was so laudable sixty years ago. Uniting on only essential matters such as defense, security, and coordination of a customs area, it would leave the remainder to national sovereignty.

As we celebrate the Treaty of Rome, Europeans and friends of Europe should return to the sanity and legitimacy of the Europe that the treaty defined.

The Brexit Deal Is "Unconditional Surrender"

In the darkest days of 1940 and 1941, during the blitzkrieg and the Battle for Britain, Germany demanded one thing: unconditional surrender. The invasion of the British Isles was called Operation Sea Lion, and it was about to commence and end democracy and the lives of the free British people.

Today, in a new Battle for Britain, there may be no bombs dropping or dogfights in the air, but the barbs coming from Berlin and Brussels over Brexit amount to virtually the same thing.

Top German MEP Hans-Olaf Henkel, a former head of the Federation of German Industries (BDI), in agreement with Michel Barnier and Guy Verhofstadt, said that he believes that Berlin wants "unconditional surrender" from Britain on everything from the European Court of Justice to the divorce bill. This attitude may lead to talks collapsing or worse.

In December 2018, the UK Parliament will vote on the poor deal PM Theresa May has negotiated with the European Union. It is a disgrace that gives away the entire store and relents on all the promises made in the referendum and in her own election manifesto. It probably will be turned down by a very large majority of members in Parliament from every political party, including her own Conservatives.

No one knows what comes next. There is no plan B. Indeed, there is sufficient reason to believe that Angela Merkel's overly dominant Germany is the real reason for the demise of the critical and long-lasting transatlantic alliance and the fallout over Brexit. Germany and France have said that any country seeking to leave the European Union "must be punished."

The situation in the United Kingdom is a total humiliation and, as Brexiters have stated, would make Britain into a "vassal" or, worse, a "slave state" to a dominated by Germany.

Germany's culture, as evidenced in its recent election, is an odd combination of pride and gone are the common Atlantic values of the past.

Peace, security, and economic growth have been sacrificed for raw German ambition camouflaged in European clothing. Britain has been usurped and defeated.

It turns out the British television series SS-GB may not be so fictitious after all. It is November 1941, nine months after a successful German invasion of Britain. Winston Churchill has been executed.

King George is a prisoner and has not been seen in public for some time. His wife and his daughters Elizabeth and Margaret have escaped, and the Duke of Windsor, who had earlier abdicated as Edward VIII, is in exile. A British government in exile exists but is not recognized. Swastikas furl in the wind all over London; the Germans run things.

Fast-forward in time to nonfiction. Today, before it is too late, the United States and the United Kingdom—the Europeans too—have to step up and call Germany what it is.

The transatlantic alliance in this century demands honesty and burden sharing as well as common principles and purpose.

Brexit is not about unconditional surrender to a foreign power. The United Kingdom needs to take back its money, its borders, and its laws. That means honoring the vote of the referendum to leave the European Union—its single market, its customs union, and the European Court of Justice. Nothing else will suffice.

European nations that value freedom should come to their own conclusions, but we Americans should not appease or deny reality any longer.

Brexit Betrayed and Denied

Independence Day in Britain was supposed to happen when the United Kingdom left the European Union. The United Kingdom voted in a referendum three years ago to leave the European Union, but it didn't happen. Big Ben did not chime.

Freedom and sovereignty have been postponed or ignored as Parliament and the most incompetent prime minister in all of history have been unable or, more truthfully, unwilling to deliver what the democratic vote insisted on.

Why?

There are four reasons Brexit has been betrayed. Let's inspect each one of them so that we can comprehend what comes next or doesn't.

1. **Capitulation to an adversary.** The European Union is an evil, dominating socialist supranationalist entity that bullies everyone and everything that stands in its way. It sought to punish the United Kingdom for voting to escape its clutches, and it won. The question is, Why did the Remain-oriented prime minister allow this to happen? Why did she fail to hold up her end of the bargain? Was she compromised? Did she ever want a real break with Europe? It appears not. What she did deliver after three years of diplomatic hogwash was a horrible, wretched deal that almost no one wanted.

2. **An intransigent elite in Parliament that loathes the public.** In both the Conservative Party and the Labour Party there is an elite so out of touch with the normal members of British society that they actually laugh at and hate the people they are supposed to represent. They think themselves more knowing and better than the common person. When asked to vote on eight Brexit options all over the landscape, they voted no, no, no, no, no, no, no, and no. They also turned down the PM's deal on meaningful votes three times, offering up instead a crisis of constitutional proportion.

3. **The media and the pundits lobbied in earnest to undo the vote to leave.** Before the referendum and for three years since nearly all the mainstream media and most of the think tanks have unloaded on the stupidity of the voters, their backwardness, racism, naïveté, and failure to take dire economic predictions seriously. Campaign Fear was launched to scare the people, but it backfired, so they doubled down. BBC, the state-owned television and media monopoly, was resoundingly against Brexit, and so were all but two newspapers. *The Financial Times* was so globalist in its slanted opinions that it looked to be literally run and financed by the Brussels

dictators. In turns out that it was. The same people wanted a second (and possibly third and fourth) referendum, doubtless to overturn the desire of the citizens of Great Britain and Northern Ireland.

4. **Economic arguments were used to trump freedom.** Over and over the public was fed a line that Brexit would hurt them, most of all in their pocketbooks. Jobs would be lost, economic growth would decline, and all investment would flee the British shores. London would cease to be a major capital market, and Britons would see the loss of power, prestige, and wealth. Technically, it was all a "crock of shit," and the economic models, based on Keynesian quantitative black boxes, were erroneous, if not entirely biased. There were no facts in them, just faulty assumptions and overt political bias. None of these arguments took seriously the weight of England's common law traditions, its long history of democracy, and its unique position among nations, including the commonality with America on liberty. In other words, freedom was sacrificed on the altar of faulty economics.

Today we have a situation in which Brexit has been betrayed and put on hold, softened to be meaningless, and possibly denied altogether. Until . . .

Boris Is Now the UK Trump

Boris Johnson, the charismatic, highly energetic, and eccentric Conservative member of parliament and former mayor of London, has become prime minister.

He is what in Britain they call "brilliant." I've run into him numerous times at my club in Pall Mall and will attest to Bojo's incredible intellect and clever wit.

He speaks his mind. He is exceptionally clear and coherent. His track record is flawless: Crime in London was slashed until Sadiq Khan, Boris's successor as mayor, took over.

The early polls put him far ahead of the other ten contenders for the post, and he is an odds-on favorite to become the next prime minister.

He should have been made prime minister three years ago after he led the winning EU referendum campaign to leave the European Union.

Making up for lost time, Boris is promising a huge tax cut on Britons making up to £80,000 a year. This is sound economics for Britain.

Michael Gove, who is again challenging him for the top post, stabbed him in the back once. He is a winner, and so will Great Britain win.

His tagline this time was direct: Back Boris.

Boris is a historian and has a knack for writing. His book on Churchill allowed him to channel that famous patriot and warrior who he resembles in many ways.

Boris was born in America and has a strong affinity for the United States, freedom, and the U.S.–UK Special Relationship. He gets on well with his American governmental counterpart, one Donald J. Trump.

As a one-nation conservative, he seeks to keep the United Kingdom united and wants what he calls "an opportunity society" with "no one left behind." He will bring back stop-and-search nationwide to combat the appalling rise in knife crime; London just passed New York in murders per capita, a horrifying development.

The Etonian, educated at Balliol College, Oxford, reeks of class and aristocracy and was the president of the Oxford Union debating society (Gove was his campaign manager). Yet he is adored by the working classes and won twice in London, which is multicultural and Labour left.

The Conservatives badly need a winner.

As a journalist, having started with *The Times* and then moving on to be *The Telegraph*'s Brussels correspondent before editing

The Spectator, Boris knows how to cajole and manipulate the media. He is expert at doing his own PR—just like POTUS.

Bojo is a brand that we will be seeing a lot of on the world's stage. A strong Eurosceptic, Boris is a thorough Leaver, which means that the one thing he is promising over everything else is that after three years of muddling, Britain will depart the European Union on October 31, 2019 with or without a deal.

Here is the deal he should offer now: Put the horse in front of the cart. Start all over. Say that a free trade deal based on that of Canada and the European Union is the starting place. Cement it. Done!

The following year will hash out all the pluses to add. But there is an agreed deal from the start. This solves everything. It is a deal-based managed Brexit.

The withdrawal agreement can be rewritten in fifteen pages, spelling out a simple exit. No need for an Irish backstop. Payments should be made in full based on agreement, not in advance.

This solves everything and allows Britain to leave and still have a strong trading relationship with the European Union and soon all the other countries that want to make a similar deal, with the United States coming first.

Boris Johnson is an entertaining, humorous, and extremely popular leader and is the best thing for the United Kingdom and its people. He made London work, defends capitalism, and is all about national sovereignty and unity. He is America's best ally and friend.

In an interview, just before visiting the United Kingdom, Donald Trump endorsed Johnson for the role, saying of the election: "I actually have studied it very hard. I know the different players. But I think Boris would do a very good job. I think he would be excellent. I like him."

Hey, Dude!

At roughly 2 p.m. on July 24, 2019, Alexander Boris de Pfeffel Johnson became prime minister of the United Kingdom of Great

Britain and Northern Ireland. Number 10 Downing Street now has a full-throated, committed, and energized Brexiteer in charge.

He committed again in his first speech to deliver Brexit by October 31, "no ifs, ands, or buts." To that single promise he will be held accountable.

In a massive change of government that is unprecedented, the new PM put an entire team of firm Brexit stalwarts in his cabinet, changing everything.

The vision he announced is spelled *DUDE*.

- Deliver Brexit
- Unite the country
- Defeat the Labour Socialists
- Energize the nation

This is a new can-do spirit that will make Britain great again, a do-or-die mission to make sure the referendum vote to leave the European Union comes to fruition.

President Trump was one of the first world leaders to welcome Bojo, as he is known in Britain, and thinks he will be "great."

Already, we see a slipping away from the horrible, negative, and surrendering attitude of his immediate predecessor and the emergence of a true, robust leader. European Union beware!

With a maniacal mentality, Boris is on a sprint to make up for lost time and the abysmal administration of Theresa May. He has his work cut out for him. It will not be easy.

But it is doable if he does these four things, and he knows it:

1. Go to Washington first and meet President Trump. Seal a U.S.–UK free trade deal. Start formal talks tomorrow. This will send a signal to the evil EU negotiators that the future lies elsewhere.
2. Appoint a new UK Ambassador to the United States first thing, one who is his man in DC. He cannot be a stale, unreliable, duplicitous civil servant but should be a deal maker

businessperson with Brexit credentials and ties directly to Johnson and a friendly attitude and access to Trump.

3. Get ready a full-fledged, highly organized PR and campaign team immediately to sell the deal and take control of the situation, including a team of expert external advisers to get this over the line. Do not wait. Go on the offensive.

4. Announce that there is a deal. Put the deal in writing, and after seeking and getting Trump's endorsement, then and only then go to Brussels and present it to the EU cronies as a take-it-or-leave-it offer. It will be a Canada-Plus free trade agreement. It should be a fifteen-page withdrawal (no backstops) statement wrapped into one clear and cogent document, and the 39 billion quid will be paid in two equal installments: one on agreeing and the rest on the enactment of the formal FTA.

This is bigger than the Olympics. This is Johnson's time in the sun, and all of the world is watching. We in America are with you. Stand firm.

Boris was a classics major at Oxford, so here is what he needs to pin to his door:

Vos Confirmate Corda Motto.

7

Trump's Adversaries

The media is, really the word—I think one of the greatest of all terms I have come up with is fake.

—President Donald Trump

What Happened to CNN?

Donald Trump has very rarely run away from a fight. Instead, he heads right into them. He has a knack for knowing who to pick on, when, where, and how. His list of adversaries is long and growing, and they all want to bring him down, depose him as president, or defeat him politically. You can't comprehend Trump's foreign policy without a scorecard on who opposes him. He counter-punches, often quite effectively.

That list includes CNN, *The New York Times*, Germany and Merkel, the European Union, globalism, Russia, Clinton, the deep state, "shithole countries," and the new Marxists in the U.S. Congress, among others.

Let's review his nemeses and see how they shape, distort, or cover (well, fail to cover) his foreign achievements.

Atlanta was a quaint Southern town, but it was metamorphosing into something very different and more impressive by 1992. It was getting cosmopolitan and downright worldly. It had won the Olympic bid scheduled for 1996 (secured by Andrew Young at—you guessed it—Davos). Segregation was over, and grits were hard to find.

One company had come to personify the newfound swagger and embody the spirit of the New South. That company started as a small-fry radio station with a big signal and grew into the powerhouse and the most watched network on cable television.

Its format was unheard of: All News, All the Time.

Boy, has that changed! After the Gulf War, Ted Turner, the cocky CEO and founder, bragged that he had won. CNN represented raw media power as it had never been witnessed before.

When you met Turner, the smile, the pencil moustache, and the ability to speak his mind instantly mesmerized you. In his upscale restaurant, he served bison steaks and talked about his growing empire worldwide.

Turner could get mad as hell and was even known to throw phones, but when he wanted something, he went after it like an untamed Georgia bulldog. Since he owned the Braves, he would sit in the dugout, and when Chipper Jones hit a home run to win the game, they brought him the ball.

Tom Johnson, who ran CNN, was a senior TV journalist who had been Lyndon Johnson's press secretary. He was a class act and a real journalist. He was also mentally ill, as he later divulged in a most honest account of manic depression. He knew his way around Washington but often was hidden away as if he were battling something. It turns out he was in deep depression.

The best anchor at CNN was the colorful and ego-driven Lou Dobbs. His star was ascending, and he wanted Ted to make him president of CNN. He was, in other words, as Lou often does, posturing. He thought a lot of himself, and his people in New York at the offices across from Penn Station were both afraid of him and oddly devoted to him.

I was never sure which came first. I liked Lou a lot, and he was a good head.

He eventually left because he couldn't take CNN anymore and went to FOX.

CNN became a powerful media company with a large international footprint, and it did legitimate journalism. It was basically honest and fair. It was respected.

Then something happened. In the Bush 43 years and leading up to the CNN-anointed Obama monarchy, the network stopped doing journalism and started becoming an activist political agitator.

When Jeff Zucker, a total hack, took over as CEO, it bent all the way. They adored Obama and fawned over him like sycophants. He could do no wrong even if he accomplished little and became an apologist for America's enemies.

By the time Trump appeared on the scene, CNN was a full-scale trenchant leftist company with only one dominant point of view. It was a propaganda machine for the most left-leaning Democrats.

Trump was a "character" it covered and mocked. This helped them raise their dismal ratings but was not to be taken seriously. After all, he couldn't win! But he did.

Now they were not just perplexed but irate and sought to destroy him immediately. They wanted nothing more than to delegitimize his voters as "deplorable" or "deranged."

Their fake news came to be the very definition of what has become (less than) journalism in America. It isn't even fact-founded opinion. It is more like the ideological attacks one finds in Europe, where the press is not seen as an unbiased fourth estate but as a political actor with a sharp ideological agenda. The European system isn't worse or better; indeed, American newspapers are similar in wearing their bias on their sleeves. Nationally broadcast TV news, however, was a different ball game, at least until cable news outlets like CNN came to the fore.

Objective surveys done at Harvard show that CNN coverage of Donald Trump and his administration has been 93 percent negative. Is that just a slight bias, or is it more deceitful? CNN is now the epicenter of all Trump-hating and a de facto professional progressive opposition party.

Jim Acosta, CNN's White House correspondent, is in a league of his own. His rude behavior, castigating smug attitude, and defamation-violent behavior finally caught up with him when he pushed a young intern at a briefing. It cost him his credentials, something that was long overdue. Anchors such as Chris Cuomo (son of the late Democratic New York governor and brother of the current New York governor, which presents no conflict) are a literal joke. "Let's get after it" is his tagline.

Really? "It" is certainly not the truth. CNN talk show panels are so slanted and one-sided, they don't even warrant comment. They are laughable and disgusting diatribes. Why would anyone bother to watch them?

Uneducated Don Lemon is a reverse racist who makes slurs (all white men are terrorists) instead of reporting. Anderson Cooper is a pathetic pawn for the LBGTQ cultural and social justice warriors. Jake the Fake Tapper is hardly "leading" on anything, and after appearing on his show, one White House official said, "You should be ashamed of yourself."

This is not mere partisanship. It is just one thing: blatant propaganda. CNN has become the *Pravda* of the socialist left. With shoddy reporting, lies that make Pinocchio look like he has a small nose, and inaccuracies that fill directories, this is news?

It is nothing but hatred that is driving the country apart on the basis of identity politics.

CNN has become toxic. There should be a health warning stating that the channel is bad for one's health.

Becky Anderson, its Middle East crony, who falls in line with the Al Jazeera line more or less, once asked me on her show *Connect the World*, in all seriousness, and I quote, "Don't you think the WHOLE world should vote in American elections?" She actually thought they should! By the way, she is British but lives in Abu Dhabi, which she just adores.

The CNN worldview is patently globalist, far left, and increasingly supersanctimonious.

They are a case study in "virtue signaling." The use of profanity, lewdness, anger, racism, scatology, and threats pervades the airwaves. They have said they want to kill the president, decapitate him, and crash his jet.

CNN has become the "enemy of the people," according to Trump. He suggests that you not watch them, support them, or buy any products they advertise. They are "fake." Maybe as a result CNN will die, go away, or simply go broke.

The "Failing" *New York Times*

Many of us grew up reading *The New York Times* as the paper of record because our social studies teachers in high school and college mandated it. Many of us stopped reading it years ago as it became overtly biased and predictably liberal.

Trump follows it and calls it a scandal and "failed" because it is financially handicapped and has lost readership.

This is not a real newspaper. It is a propaganda organ for the anti-American postmodern radical who loathes Trump, any traditional values, the family, and what used to be referred to as good taste.

The headlines were ludicrous, not journalism but outright attacks. The photos were all of shaming, refugee suffering, and

Trump mockery. The so-called far right everywhere, especially in Germany, was excoriated because—can you believe this?—they are upset about immigration. What makes them "far" right? No answer was provided, but "neo-Nazi" was used repeatedly to describe them. *The New York Times*'s far left view of the world was never called out as such until Trump came along.

On page 1 of *The New York Times* they now have an "opinion" column with perspectives "in hopes of promoting constructive debate about consequential questions." Except that all the articles are from leftists. Where's the debate? It is the same thing in our universities. This is diversity of opinion?

There were articles about damaging climate change and pending environmental disaster and the poor puffins that are suffering in Iceland as well as racist chants about whites at public schools and blacks who "stupidly" like the economics of prosperity. Far be it from anyone to think differently than the almighty *New York Times*!

The international accounts were against America and capitalism for the most part. Well, there were some advertisements for luxury goods. One long treatment was on the vanilla bean riches that are destroying Madagascar. I am sure the poverty-stricken farmers there feel the same way.

Of course, the funeral of Saint John McCain got the most attention as the establishment hailed its boy, failing to mention that the same mainstream media excoriated him as an extremist and racist when he ran against the anointed one.

They praise him now because he came to love Obama, voted to keep Obamacare and various liberal causes, and was an ardent Never Trumper.

He was no maverick. In truth, he was a warmonger globalist who never found a war he didn't like. He was foul-mouthed, hot-tempered, and spiteful. May he rest in peace. His first wife, whom he dropped when she was gravely ill and with child, did not have kind things to say about him. Surprisingly, that didn't make it into *The New York Times*.

But *The New York Times* adores McCain now and wants to enshrine him. There were full texts of eulogies and pictures galore of the bipartisan liberal elites—Bush, Clinton, and Obama—and his senatorial partner Lindsey Graham.

There was plenty of Trump coverage in *The New York Times*, all of it negative. His tariffs won't work, his loud rallies are for "deplorables," and he planned to buy dirt on himself from the sensational *National Enquirer*. He must be impeached soon.

The business section of *The New York Times* would better be called "antibusiness," for that is what it is. Big tech is not biased in the least, we need a carbon-free future, and companies are evil if they make a profit. Oh, we don't believe in God any longer.

The New York Times opinion pages are a joke. One rant was on the religion of whiteness, and another by an Obama sycophant was on "we are not a 'cabal,' just critics of Trump." Plenty on Judge Kavanaugh and Guantanamo, which we all know is a blight on American history. They even had the audacity to run a celebration of the Soviet space program on the fiftieth anniversary of America's landing on the moon, our triumph in the space race

The sports section in *The New York Times* is less about scores and games than about politicization. The NFL is again on its knees, but there was an elitist story about the Formula 1 race. Liberals like speed? Ironic that they attack oil and gas on one page and are fascinated by fast cars on another. Just another cultural contradiction of postmodern liberalism.

The New York Times still believes apparently in "meaning." Living longer, healthier, happier lives is a good thing, they seem to think. Maybe science can provide the answer? *The New York Times* is disillusioned on that and seems to suggest nihilism as the better antidote.

Many conservatives who used to read *The New York Times* have given it up. They don't buy it, don't read it, and don't advertise in it. It is most certainly not "all the news that's fit to print." Its coverage is advocacy, opposed to everything Trump.

The Deep State: Out to Get Trump and Kill Democracy

Sometimes art truly does imitate life. *Deep State* is a fictional television miniseries about a retired MI6 agent called back to do just one more job. Sound familiar?

In the real world, the deep state is synonymous with a shadow government: a permanent yet formless administrative state that exists in contrast to the tangible public structures we've all come to know. This deep state is secretive. It entails a fluid network that includes intelligence agencies such as the National Security Agency (NSA), FBI, CIA, and Defense Department—agencies that run on secret surveillance, in-the-know intel, and cryptic communication. Agencies that play for high stakes, that are willing to do anything to make sure they don't lose it all. This deep state isn't your local town council or the department of agriculture. In other words, it ain't your grandpa's government.

The term has been thrown around in political circles for years, but it quickly reentered the national discourse in early 2016 when Trump talked about a cabal—a secret political faction—that operated in Washington, D.C., and consisted of unelected officials. That "swamp" had to be drained, he insisted.

Back in 2014 Edward Snowden, the NSA whistle-blower, exposed the reach of government surveillance, saying: "There's definitely a deep state. Trust me, I've been there." Internet activist and founder of WikiLeaks Julian Assange, who has gained international recognition as an advocate for truth, publicly released a trove of classified CIA documents that have been dubbed the "deep state files."

After an arrest in 2010, Assange lived under political asylum granted by Ecuador. Currently, he is in a London jail, awaiting extradition to the United States. Clearly, the stakes when one is going against the deep state are high.

Perhaps it is Mike Lofgren, a former congressional aide, who accurately captures the essence of the deep state best, calling it "a hybrid association of elements of government and parts of top-level finance and industry that is effectively able to govern the United States without reference to the consent of the governed as expressed through the formal political process."

Its origins echo the long-standing politico term "military-industrial complex," first referenced by President Dwight D. Eisenhower in his 1961 farewell address, in which he discussed its potential risks: "In the councils of government, we must guard against the acquisition of unwarranted influence, whether sought or unsought, by the military-industrial complex. The potential for the disastrous rise of misplaced power exists and will persist."

Some believe that the military-industrial complex makes up only the private part of the deep state. However, it also involves leaders in finance and technology who are tied to the intelligence community and the defense establishment.

In his book *The New Freedom*, published in 1913, Woodrow Wilson, U.S. president during World War I, had this to say: "Since I entered politics, I have chiefly had men's views confided to me privately. Some of the biggest men in the United States, in the field of commerce and manufacture, are afraid of somebody, are afraid of something. They know that there is a power somewhere so organized, so subtle, so watchful, so interlocked, so complete, so pervasive, that they had better not speak above their breath when they speak in condemnation of it."

Make no mistake: The deep state is the central actor in the Red November plot to destroy the president. Without it, the whole thing would not exist.

The elements of the deep state work together to fulfill their collective yet sometimes conflicting political agendas in hopes of extending its ever-growing reach. To do this, they orchestrate either for or against a political candidate come November.

They were and are against Donald Trump, as is evidenced repeatedly in the cowardly op-eds in the failing *New York Times* that demonstrate the resistance to and thwarting of democracy in this administration. This is the deep state in spades!

Tenured Radicals and Leftist Universities

Living in these times means having to endure a steady stream of appalling news out of academia. Trump sees the university as the font of much bad thinking and the origin of the crippling of America, if not the West. The march through the institutions that began after the Kent State massacre is complete: Everywhere you go, whether at home or abroad, the corps of professors evinces a worrying left-wing orthodoxy. No diversity is allowed.

The reason for the rise of the West, more triumphantly known as Christendom, was grounded in the life of the mind. This foundation of faith was undermined by the development of anti-Christian rationalism and the Enlightenment, culminating in the materialistic new religions and ideologies of destruction that took over the universities, killing God and destroying civil life and society in the process.

Trump is an Ivy League graduate but has come to see that the university, outside the sciences and some business courses, is categorically against him and his ilk. They oppose all he does: his policies and his positions, his people and his plans.

The problem has become so grave that Jonathan Haidt—no right-winger, to be sure—established the Heterodox Academy (HxA), an effort to provide a home for academics who stray from the party line. Tenure, that institution specifically devised to ensure that dangerous ideas are sounded out, has not saved some of the greatest minds of our time from left-wing mobs, both digital and physical.

The HxA surveys give us a wealth of data to consider. Conservative students feel intimidated about speaking their minds. Of the 4,000 or so universities in America, you can count the predominantly conservative ones on two hands; you might even have a few fingers left over, depending on how strict your definitions are. Political correctness is nearly permanent, and safe places and silly ideological studies and gender majors have come to define colleges today.

Gone are the days of the Greco-Roman trivium: rhetoric, grammar, and logic. Today's curriculum, especially in the vast majority of schools that require liberal arts credits for graduation, focus on the softest of social subjects that do little more than pay for the activism of the professors who teach them. The intersectional (gender/race/poverty) lens has infected traditionally sound disciplines as well. The decline of history, previously one of the great sweeping paths of education, is a notable casualty.

Adding insult to injury, not only is the modern university doubling as an ideological madrassa, the price tag on college degrees has outpaced inflation by a factor of 4. The undergraduate degree is widely seen as the price of admission to the workforce, forcing young Americans to endure a multiyear socialist indoctrination as table stakes for the highly paid white-collar jobs that college traditionally has led to.

Lest you think the worst part is the universities' failure to place many bright minds in the job market, it gets even worse: If you dodge the ideological purge, you'll be faced with human resources departments packed with thought police. Entrepreneurship, a traditional route to prosperity and financial independence in America, is largely intermediated by the Silicon Valley venture fund clique, another famously liberal set.

How can conservatives and Trump supporters turn back the clock on this terrible state of affairs? To quote President Reagan: Starve the beast. And that is what Trump has set out to do.

There is no reason why the blank check universities currently get from the government should be the status quo. Stricter standards should be in place to ensure that grant money is used for the research it was meant for, not for hiring yet another degree mill drone to work a few hours a week or more overpaid administrators.

Echoing Lenin, the vanguard of professional activists has looked to where the state-financed spots are and latched on to the teat. Academia has become a path to political office, as Elizabeth Warren has shown. She also used her fake identity status as Native American (or not) to climb the greasy academic pole, where affirmative action routinely discriminates against smarter students in the name of representation, as if every cohort of American high school graduate were the same.

President Trump has organized his young supporters and encouraged them to speak out. This won't be enough. The market must be allowed to work its magic, the invisible hand allowed to reallocate the myriad resources currently being wasted on the sort of cultural output you'd expect from Soviet academics.

The product of the 1960s and its offspring, these tenured radicals have infested the life of the mind and ruined the university. They have politicized everything and used their lite Marxism and chic doomsdayism to foster an ideological cult in the country.

When candidate Trump unveiled his 2016 motto—Make America Great Again—many opponents asked: When did America stop being great? Most professors said it was never great.

Which era do you want to go back to? Every Trump supporter has a different answer. To make the university great again, however, it is necessary to undo the 1960s. As Allan Bloom wrote in *The Closing of the American Mind*, if we continue down this and ruinous path, the country will suffer further decline in the output of both scientists and philosophers. The culture eventually will be be destroyed.

There is still time to make universities great again.

European Federalists

Although many believe that there is unparalleled and dangerous uncertainty in U.S.–European relations in this era of Trump, there is reason to believe that an ascendant and unbounded Germany is the real reason for the demise of the critical and long-lasting transatlantic alliance.

The risks—political, economic, and cultural—of the demise of the Western alliance that has stood the test of time and the seventy years of postwar challenges comes not just from *external* risks but primarily from *internal* factors that suggest a significant and seismic shift. This is an earthquake of unprecedented proportions. It is not a topic on the G20 agenda, but it should be lurking in the minds of its leaders.

Change is part and parcel of international relations whether you are a realist or an idealist. Patterns move, politics is by definition fractious, and competition is dynamic. Much has been said about the so-called speed of change in these dramatically technological times. Doubtless, it is trite to say that the speed of change is accelerating. Technology will cause havoc in governments and economies in the decades ahead. But the significance and scope of change is what is more apparent in the rapidly diminishing U.S.–European marriage cum divorce.

From the U.S. side, the current president, a true outsider, may be pedantic, pugilistic, petulant, patriotic, and populist, but he is nonetheless president of the United States of America. And the United States, though not a typical hegemon, is the only global superpower and in effect a G1. It would be a tragic mistake to ignore, let alone obstruct and condemn him, or, as Germany appears to be doing, castigate him and risk everything and leave the relationship in tatters.

If you go to all the European capitals and talk with the people and not just the elites, you quickly realize that there is a vast diversity of political opinion that is nowhere near the federalist consensus the elites claim. In fact, in many European countries the nationalist–populist elements are at 30 percent or more in the polls and rising. If you put any two-country letters in front of the word "exit," you have a potential movement to leave the European

Union, the euro, or both. Europe is in chaos even if it pretends otherwise. Brussels is in denial mode and therefore hyperdefensive. But the European Union is objectively in decline and has lost power, and the world is pivoting elsewhere, namely, to Asia.

The North Atlantic Treaty Organization (NATO) had a sound purpose, but that rationale has become "obsolete" to quote presidential candidate Trump, even if he now is convinced that we may need to reinvent it for future use. The original Eurocentric reason behind NATO was supposedly to keep Russia (well, the USSR) out, to keep the United States in, and to keep Germany down. That all worked until the Berlin Wall came down.

It has not worked in the postcommunist era; actually, it has utterly failed.

Russia is not the USSR; the United States under Trump is more impatient and isolationist, looking to its own greatness; and Germany is the dominant reunited bullying European power in every sense of the term. Can something so obsolete be reinvented? Can its structures be reengineered? Should it have an altogether new mission? Should it have a more regional basis? Should it look at new threats and truly take on Islamic terrorism and cybersecurity?

Perhaps, but it also has to be paid for, and as Trump keeps saying, only seven of its twenty-eight members are carrying their freight by paying the agreed 2 percent of their GDP for common defense. Germany is the biggest laggard at 1.2 percent even though it has the most robust economy and a huge current account surplus. In effect, American taxpayers, by paying so much (70 percent of the current budget), are essentially subsidizing European welfare states, particularly the German one. It can't continue, and Trump has read them the riot act. Our patience has worn thin, and the new sheriff is not taking "no" or "later" for an answer any longer.

While German magazines (*Der Spiegel*) despicably portray a severed Trump head on their covers, Germany marches to its own dangerous drumbeat, dragging the entire European Union along for the ride. Europe is wary of German zeal because of past experiences that are fading from collective memory—just look to Greece—but there is nothing the European nations can do about it.

Peace, security, and economic growth are being sacrificed for raw German ambition camouflaged in new European clothing and the blue flag with gold stars. Germany uses the devalued euro to benefit its own industries and exports to the detriment of others.

Fast-forward in time to today. Before it is too late the United States and the G20 have to step up and call Germany what it is. The world and the European continent should not be forced to live under the German eagle used in an earlier emblem known as the *Parteiadler*.

Should anyone in his or her right mind trust the Germans?

Many respect German order and science, and it behooves us to realize that the Germans have always wanted to rule. They are good at bossing others around and making demands. Sometimes it seems that they just can't help themselves.

The transatlantic alliance in this century demands honesty and burden sharing as well as common principles and purpose, according to Trump. The interests of Germany alone should not dominate it.

A Trumpian Letter to Jean-Claude Juncker

All Americans must condemn the statements made by Jean-Claude Juncker, president of the European Commission, in 2017. Anyone attuned to world affairs will be aware of his statement at the European People's Party congress in Malta in which he declared that President Trump's support for Brexit was grounds to call for Ohio to be independent and Texas to leave the United States. There are a number of problems with this perspective that illustrate the faulty paradigm infecting EU institutions and the people who populate their ranks.

Whereas Texas and Ohio are states bound to the United States under the Constitution, the United Kingdom is a sovereign and independent nation-state with membership in an intergovernmental organization (the European Union) that it wishes to rescind. A sitting British prime minister ran for reelection promising a referendum on membership in the European Union and won a majority in his country's parliament. David Cameron chose to keep his promise and put the decision to a referendum, and the result was decided. It is a fait accompli. There are no longer pro- and anti-Brexit camps; it is no longer up for discussion.

The United States cannot see the Brexit negotiations through the adversarial lens that many Europeans insist on imposing on it. Britain is a sovereign democratic country with the freedom to decide which road it wishes to take in the future. The European Union is not a cohesive sovereign state. These are matters of fact, not politics.

It is not appropriate for sovereign countries to tell one another what to do. For this reason, President Trump's position on Brexit—wishing our allies the best—is sound. Regrettable as the development may be for the other member states of the European Union, the acrimoniousness surrounding the debate is worrying and should be toned down.

It is the height of irony that figures such as Juncker are questioning American leadership in our defense of democracy while objecting to the result of a democratic exercise such as the Brexit referendum. Democracy is messy and often disappoints, but disagreeing with the result of a democratic contest is no reason to object to democracy itself. Sadly, many of the complaints about Brexit skew dangerously close to questions about the process: who was allowed to vote, turnout figures, and how much the margin of victory was. For better or worse, the question has been decided. It is nonsensical to try to dismantle the process and its result. The United States does not presume to tell any of the remaining twenty-seven EU states whether they should remain in the club, but we extend the same guarantees that we always will: America will defend democracy where it exists.

The alarmism surrounding Britain's exit has reached proportions unworthy of calm, thinking people. The defense guarantee of NATO and the friendly relations reserved for systems of government similar to that of the United States will remain intact for the United Kingdom. It is unfortunately a political imperative for federalist-leaning politicians and groups to cast doubt on any objections to their project.

Transforming the current international organization known as the European Union into a proper sovereign entity is the declared aim of many figures in European institutions. This is not objectionable in itself, but it remains to be seen whether it can garner democratic support as an idea in the countries they wish to turn into subsovereign entities. The United States is of course neutral in this debate.

We assume President Juncker spoke in jest, as the case of a U.S. state is not analogous to that of a sovereign entity such as the United Kingdom or his native Luxembourg. President Juncker is undoubtedly aware of this.

Secession is an extremely sensitive topic in the United States after a war in which 620,000 American soldiers died, Union and Confederate alike. They were all Americans, and the Civil War remains the most lethal conflict in American history. It is beneath Mr. Juncker to allude to such a tragedy so lightly. He should know better.

President Abraham Lincoln, who had the unenviable task of leading a divided nation into war against its own countrymen, said, "A house divided against itself cannot stand." Western civilization and those who represent and cherish it surely will preserve the values and freedoms it affords to the common humanity it governs. If only we can avoid the vile use of one another for political purposes.

How the Media Got the Trump-Russia Dossier

Hint: David Kramer, an aide to Senator John McCain, passed it to BuzzFeed.

The late Republican senator from Arizona had been in office since 1987. He is perhaps best remembered as the losing candidate for president in 2008, when he went down overwhelmingly in defeat to Barack Obama, who surprised everyone by snatching the Democratic nomination from Hillary Clinton. One of the great ironies of American politics is this commonality between Trump supporters and Obamaniacs: They both hate Hillary, and they both hated John McCain.

As a young Naval Academy graduate McCain was a less than brilliant student, graduating at the bottom of his class. But because of his family pedigree—his father and grandfather were both accomplished admirals—he was able to secure a coveted spot as a naval aviator.

Flying missions in the Vietnam War, he was shot down, captured, imprisoned, and tortured.

As a hawkish neoconservative politician, McCain earned a reputation as a "maverick." It was something the hot-tempered senator sought and relished.

His colleagues and staff considered him most disagreeable.

As a member of the Keating Five scandal, McCain skirted the law and redeemed himself in an all-out effort on campaign finance reform. This became his signature piece of legislation.

McCain chaired the Senate Foreign Relations Committee, where he developed a taste for personal diplomacy. He vehemently opposed pork barrel spending at the Department of Defense. He liked to grandstand and was a huge favorite with the mainstream press. In other words, he became a liberal.

In 2015, Senator McCain in his fifth term became chairman of the Armed Services Committee, something he longed for as a capstone to his long political career. From that perch he would travel the world, meet with global leaders and generals, and pontificate on U.S. policy. He was, some said, his own state department of one, and he loved the attention.

On November 8, 2016, after Christopher Steele, a former MI6 agent, had passed his Trump-Russia dossier (paid for by Hillary and the DNC) on to both the MI6 intelligence service in the United Kingdom and the FBI, Sir Alan Wood, a former UK ambassador, was at a meeting attended by Senator McCain: the annual International Security Forum in Halifax, Canada. The ambassador confidentially talked about a report that compromised the incoming president and got McCain's full attention.

How will history judge his interference in the election? Leaking the Steele dossier, the story goes, was much harder than expected. Even the mainstream, virulently anti-Trump media turned down the leaks. Reduced to publishing it on BuzzFeed—an outlet known for time-wasting online entertainment, aka clickbait—McCain and his flunkies should have known that the story would fail to hold water.

McCain wanted Hillary to win, and it bears remembering that Arizona's electoral votes went to Hillary in a state where both houses of the legislature, the governorship, both senators, and most congressmen were Republicans. The political machine clearly wasn't as well oiled as it usually is.

McCain also failed to swing the election. Confronted with a system much harder to rig than those he was used to (his exploits overseas are a matter of much speculation), he refused to accept the result and became a thorn in the White House's legislative agenda. In a redux of 2008—the only real legislative consequence of which was Obamacare—the losing presidential candidate (McCain) held the deciding vote. He single-handedly saved Obama's legacy. For now, anyway.

It is arguably the greatest flip-flop of the century. McCain voted against Obamacare when it was on the docket in 2009. McCain was reelected (twice!) on a platform calling for the repeal of Obamacare when it was the main issue in American politics.

No wonder the liberals all loved him and Trump didn't.

Mrs. Clinton—the Opposition Knew

Hillary Clinton knew about, approved, and paid for the Trump-Russia dirty dossier from the beginning and hid that fact from the press.

The Democratic candidate for president in 2016 was an experienced pro who had seen her way through many political campaigns, including contentious primaries against Obama, for the U.S. Senate in New York, in Arkansas, and of course twice for her husband, Bill, the forty-second president.

Clinton had a reputation for toughness and a harsh spirit with a knack for details and a large ego to match. Some saw her as conceited and a Yale Law School feminist know-it-all. Others, who worked with her, had a more benign view but nonetheless readily admitted that she made all the decisions.

Nothing got past her, her grip, or her two cents. There wasn't a policy, a message, or a statement that went out that she did not see and approve. In fact, she often revised things two or three times, slowing down the well-oiled machine. But she wanted it that way. She didn't want to lose, damage her image, or, most definitely, lose control.

Throughout the primary she milked all her contacts in the DNC, in the media, and in the government. Hillary knew just about everybody after her decades in government and kept close track of what they said about her, what they owed her, and how much they contributed to her. She had a list of no-gos and of people she flatly refused to see, hear, or listen to. If you crossed her, you were off her good list. Toast.

She worked every angle and source and played nice when necessary, putting on a smile and even a grandmotherly look, complete with a light blue extra-wide pantsuit.

The woman card was the ace up her sleeve, or so she thought. How could any woman seriously vote against her? Didn't every woman want to break that impenetrable glass ceiling and see her become the first female president?

In the primary she had a pesky leftist nemesis named Bernie Sanders as her sole opponent. He was an independent (actually socialist) senator from the green state of Vermont. His politics were left of left, and he liked to promise just about everything, all for free.

Hillary had to bend her progressive views to get the nomination, but as a Clinton she could be a chameleon and do anything to win the big prize. From the start, she stacked the cards against poor Bernie, whom she slandered and maligned just slightly so as not to lose his kooky and especially his young followers.

Clinton aligned the Democrat superdelegates to her cause and put all her people into the DNC and its organs so that she could not possibly lose. She owned the party. Even Donna Brazile in her tell-all book after the election said, "Clinton cheated."

That was news! Clinton had cheated before and had lost in the primaries to that useless and inexperienced community organizer and black senator Barack Obama, and it wasn't going to happen again. Her side even said that he was not born in the United States. Oh, no.

Once she secured the Democrat nomination crookedly, she figured there was no way she could lose the general election, especially to a buffoon like Donald Trump. After all, his entire base was a bunch of deplorables, irredeemables, and the rankest members of society clinging to their guns and religion.

Hillary had her own theories about the vast right-wing conspiracy and its ilk, and there wasn't a chance in hell that she would not get back to 1600 Pennsylvania Avenue because of them. She knew all the nooks and crannies in that house, and this time the Oval Office would be hers alone.

To tie down all the pieces, Clinton brought in a top-notch team and hired her old pal John Podesta to chair the very organized and overly planned campaign. They would take care of it this time. No holds were barred, and nothing was to be left undone.

The dirt on Trump would be easy to secure, and so she hired the Fusion GPS boys to dig harder, to get more. Using the DNC and a private law firm as the go-betweens, she figured she was covered and didn't need to know everything or how, just the dirt, and the more the better.

It was both oppo research and an "insurance policy"—just in case.

Giving approval to everything her campaign did was not unusual for such a deliberate, maniacal, cannot-fail candidate. Behind her were still wayward Bill, who was a tad old and rather clumsy, and her daughter, Chelsea. Her surrogates were legion, and there wasn't anybody in the media, with the possible exception of one or two people at Fox News, who thought she wasn't a shoo-in to win.

All the newspapers endorsed her, all the pundits kowtowed to her, the pollsters all predicted her victory, and she said she won the televised debates. The only question was how much she would run up her tallies and numbers in the Electoral College. How big a landslide could it be?

Sure, she had a record of coyness and sometimes did not follow through on her promises, but her ratings were astronomical and her field game was second to none. They would turn out the vote and make identity politics work like a charm. In Las Vegas the odds were eight to one she would win.

Getting the word out on how bad Trump was was absolutely imperative. Trump was a sleaze in Clinton's eyes. Wouldn't the overall electorate agree with that, even the dumbasses she so loathed? She would hold nothing back. She would throw everything at him from disgraces, to scandals, to character flaws, to Russia.

The Obama forces, even if there were past "histories" between them, would help elect her as a kind of third term for Barack, who had achieved so little in his eight years in office. His cronies would be her cronies. They would do her bidding. They would protect her and most certainly fail to indict her. They would use the deep state, where needed, to do her work behind the scenes.

At the center of the whole design was the grand conspiracy called the Trump-Russia dossier. She paid for it and approved it from the get-go. It was good as gold. McCain, who was no fan of Donald Trump, dispatched a senior aide and former state department official to London to meet Christopher Steele in person and get briefed.

He was given a copy of the dossier and returned in twenty-four hours to Washington, D.C., where he gave it to McCain. It is now known that Glenn Simpson of Fusion GPS met that day with McCain and gave him a full copy of the dossier.

Senator McCain did not like what he read, and so he set up a meeting with FBI Director James Comey, which took place on December 9, 2016. Kramer also gave a copy to BuzzFeed, according to court filings.

The meeting with BuzzFeed took place on December 23, 2016, and he saw the BuzzFeed journalist Ken Bensinger.

The entire dossier was published on January 10, 2017. Kramer was its source. Kramer also met with McCain's chief of staff to discuss the contents of the dossier. He went to see Victoria Nuland, who was the assistant secretary of state for European and Eurasian Affairs for Secretary of State John Kerry. She sent him to meet with Celeste Wallende, President Obama's Russia expert on the National Security Council.

This is how the Russia hoax got started and circulated across all of Washington and the media.

McCain was no friend of Trump's and did not back him in his primary or general campaigns. He saw Trump as dangerous, isolationist, and a challenge to the entire establishment.

"Upon examination of the contents, and unable to make a judgment about their accuracy, I delivered the information to the Director of the FBI. That has been the extent of my contact with the FBI or any other government agency regarding this issue," the senator said in a prepared statement.

Sure.

Shithole Countries

In the Oval Office during a debate about his immigration policies, the president asked, "Why do we want all these people from 'shithole countries' coming here?"

As they went over a list of countries, when they got to Haiti, he pondered out loud, Why do we need them? What do they add? Don't we really want more qualified people from places like Norway?

Those remarks lit a fuse, and the mainstream media made Trump look like either a callous observer or, worse, a racist. They had never heard such "frank" talk coming from a U.S. president.

They must not have been listening to the taped words of Richard Nixon during Watergate or the salty language of Lyndon Baines Johnson, who had a penchant for cursing.

Are they naïve or just ignorant? Is their animus against Trump so great that regardless of what he says, they and all the late-night comedians mock him and constantly decry his sensibilities?

All this goes on while his large and conservative nonurban and nonurbane base congratulates him and appreciates his coarse frankness. He is saying precisely what they say and think at home.

Trump uses rhetoric, even vulgar words at times to speak the truth. It is not polished or eloquent so much as it puts into words rather boldly what real people actually think. He often calls people names, makes fun of things, and trivializes things that are held sacrosanct.

The media is two-faced about all this. On the one hand, they critique him without end in language that is not becoming. On the other hand, they love him because he makes news and keeps their ratings high—24/7 the news is all about Trump.

"Shithole nations" is not a technical term or a category deployed by the United Nations, the World Bank, or the IMF. Social scientists generally don't utilize it in their academic analyses or lectures.

But honestly, we rank all sorts of things in politics and economics: most violent societies, wealthiest countries, most TVs per capita, most Internet connectivity, highest economic growth rates, and best life expectancy and health.

The reality is that when you look at most of these things and label them, the same countries are in the bottom quartile. They rate lowest on just about everything. They are not only the least developed, they are not places people want to travel to. In fact, most of their own citizens would prefer to leave their borders for a better life.

It is surely not a nice thing to say out loud, but then again, it was leaked. No president had said it before, but then again, there has never been a president quite like Donald Trump. He might as well have said it in a press briefing.

Some people and countries are offended. So be it. The truth is that there is no magic dirt in our city on a hill. It was built by the sweat and tears of generations of Americans. Leaving your country is not the way to make it better. If it's so great over there, why do they leave?

The New Marxists in the U.S. Congress

It appears that it has all of a sudden become very fashionable to be a Marxist in the U.S. Congress. We have an increasing number of Democratic representatives and some senators willing to accept the mantle of Marx and rallying around outright socialism.

The list includes, among others, Alexandria Ocasio-Cortez (D-NY) and Rashida Tlaib (D-MI) as well as Senators Bernie Sanders (I-VT), Harris (D-CA), and Warren (D-MA). Others appear ready to follow.

This is a new phenomenon in American politics. Although communist and socialist parties have been around for many decades, they never had electoral success or a following in Congress.

Long a part of the European political landscape, Karl Marx and Marxists appreciated the importance of the connection between leftist progressivism and the economy, and they emphasized the connection between economic phenomena and other social institutions.

As government interventionists, they long argued for nationalization of industry, redistribution of wealth, class warfare, and greater state control over all of life. However, their analysis was flawed by (1) a dubious philosophical and historical thesis that claimed to be able to predict the determined future and (2) a politicized agenda. Both led to a host of predictions, all of which turned out to be patently false.

Marxist policies, wherever they have been practiced, from the Soviet Union to Cuba and from Venezuela to North Korea, have led to bust and dictatorship. Untold suffering has resulted, along with massive economic underdevelopment and millions and millions of lost lives. The abundant evidence demonstrates that Marxism and its variants—Russian, Chinese, and others—are utterly disastrous for humanity.

Oddly, the worst part of their intellectual legacy may have been the term "capitalism" itself. This is a theoretical term for Marxists, not a descriptive one. To use the term is to accept a lot of objectionable theoretical baggage. Among that baggage is the claim that all social phenomena, including religious beliefs, are products of underlying material forces.

Using the term "capitalism" is misleading and distorting. This Marxist term is an attempt to capture what some have called the logic of modernity, but it fails to do so economically, historically, or culturally. Marx was just plain wrong, and Marxism has wreaked havoc and death wherever it has reared its ugly head.

The new Marxist Democrats are running on a platform of Medicare for all, a $15 minimum wage, a 70 to 90 percent tax rate, an end to all PAC money, the end of the petroleum industry, and "social justice." These new American socialists are out to transform the United States, making our country a foreign and unrecognizable place.

Republicans, conservatives, and Trump would be wise to nip this in the bud and call out this ilk for what they really are: un-American. If Democrats were wise, they would do the same thing.

President Trump made this clear in his 2019 State of the Union address when he said forthrightly that he was "alarmed by new calls to adopt socialism" in the United States. It was a statement that prompted some boos from the audience. The president continued: "America was founded on liberty and independence—not government coercion, domination and control. We are born free and we will stay free. Tonight, we renew our resolve that America will never be a socialist country."

Thanks be to God. Trump will not suffer fools, and his foreign policy is against socialism wherever in the world it appears.

Epilogue

UNDERSTANDING AND LIVING
WITH TRUMP AS GEO DEUS

I've always won, and I'm going to continue to win.
And that's the way it is.
—President Donald Trump

Predictions for a Coming Trump World

The year 2019, like most years that end in a 9 (look back in history), has been a year to remember.

NB: As authors, we're not Nostradamus and have no crystal ball. These predictions are based on analysis and perspective guided by trends. Like any such views they are a baseline, and high and low alternatives are also plausible.

The years ahead will provide lots of intrigue, controversy, volatility, and danger with Trump in charge. There are ways to play it and come out ahead or to be damaged, perhaps severely.

The pundits are all focused on the "fall of Trump," which won't happen, but there are other traps and challenges galore.

Here then, from our strategist-scholar-diplomat perch is a list of the things we predict for the years ahead. That includes a second four-year term in which Trump's hold on the world increases and his effect is magnified.

Keep watch and beware: This is truly Trump World.

1. Trump will remain in office and keep America great. A border barrier of some sort and some length will be built. The impeachment campaign will fall flat on its face, and the Mueller report will be seen to have ended with a whimper and an aggressive rebuttal. Trump is in the driver's seat in America and everywhere it has influence, which is everywhere.

2. Brexit will happen (no thanks to Mrs. May, only to her nemesis and Trump ally Boris Johnson) and the United Kingdom will leave the failed European Union in a clean break, perhaps at a slower pace. Brexit jump-started the entire movement to reject globalism, of which Trump is the crowning achievement. The new Trump world of sovereign nation-states will proceed ahead on free trade rules, and the economy will hardly suffer an iota; quite the contrary. All this will prove Trump and the sovereigntists right and lead to less multilateralism and more exits from the failing European Union.

3. As the United States departs from Syria, Iran and its proxies will try to fill the power vacuum, starting a larger regional conflict involving Israel. It will not end well for the Iranians, and their regime will suffer, as will the ayatollahs. Oil prices will shoot up to almost $80 a barrel. Trump will have a double victory because Iran will be whacked down and his energy independence strategy will prove a boon to the United States economically and for energy security. Regime collapse is in the air.

4. The global economy will retract as Europe slows under the dead weight of the euro, slow growth, and increased trade tensions. The United States will be the only strong nation left,

growing at 3 percent or more a year and witnessing yet more job expansion. The Dow Jones will shoot past 30,000. America is the best safe haven, and Trump will take credit for that as he demands that the Fed lower interest rates.

5. China will cry uncle after its leadership realizes that it is doomed facing an adversary like Trump. They will capitulate on nearly everything from tariffs, to nontariff barriers, to intellectual property and tech transfers. The so-called Asian century will be postponed indefinitely, thanks to Trump playing hardball. Supply chains will be reshaped before our eyes. It may take a depression in China for this to happen.

6. The European Union will continue for another term with the globalist inertia of the 1990s. There's not a lot of gas left in that tank, but the hope of a reformist bloc after the 2019 election has not materialized. If the populist parties coalesce to form a supergroup, they will take over one of the main institutions and learn to govern. The old European project will be discarded, and a smaller, leaner prosovereignty European Union will take shape around a common market. Trump's transatlantic policy will find more and more support. Places such as Hungary, Poland, and Italy will have their own Trumps.

7. Thanks to American innovation, new breakthrough drugs will come to market that provide wonders ranging from the prevention of cancer to the elimination of diseases such as malaria, Ebola, HIV, and Alzheimer's. Trump will take a bow and be congratulated by people all over the world for freeing up the Food and Drug Administration and drug discovery. Innovation will be hailed as the American centerpiece.

8. Automation, robotization, and blockchain will continue apace, changing forever the way business is done, workers work, and things are made. White-collar jobs will be dramatically affected, not just blue-collar ones. Trump's global economic plan will both accelerate this process and help minimize its effects on American workers, his base.

9. Social media will become even more totalitarian by policing "hate speech," censoring anyone they disagree with (which means conservatives), and monopolizing our lives, wallets, and minds. The backlash will begin. People will drop out, go local, and go offline, and governments, including the Trump administration, will regulate and commence antitrust actions against FAANG. This will be applauded at home and in foreign places.

10. Outer space will be back in vogue, with many countries jumping into the next frontier. The United States under President Trump will launch its Space Force as a new military service, set a time to go to Mars, and return to the moon. You too can go to space if you enlist in the Space Force. Uncle Donald needs you to fly to the moon.

As the French poet Victor Hugo reminded us over a century ago in *Les Misérables*: "The future has several names. For the weak, it is impossible; for the fainthearted, it is unknown; but for the valiant, it is ideal."

With Trump as leader of the free world, America will prosper and be in the fast lane. He will work to keep America great and make it greater yet.

The Reign of Trump

There are those who seek merely to decry Trump, and there are those who call him "chaotic" or worse. His opponents truthfully want to destroy and perhaps even impeach him now that he is winning. And some in the establishment and the old guard fear that he has totally taken over the GOP.

Donald Trump and the political phenomenon he has created are both understandable and formidable. He is not going away.

How do you understand Trump and his effect on the world?

Three kinds of people are involved in politics: theorists, unprincipled actors, and principled actors.

Theorists of both the right and the left and many lesser minds in academia and the media conceive of politics as putting into practice a preconceived theory, an ideology that supplies a formulated end in advance of the historical facts. To be educated into this ideology is to be taught how to expound, defend, and implement a strict ideology.

What it maintains is that what was carried out previously under the aegis of politics can now be accomplished through intellectual discourse alone. Political actors who do not play this game are either fools or scoundrels. Theorists expect politicians to be imperfect but deferential versions of themselves.

The theorists like to be consulted, and although they pretend that they have no ego (it's all about the theory), they are most devoted to their own prestige. Republican theorists pretend that Reagan was one of them; he was great at giving speeches, but he did not write them and was constrained by abstractions. Lincoln could write and give speeches, but he too was not constrained by any theory.

Politics, however, is not the application of theory to practice. Politics is not about theory. It's about addressing and responding to current but inherited issues, not timeless universal concerns. This is, by the way, a form of conservatism when it is principled. At best, one hires theorists to write set speeches, but speeches are rituals, not theories.

Politics can be practiced in one of two ways: principled or unprincipled.

The Clintons were unprincipled. They lacked a vision, and when pressed to express one (e.g., make me the first female president), all they could say was that it's all about me. They had no life and no accomplishments outside of politics. The game of politics was all they knew. They had little talent for anything else, and unless they were political winners or celebrities, their lives were empty. Therefore, they did or said anything to win. They also made a living or a fortune from politics (pay-to-play schemes).

Principled political leaders do not see politics as an end but as a means to create, maintain, or defend a way of life. It's the way of life that matters. They are achievers in the real world (poets, athletes, businesspeople, engineers, etc.). They do not need to be president to feel fulfilled; they have a life outside of politics (like the U.S. Founders, not like the current permanent political class).

Donald Trump is such a principled political leader. He has been successful at almost everything he has done in the real world. If he does not win, he will go back to that real world. But he *will* win.

He has a vision: Make America Great Again. It sounds corny to theorists who are too embarrassed by America's might and potential achievement, and it grates on the hate-America crowd and Obamaites or those who think they are victims, but it resonates with most Americans.

Trump exudes a self-confidence that comes in part from past achievement. His assertion of self-confidence comes from what he has done. "I'm number one in the polls" is an achievement; the winner in his world is not the guy with the cleverest comment but the person who achieves the most. Even making money is a sign of such achievement, not an end in itself.

He is appalled at most of the current practitioners and competitors (with good reason) and thinks he is better than the rest, especially the Dems. Why run if you do not think you are the best?

More important, his medium is the message. His form and content are identical, and he tells it like it is, which is refreshingly appealing. This is a style that mere theorists do not understand.

To exude confidence not only inspires others but becomes a self-fulfilling act. To make America great again, one has to believe that one is a partial expression of that very greatness. He wants all Americans to be included in that success, and that is why his reach extends beyond one party, class, race, gender, or region to all citizens.

He loves and welcomes the challenge. After all, Trump is essentially an entrepreneur.

What, then, are the current inherited issues that the American political actor might face in a second term of a disruptive presidency? How could it be anything but disruptive?

There are three: the economy, security, and civilizational identity. Watch each in order to understand the coming years in the reign of Trump as Geo Deus.

On the domestic economy, Trump has always been probusiness and free market. His tax plans have proved competitive with those of any other Republican to hold office. Everyone agrees that infrastructure needs to be addressed. Trump is a builder, and he rightly expects to get this done efficiently. Hasn't he always? He also addresses the one economic issue that most Republicans like to avoid: the income gap, which is also a serious social problem. Trump reassures blue-collar workers that he has their back; his tax plan takes this into consideration, and his global economic strategy takes it seriously. A second term will see an infrastructure bill on a bipartisan basis, personal income tax cuts, and more economic growth to the benefit of all.

With regard to the global economy, he understands that being libertarian in a mercantilist world is stupid. The libertarians and even the neocons may be correct in theory, but the world has not caught up; the current issue is how to deal with the fact that others are taking advantage of U.S. largesse and most of the world is not yet capable of being free. Articulate theorists from the developing world are not evidence against this. His policy is simply America first. This is not reactionary nationalism but a reasonable response to failed cosmopolitanism. It is what is expected of a U.S. president! So too is border security as a first rule of national security. A second term will see a standoff on border security and a compromise on building the wall or fence, a win on China trade, and getting others to pay more of their fair share.

On domestic security, Trump sees his responsibility as preventing dangerous people from entering the United States, hence the southern border wall and the Muslim visa prohibition. Trump is not counting on the votes of illegal aliens present and future nor is pandering to groups that see themselves as victims. He is instead the leader of all those who want to be successful. He is not anti-immigration at all; he wants immigration to be for the benefit of America and Americans. America has a successful and proven formula. If you want to be a part of it, become American. Come here legally to become American; don't try to turn the United States into Mexico or impose sharia law. A second term will see merit-based immigration and law and order defeating the triple threat of jihadists, socialists, and the media—his enemy of the people.

On global security, Trump advocates an overwhelmingly powerful military. There are to be no foreign adventures unless there is a clear practical objective that is obtainable (perpetual peace, world government, and the like, are neither clear nor achievable in the foreseeable future). He does not announce doctrines: Why be hampered by abstractions? The United States does not have to apologize for making the world free and prosperous; if it had not been for the United States in World War II and the Cold War, no country in the world would be free or prosperous. Of course, the United States sometimes does dumb stuff, but the lack of overall gratitude and hostility should teach us a lesson. A second term will see a rollback in Syria and Afghanistan; the resurgence of our military to new levels and sophistication, including a Space Force; and the disentanglement of bad or worn-out alliances and over-extensions. America first means American citizens must benefit.

The Middle East is no longer important economically. Between fracking, renewable energy, and new technology we are now the center of the energy universe. Surely the Saudis recognize this. The old Cold War strategy is no longer applicable. We should wish them well but not get bogged down in their perennial conflicts.

Yes, we should support Israel more because it is our only ally in the Middle East, but we should focus on U.S. interests.

We come now to civilizational identity. In his book *Who Are We?* the late Harvard professor Samuel Huntington warned us about the "clash of civilizations." The greatest current threat to the United States is radical Islamism, the jihadist attempt to win the conflict over who defines the coming global culture. This is the new version of the Cold War. Trump dares to voice his deep concern. He has the courage to stare down the political correctness crowd on this issue. He understands that we are citizens of the United States of America, not of the make-believe world of rootless, open-border, cosmopolitan globalists or one-worlders.

Understanding Trump as Geo Deus is not all that difficult. He resonates with reality, not some worn-out theory or dated ideology.

He is a pragmatic deal maker. He is a *real* American. He is actually making our country great again, and that is most laudable.

If you watch Trump unfold along the lines described here, you can see how he thinks, what his economic models imply, what political philosophy and foreign policies are part of his agenda, and who he sees as his adversaries.

Trump is truly a Geo Deus, a de facto emperor (with clothes) with an all-powerful rule over the country and the world.

Index

About the Authors

Theodore Roosevelt Malloch is a scholar-diplomat-strategist. He was a Professor at Oxford, Henley Business School, and Yale as well as CEO of the thought leadership and strategy firm, The Roosevelt Group. Dr. Malloch was a foot soldier in the Reagan State Department and served on the U.S. Senate Foreign Relations staff before taking the top American job in the UN Geneva, where he had a front row seat on the end of the Cold War. Malloch has a PhD in international political economy from the University of Toronto and has been awarded four honorary doctorates, one for his contribution to "civil society." He was an early backer and remains a firm supporter of President Trump, who considered him for high appointive office. Author of seventeen books, mostly on business and economics, and a memoir, *DAVOS, ASPEN & YALE: My Life Behind the Elite Curtain as a Global Sherpa*, his last title was: *The Plot to Destroy Trump*. Malloch appears regularly in the media, as a keynote speaker, and on television around the world.

Felipe J. Cuello is a Republican consultant and policy analyst. He is an alumnus of the United Nations University, where he specialized in migration and development. Felipe was a junior official at the European Commission in Brussels, when he defected to the Trump 2016 campaign and was a member of the Defense and Foreign Policy coordination unit for the Presidential Transition Team under a 3-star General. He currently teaches public policy at the graduate level with the Pontifical University of Santo Domingo (PUCMM) and consults for campaigns in the United States, Europe, and Latin America.